Multidisciplinary Perspectives on the Psychology of Exclusion

This new volume considers one of the most pressing topics of the generation: the sense of social exclusion, rejection and loneliness experienced by many adolescents and young adults. It offers insights from psychological and biochemical research, explaining the role of the brain, mind and body in the development of a sense of belonging over a lifespan.

Illustrated with examples of the consequences of exclusion drawn from the author's clinical work, this important work surveys the latest research in the field and introduces an innovative framework for understanding the development of a sense of belonging. Wilczyńska considers the effects of social exclusion, exploring its consequences for mental health, particularly amongst young people, and reveals how transgenerational trauma imprinted at the early stages of human development impacts lifelong development.

Including a foreword by Philip Zimbardo, *Multidisciplinary Perspectives on the Psychology of Exclusion* is essential reading for students and researchers of developmental psychology, social psychology and sociology. It will also be of interest to practitioners and policymakers working with children and young people to understand and mitigate the effects of social exclusion and loneliness.

Agnieszka Wilczyńska is a Professor of Psychology at WSB University, Toruń, Poland.

Multidisciplinary Perspectives on the Psychology of Exclusion

From Rejection to Personal and Social Harmony

Agnieszka Wilczyńska

Routledge
Taylor & Francis Group
LONDON AND NEW YORK

First published 2020
by Routledge
2 Park Square, Milton Park, Abingdon, Oxon OX14 4RN

and by Routledge
52 Vanderbilt Avenue, New York, NY 10017

Routledge is an imprint of the Taylor & Francis Group, an informa business

British Library Cataloguing-in-Publication Data
A catalogue record for this book is available from the British Library

Library of Congress Cataloging-in-Publication Data
A catalog record has been requested for this book

ISBN: 978-0-367-64466-6 (hbk)
ISBN: 978-0-367-62789-8 (pbk)
ISBN: 978-1-003-12464-1 (ebk)

Typeset in Sabon
by MPS Limited, Dehradun

Contents

Expanded table of contents

Acknowledgements

I would like to express my deepest gratitude to my teachers and mentors who have inspired me and bolstered my enthusiasm for writing this book and made it a palpable change in my life. My sincere thank you goes to Professor Phil Zimbardo, whose invariably edifying attitude to other human beings has supported my creative solutions and my resolve to produce this book in extremely challenging times. I also want to thank Dr Fabien De Meester for sharing his expertise in biochemistry and physics with me and for the many years of commitment to our mutual project, which is intrinsically devoted to the reinforcement and development of humanity. I would like to express my deepest love and respect for Ewa Kwiatek and Bartosz Kwiatek for their openness, generosity and wisdom in sharing their feelings, reflections and insights with me. Without you, this book would never have been written. I also thank my parents, sister and other relatives, as well as all the past generations without whom I would not have been able to explore the practical dimensions of intergenerational transmissions that I address in this book. Thank you, Ulcia; thank you, Kasia; thank you Mati – for the friendship that binds us and for your unwavering support. I love you, and I feel that I belong in our world despite my distinctiveness, otherness and individuality.

Foreword

Every day, every night, in every country around the world, children cry out for help, with silent voices, but no one hears them. They tell us that they are being shunned, bullied, ignored and socially excluded – both by adults and other children. Some are shy. Many become introverts. All hide away from the glaring light of social interactions – even in their own families. Although equally intelligent as most other children, they typically do poorly in school because they cannot concentrate on the class lessons, because their primary focus is internal – on how to deal with their excruciating social pain. Some could be helped by counsel from wise therapists, but their problem does not fit standard criteria for mental illness. Moreover, they cannot ask for help, and their families never recognise their desperate needs for professional care.

Fortunately, someone has been listening for decades and doing her best to help many of these socially excluded children find new paths toward becoming socially included. She has aided literally thousands of these children in her unique therapy centre in Gliwice and Wroclaw, Poland, and also has created a research centre to investigate thoroughly the causes, consequences and best conversion treatment strategies. That person is the author of this amazing new book that presents her life's work and new hopes for all the socially excluded – Professor Agnieszka Wilczyńska.

I have known 'Agnes' for many years – as a research colleague, visiting her clinic, sharing ideas about my earlier work on shyness and constantly encouraging her to collect the breadth of her knowledge in a popular book – for parents, teachers, students, therapists and researchers. HERE IT IS! And it is superb in every way. Her writing style reflects her personality – friendly, charming and accessible. Readers are treated as her companions on a special journey of discovery of vital aspects of human nature. She takes us from the dark side of loneliness and despair of so many of our children to the bright side of how best to enhance their sense of belonging and social inclusion. Readers will discover a unique mind-body approach through which to discover a new future of psychotherapy.

I believe that this book will become one of our decade's most important contributions.

Philip G Zimbardo, PhD, Emeritus Professor, Psychology, Stanford University, Author of *Shyness: What It Is, What To Do About It* and *The Shy Child*

Preface

On social exclusion, the bad and the good

A warm welcome to all the readers of my life's work, research and therapy on social exclusion. You are soon going to learn about the numerous negative developments in the lives of individuals who have been socially excluded/shunned by adults or by other children.

For these youngsters, social exclusion is bad; for some, it is the worst thing imaginable.

Just as I am finishing the writing of this book a few days before Easter 2020, a pandemic is soaring around the world. In this new era of the coronavirus pandemic, social exclusion has suddenly accrued a novel and positive meaning. In order to limit the transmission of the deadly virus, it is imperative for all of us everywhere to stay away from all other people, including from family, friends and colleagues. The recommended distance to be kept between individuals practically at all times is at least six feet.

All over the world, authorities and centres of disease control urge all citizens to strictly abide by the rules of social distancing. It is on everybody's lips now. Social distancing means not going to any public events, ceremonies or family gatherings for any reason whatsoever. In many ways, the practice of social distancing involves what we can call social exclusion.

Emphatically, in this case, voluntary social exclusion is good for our physical health!

I sincerely hope that we will all soon see the successful end to the pandemic, which poses a grave threat to our psychological health, our well-being and our lives in general.

The coronavirus pandemic has triggered a series of global social developments on an unprecedented scale. What seemed to be immovably entrenched social rules are crumbling. New principles of living together and even new values are being formulated nearly overnight. People are staying locked up in their homes – filling their time with remote work, watching TV shows and keeping in touch with others via the Internet. Those who are more self-conscious engage in self-development, self-reflection and reexaminations of their relationships with others.

We have no way of knowing when the pandemic will finally subside and what our reality and lives will look like when it eventually does. Will we morph into nationalistically sealed, scared and sterile societies seized by fears of another epidemic, or will we open up to new values in harmony with ourselves and the world? The rigours and restrictions launched by most countries are supposed to limit the spread of the virus as much as possible, but we know today that, in order to prevent similar outbreaks in the future, we must take care of people's general health and bolster their physical and mental resilience. Universal lockdowns, walling up the world and disinfecting the entire planet are certainly pointless – if not downright impossible.

Human physical immunity is intimately connected with mental health. Today, however, people are afflicted with depression and anxieties which reduce their choices even further and cause them to give up on close relations in order to avoid more harm and suffering. Where good human relationships and the sense that we are the masters of our time end, stress begins. Loneliness has become a cultural plague. In several countries worldwide, the proportion of one-person households has risen to 50%. Research findings unambiguously show that loneliness produces serious ramifications for people's health – whether they live alone by choice or by necessity.[1] Enforced during the pandemic, self-exclusion has made all of us experience firsthand what individuals may feel like when they are isolated, excluded, faced with a chaotic present and an unpredictable future, having depleted possibilities of choice–making and being unable to rely on others' genuine support other than communicating via a computer screen. The stable ground – our previous autonomy and bonds with others – has been snatched from under us, and we have been robbed of self-efficacy and of possibilities to cope with and in the external world. We have no way to escape, and we have nowhere to escape to.

Without stirring outdoors, we can consult experts on any imaginable matter, have a cup of tea with a friend, watch a theatre performance or see a doctor about one or another health complaint. All this is within hand's reach, but at the same time, mediated by the screen. I can imagine that if our human communication indeed becomes reduced solely to this virtual world, then it will soon no longer matter to us whether what we see on the screen is a real human being or an indistinguishably similar avatar.

Community belonging is a prerequisite for the survival of humanity. The presence of a loved one is powerful enough to alleviate anxiety and relieve mental and physical pain. The feeling that 'one is not alone' makes one secure, triggers one's energy to do things and fosters a space for multifarious transformations. Loneliness and exclusion are tantamount to individual social death and, in the long run, to the end of humankind. Our planet might potentially be equally well-run by a perfectly programmed organic computer – a species which will succeed humans and organise life on the Earth better than we have done. However, this is not what we want, even though such a scenario appears more and more possible these days.

Nevertheless, I believe that a considerable portion of humanity will cope with the new challenges quite successfully – especially those who have a capacity of adapting to unfamiliar conditions and are confident that they belong to a community that protects, supports and appreciates them. With such a backup, they act with resolve, conviction and trust, caring for themselves and for their communities.

Self-isolation makes us experience acutely and directly what exclusion is and how precious belonging is. Extremely trying though the present situation may be, it offers us an opportunity to profoundly remake our societies and to build a better future based on joint actions and changed relations with others. The pandemic has also made us realise what we seem to have long forgotten – namely, that we are all interconnected and dependent on each other.

At this point, we know very well that many people will need help after these difficult months of isolation. People – individuals – will need to believe that they are not deprived of others' support and that they are needed, important and valued. This will be particularly needed for the young generations who may be most vulnerable to the consequences of the pandemic. Engrossed in grappling with everyday problems, parents are unable to support children and adolescents in coping with traumatic experiences and constraining situations that inexorably made inroads into their young lives.

The primary intention of this book is to help people develop new resources by recognising the obvious – that is, that they belong to a community, a planet, a universe, and that this promotes their self-realisation both for their own sake and for others.

The new phospholipid concept of body and mind discussed in this volume considerably augments our knowledge of how human memory, consciousness and self-consciousness work.

I believe that this book will help my precious readers understand the mechanisms behind the establishment of human relationships and the genesis and therapy of relational traumas.

We are champions when our brains are fuelled by genuine love as an operating manual that comes straight from our hearts.

Note

1 The research study carried out by the Florida State University College of Medicine in 2018.

About this book

An overview of chapters

Multidisciplinary Perspectives on the Psychology of Exclusion is a study that explores social exclusion from the perspective of psychophysical and memetic human functioning. The framework which underpins my argument foregrounds interactions between individuals and their environments and describes mental properties in neurochemical, physical and above all cultural terms. These aspects of experience are discussed in relation to individuals' current lives, but they are also associated with early childhood traumas and intergenerational transmissions.

Research on social exclusion shows that – as long as individuals fail to notice that certain mental states and the related perceptions and approaches to reality develop in ways unnoticed and unrecognised by them and their communities – the same response mechanisms continue to operate. This happens because schemas and programmes formed on the basis of the primary information which is recorded in the body/mind filter the incoming information/data from the environment from then on. Understanding the properties of the mind and molecular mechanisms may further the design of breakthrough therapies and consequently contribute to reinforcing people's psychic stability and harmony. The multidisciplinary perspective applied in this book has been prompted by the author's years-long investment in both psychology and neurochemistry.

The last stages of writing this book coincided with the enhancement of people's sensitivity to social relationships in the wake of social isolation regimes implemented worldwide due to the Covid-19 pandemic.

The degree of people's engagement and acceptance of the rules in place varies across society, ranging from codependence (i.e. complete approval and participation) to independence and attempts to find a way beyond the supplied information. Multiple forms of counterdependence are symptoms of people's negation or abnegation of the existing world. This is how people differ in the extent of their social commitment to the solving of humanity's problems. This is also why this book was written and you, my dear readers, have made up your minds to read it.

The book addresses social exclusion at the individual level. In fact, every human being needs to feel as a wanted part of society or any other group. This need is met in a variety of ways, or it remains unsatisfied.

The human being of our times – more sensitive than ever before, acutely tested by life histories of his/her family, ancestors and entire nations and cherishing the innermost need to belong and be included – still remains a partial enigma. The challenges which were once the engine powering social development through competition today trigger insecurity, withdrawal, increased mental disorders and dire loneliness across the globe.

The Introduction presents social exclusion as such – a condition that has been or is being experienced in various degrees by each and every one of us. People and nations are affected by traumas linked to religion, war, poverty, destructive or constraining stereotypes and various systems of government. Besides, every individual is shaped by his/her personal life story, including episodes of, for example, growing up in a helpless or dysfunctional family. The ways in which such experiences contribute to exclusion and to the sense of exclusion are discussed throughout this book.

Viewed in this way, people are like metaphorical pieces of a jigsaw puzzle which fit into a certain part of a bigger whole at a given time and in a given space. The difference is that their shapes need not be unambiguously defined; instead, they are being formed in these contexts. This enables people to alter their contours and colours and, in this way, to fit into another part of this whole. The jigsaw puzzle is a metaphor for the world as an arrangement of various human stories and events, both of those that are grim and limiting as well as those that are cheerful and development-boosting.

The propensity to experience exclusion depends on people's individual biological-physical setup (genes) and their emotional sensitivity to the impact of external histories (memes). The latter (i.e. sociocultural and psychological influences) are decisive and have a capacity to affect the former at the cellular and genetic levels – epigenetic changes. As emphasised at the very beginning, childhood and adolescence are critical periods for the development of the sense of belonging or exclusion. Patterns of functioning and coping arise and take shape in response to early-life events and under the influence of upbringing. These patterns become enciphered and recorded as codes in certain biological structures. Such codes remain partly intact and relatively stable until they are restructured and deactivated. Individuals' impaired involvement with society is usually the last act of exclusion, of which they are not always aware. It is challenging to decipher the programme in adulthood, because, usually, nobody remembers the code any longer.

The study case of Mark described in this part captures the ways in which social exclusion is generated by individuals' internal systems of unrecognised schemas and programmes.

Part I

The first part of the book features a survey of the literature and research findings and outlines phenomena associated with social exclusion in today's world.

The social rules which have been endorsed so far have become unfriendly to individuals and societies in several respects. These do not promote people's feeling of being part of a community; instead, these fuel loneliness and social distancing. Self-exclusion has become a measure to which people resort in order to protect themselves, not only physically against the dangerous virus but also mentally against being hurt by the pain of exclusion, rejection, disregard, underestimation, dysregulation and wounding – all of which are so endemic in our world.

Social exclusion is depicted here the way it is seen by individuals and by society and the way it is conceptualised in psychological and social theories. Individual, situational and systemic aspects of social exclusion are portrayed alongside the author's multidisciplinary approach, which guides readers across the two concluding parts of the book.

The author's intent in writing this book was to lead readers through a certain framework of understanding on how the mind is shaped and transmitted and where it is located. Self-awareness is actually the key notion in our journey to knowing the mind, discerning its connections with the body and grasping the roles played by the human brain and heart.

According to the conception adopted in this book, the mind and the body interact through the information that they store and manage. As research suggests, the human mind – partly already formed and partly being formed – is located in the lipid structures of cell membranes throughout the body, particularly in the brain and in the heart. The mechanism of potential incorporation and removal of information from this system is discussed in detail in Part III of the book.

The chapter 'Psychosocial issues of social exclusion' devoted to phenomena observable in society describes the social schemas involved in labelling people as 'excluded'. This moniker has usually been used to designate 'unwanted others' – those who, sometimes, are also called 'deviants'. This capacious category encompasses people who break the law, as well as individuals who have different sexual preferences or those who are not eager to take part in social occasions.

An explanation of the mode in which people and groups are selected to 'function as the excluded' is offered. Situational consciousness helps differentiate between evolutionary group tendencies to display excluding behaviour and individuals' responses, which are often driven by their own experiences of exclusion.

The phenomena described in this part reflect people's loneliness in our overpopulated world. They include data on depression, loneliness, fear and self-isolation during the pandemic. The survey of research findings implies that people tend to exchange real lives for virtual lives as one of the popular coping strategies. Immersion in the world of serial shows and video games has become a specific escape from the effort of experiencing and moulding one's life. However, both film narratives and the hermeneutics of computer games only help for a brief moment. They foster new dreams and visions of felicity that fail to materialise in real life. This does not help people shake off personal anxieties and problems; instead, this removes these issues from their field of vision only for a while. In fact, the individual world and the cultural world coalesce in the human mind, being, one way or another, a continuation of the individual's personal history.

The last chapter, 'The experience and impact of exclusion', addresses the pivotal issues of this discussion (i.e. the need of belonging, the sense of belonging and major theories and psychological studies on social exclusion). This part can serve as a ready compendium of psychological research as it offers a review of the effects of and the hypothetical reasons behind social exclusion.

Over recent years, research has found that individuals' exclusion is primarily bound up with their personal and family experiences (Garbarino, 1990; Buckley et al., 2004, Twenge et al., 2007; Twenge, Baumeister, DeWall, Clarocco and Bitels, 2007; Twenge, Catanese and Baumeister, 2003). Given this, a considerable portion of this book's chapters focuses on the nurturing and raising of young people. Situations and circumstances in which they grow up mould their ways of experiencing the self and others into a relatively stable form, which is referred to as a programme or a schema.

Based on a survey of international research, a list of predictors of social exclusion is compiled, containing the types of anxious, avoidant and disorganised attachments, unworked-through traumatic experiences, past psychiatric/psychological complaints, family problems and traumas, intergenerational transmission therein, the lack of social support and negative labelling.

There is no consensus on the psychological implications of social exclusion. Some findings show a decrease in emotions and an increase in what is known as emotional numbness and cognitive deconstruction. Other experimental research findings suggest that social exclusion exacerbates aggression and reduces prosocial behaviour, which engenders what is referred to as negative emotionality. The literature also describes serious consequences of exclusion, where victims of exclusion display self-destructive tendencies and engage in criminal behaviour, including suicide attempts, assaults, mass shootings, etc.

Social exclusion is a serious threat to people's physical and mental well-being. It can manifest in the body through heightened tension in various body parts and somatic diseases (Argyle, 1987; Cacioppo, Hawkley and

Berntson, 2003; Wilczyńska-Kwiatek and Bargiel-Matusiewicz, 2008). The mental pain of exclusion is comparable to very real physical pain. These correlations are also examined in this part of the book.

Part II

The second part of the study is specifically research-focused. It reports on a research study on social exclusion and factors in coping with exclusion, which was carried out on a sample of teenagers. Social exclusion is discussed as a stress situation that teenagers confront by activating their own resources and mobilising strategies of coping with stress. For this reason, the first chapter in this part offers an introduction to the scholarly notion of stress and to research findings on adolescent coping with stress.

Children and adolescents do not ascribe significance to early childhood stress experiences and/or they do not remember the traumatic experiences that they have gone through in their lives. Their potential for resilience is depleted if their early childhood traumas were severe or systematically recurring. The strategies for coping with stress result from the resources that people still have at their disposal after experiencing such very early traumas.

The literature catalogues an array of ways in which youngsters cope with stress, depending on their volition and engagement in the coping process. Bruce E Compas, Jennifer K Connor-Smith and colleagues (2001) have described young people's coping as an aspect of a broader category of self-regulation processes. The most stressful situations are connected with relationships and school. For example, girls are more likely to fall back on non-adaptive strategies of coping with stress than boys – such as tension reduction, ignoring the problem or self-blame. Boys tend to seek other solutions (e.g. engaging in physical exercises and playing video games), but they also often ignore problems and do not reveal their feelings. As a rule, they do not admit that they cannot see how they can cope. Girls, more often than boys, own up to the fact that they have no strategy of coping with problems.

However, research results are inconclusive on whether the strategies used by young people are mostly productive or unproductive. Both types are actually employed in various situations.

Given this, the following chapter of Part II describes the research assumptions and the findings of the author's original study, which identify specific ways of adolescent coping in correlation with the types of exclusion risk. The study was conducted on a sample of public lower-secondary school students in a mid-sized town in Poland.

The study looked into a set of selected psychological variables, including characteristics prone to change in the situation of social exclusion, such as the sense of belonging, the need of belonging, anger expression, emotional intelligence, mood and coping with stress.

Based on cluster analysis, four groups differing in the kind of social exclusion were identified in the sample. Path analysis in each of the groups helped describe their strategies of coping with stress. The ways in which the respondents used their own resources in response to exclusion were defined on the basis of the analysis of statistically significant directional correlations among the studied variables – personal characteristics.

The study showed that the risk of exclusion was quite common among teenagers in this part of Europe and comprised more than 65% of adolescents. By illuminating psychological interconnections among the studied characteristics, some light was also shed on the resources used by teenagers to cope with exclusion. The four identified groups included one that was not at risk of social exclusion (i.e. the Socially Included), two groups experiencing the sense of exclusion (exclusion in the family, i.e. the Invisible Kids; and exclusion in peer-group, i.e. the Rejected, Frozen and Needy), and one group of excluded people who did not report either the need of belonging or the sense of being at risk of social exclusion. Drinking and smoking—generally, substance abuse – were the chief 'issues' reported by the latter group (i.e. the 'Unneedy' Loiters).

Among other findings, the study established that people from the socially included group coped with stress most effectively, used all their resources and applied productive coping strategies. Their need of belonging was met. In two other groups, the need of belonging was not met, though it was signalled and perceived by the teenagers. In the family-exclusion group, the frustrated need of belonging was found to cause a significant increase in externally directed anger. In the peer-exclusion group, the unmet need of belonging produced emotional numbness that thwarted any possibilities of coping with rejection – for example, in the school-based group. Those in the 'Unneedy' Loiters group did not report any belonging-related needs, and the findings indicated that their sense of belonging was satisfied by participation in minority groups of asocial type.

The chapter includes a detailed depiction of the entire research procedure and a discussion of its results. This part can serve as an important source of information for parents and people who work with young people, since it may further their understanding of the ways in which excluded children function and may also help in designing evidence-based helping strategies.

The last chapter of Part II presents the author's original longitudinal research in the form of a case study. The case study concerns a teenage girl who came to therapy straight from a children's home, where she had undertaken several suicide attempts, refused to eat and was disengaged from any social contact. For these reasons, the girl had undergone psychiatric treatment at a local mental health out-patient clinic. The case study describes the reasons for referral, consultations and the successive stages of therapy, which was conducted within the psychodynamic model. Given that the girl's attitude to involvement in therapy was complex, and she engaged in self-excluding behaviour, a detailed account is offered of transference and countertransference mechanisms. This gives readers a better insight into the therapeutic process and the patient's reactions.

The depiction of the therapist's (the author's) feelings and observations in therapy affords a closer look at how the girl self-excluded by behaving in ways that provoked others to exclude her. Magda's case shows that repeated traumatic stress triggered a particular defence mechanism – a schema which filtered all later information and life experiences, even the positive ones, therein those from therapy. This part of the book may be of special utility to therapists, teachers and educators in improving their understanding of the actions and attitudes of people who are excluded and deeply wounded by their life histories.

Part III

According to the latest discoveries in science, trauma can be transmitted as an experience of previous generations. This happens in two ways: through handing down models of emotion, behaviour and, in particular, relation-building, and through transmissions at the cellular level.

In this book, trauma is conceptualised as a process in which fear, anger and/or guilty feelings are transferred onto descendants by the generations who were directly exposed to suffering – for example, during war or other traumatic events. Polish scholars argue that almost all Poles are traumatised as a result of the experiences of World War 1 and World War 2 and that Poland's local history can indeed explain why they are prevalently pessimistic, have a negative mindset and do not trust others.

In the chapter on attachment and exclusion, a deficit of closeness is perceived and presented as an early childhood relational trauma or a potentially traumatic event. Children who do not experience close contact – which they vitally need – go through the same process of trauma as those involved in traumatic experiences of violence. The kind of mother-child attachment formed in childhood partly determines the child's future emotional disorders and is regarded as a predictor of disturbed functioning in later life.

This part of the book illuminates the ways in which particular attachment patterns may trigger the trauma of exclusion and vice versa. This perspective is adopted to elucidate an avoidant attachment and the sense of exclusion, an anxious attachment and the sustained risk of losing relationships and finally a disorganised attachment in which the person fluctuates between the passion of love and hatred.

In fact, people's functioning is determined not just by their type of attachment to the mother but by a constellation of several conditions.

Genetic and epigenetic conditions are of utmost relevance in this respect, including the receptiveness of the nervous system, emotional regulation modes, transgenerational transmission, the experience of traumas unrelated to attachment, chronobiological, chronopsychological determinants, etc.

Events that are traumatic for people are recorded and pushed into oblivion. Those experiences are imprinted in the body. How the traumas that are 'inscribed' in the body can be discovered is explained in this part of the book by drawing on the research carried out by renowned French microkinesitherapist Dr Daniel Grosjean (Grosjean, 2020).

The chapter which examines the biopsychosocial processes in the body and the mind aims to explicate the relations between people's mental functioning and physical functioning, proneness to illness and healing and/or susceptibility to changes as dependent on the type and way of the mind 'programming' at the early stages of individuals' development or in the past in general. Individual phenotypes denote the expression of memes, manifesting in people's behaviour. Like the genotype, phenotypes are subject to natural selection, which is spatiotemporal and sociocultural in this case. The genes are imprinted from the moment of conception, whereas the memes, which start to imprint themselves from the time of inception, eventually achieve a balance with the genes in adulthood. Fabien De Meester (De Meester, 2018, 2019, 2020) argues that consciousness and the mind can be studied at the level of cell membranes. In the new framework he proposed, the mind is precedent and foregrounded, while the body is secondary in terms of both the historical chronology and its rank. Memetic information about the mind is stored in every cell and affects human beings' mental functioning and bodies. Unsaturated fatty acids in cell membranes, or rather their allylic double bonds, are capable of fractally absorbing and emitting tytes of information.

This is the first explanatory framework in the field of psychology to combine psychological and biochemical approaches in order to expound the role of the mind, the brain and the body in creating the sense of belonging. This is what makes this concept unique and is the answer to urgent questions about the location of the mind and the differences between the mind and the brain.

The chapter entitled 'The mind in the body, or the body in the mind: Where is the mind located?' brings together and recapitulates the insights on the interdependence between the potentially traumatic events experienced by people and the ways they function. Its intent is to provide explanations concerning the location of the mind in the body. Recent studies that draw on biochemical and physical research reveal the function of cell membrane fatty acids in the process of building and 'storing' the mind.

Fatty acids or phospholipids, which are included in cellular membranes, can temporarily serve as a substrate of the mind. Allylic double bonds of unsaturated fatty acids form a unique electronic system that acts like a transistor. It possesses all the properties which enable the transcription of environmental and social information – as well as of all temporal and spatial information – into biological instructions. It is this information that determines human behaviour. Cell membranes spontaneously form biological matrices. These, in turn, are mathematical matrices for isothermal data (i.e. informions or tytes), which can only be transferred and recorded at a particular body temperature. The totality of processes which occur in cellular membranes makes the stored statistically significant and complex information accessible through the biological Information Technology (bIT).

Locating the mind and identifying the ways in which it is formed provide the key starting point for new research on improving the condition of people in contemporary societies. The book shows the role of the mind in shaping the sense of belonging and social exclusion. Over recent decades, researchers have been preoccupied with studying the possibilities of the human brain in the hopes of answering these yet-unexplored but important questions about the mind/psyche. The mind has long been considered immaterial and remained undefined in psychology and, for that matter, in other sciences. The commonly adopted position has also been that the brain created the mind rather than the other way around. This part of the book sheds some fresh light on these issues.

In today's approaches to human development, Charles Darwin's science of genetic transmission and Jean Baptiste de Lamarck's science of memetic transmission are set apart. However, natural selection and cultural selection do not have to be contradictory. As a matter of fact, despite certain crucial differences between the genetic (Darwin) and cultural/psychosocial (Lamarck) transmission of information, both are scrutinised in this chapter. Given this, the argument aims to outline the ways in which psychology-underpinned psychonomy should support people in their sense of belonging to a group, a community and humanity as the fundamental principle that governs the world.

Without a doubt, the framework discussed in this part of the book is inspirational and breeds a range of additional questions that still remain unanswered. I believe that the conception will encourage readers to engage in further explorations and detailed studies on these themes.

Part IV

Part IV assembles educational and therapeutic interventions designed to foster the sense of belonging in manners underpinned by the concepts discussed in the foregoing parts. The conclusions and recommendations are also formulated with parents and students of psychology, education and medicine in mind. Within my work with teachers, I have noticed that teachers themselves need to be taught how to feel relevant, how to develop self-confidence and how to be self-reliant. Social relations which are established by professionals with high levels of belonging are consciously built, and their dynamic course is harmoniously regulated as they unfold. This lies at the core of the chapter entitled 'Building self-belonging in schools: Work with teachers'.

The chapter on 'Prevention and self-soothing' describes selected aspects of approaches based on mindfulness, kindness and care as the starting points of self-soothing. Over the last two decades, there has been an increasing interest in the concepts of the compassionate mind and mindfulness. Self-compassion has been observed to help people distance themselves from self-destructive ruminations while discovering and expanding soothing and a benevolent and forgiving self-attitude.

People learn how to train their minds in order to avoid reproducing non-adaptive or harmful patterns and to achieve peace and harmony. Individuals are mindful of themselves and of their partners in relationships, are able to honour their own and other people's boundaries, take care of and respect themselves and others and obtain respect and care from others. Non-adaptive and limiting patterns of functioning arise as our organisms respond to threats. This activates protective reactions in response to the alarming emotions of fear, anger, etc. When the latter become imprinted, they transform into a selective sieve for later experiences. Modern research, therein the approach developed by Professor Paul Gilbert (Gilbert, 2005), is cited to discuss three basic systems of emotional and behavioural regulation, including the Threat and Protection System, the Drive and Achievement System and the Soothing and Commitment System. Each of these systems is associated with primary emotions, affective feelings, hormone response and behaviour response.

The chapter entitled 'Working therapeutically with socially excluded adolescents' presents findings of an experimental longitudinal study which was carried out in clinical conditions on a sample of adolescents at risk of social exclusion. Sixty F91- and F92-diagnosed teenagers (according to ICD-10) enrolled at a therapeutic facility were recruited to the research sample. All of them had experienced strong exclusion from their environments, first at their homes and families and then at their school and community systems. They displayed unstable or aggressive behaviour and emotions.

For the purposes of the experiment, the subjects were randomly assigned to three equinumerous groups: eudaimonic, hedonistic and control, with the former two having a different set of therapeutic interventions devised for them. These groups were further divided into smaller subgroups.

The eudaimonic interventions consisted in discovering and supporting the adolescents' skills and potentials related to their talents, development possibilities, abilities and/or interests. This tied in with the development of the Drive and Achievement System.

The hedonistic interventions were founded on working on the improvement of moods, the general balance of emotional sensations, an increase in satisfaction and learning through pleasant feelings. In this way, emotions and experiences characteristic of the Commitment and Soothing System were supported.

The long-term results showed that the respondents in the two experimental groups not only had failed to improve their responses but also even strengthened their attitudes from before the study. A discussion of this surprising finding is offered in conclusions from the study. It is believed to be of special interest to students of psychology and education and to all those working with excluded adolescents, the youth at risk of exclusion and young people with behavioural disorders.

Building belonging is possible across the various stages of human development. The chapter devoted to 'Positive individual human development' portrays the phases of human development, focusing on factors which buttress people's sense of belonging and thereby enhance their strategies of coping with stress and improve their self-esteem, mood and other characteristics discussed in previous chapters.

Individuals' development follows a spiral trajectory, where people find themselves at a certain level, but all their belonging-related experiences associated with other earlier levels/spaces affect them as well. Proper modes launched in childhood and continued in adulthood enable people to receptively and effortlessly engage in an array of life roles – including the roles of man/woman – which are encountered as people chose to be part of society.

For example, a lot of males still mistake controling and hostile behaviour for strength. In fact, such a behaviour originates in the weakness and helplessness of a hurt boy. Few such men experienced the care of mature parents in childhood.

Adults who seek to shake off constraining schemas that they unconsciously acquired at earlier stages of their lives can accomplish this goal in three sequential and interrelated phases of the therapeutic process. This is depicted in the chapter entitled 'Recognising memories, emotions, feelings and thinking: Transformation and thriving'.

In the first phase, the reasons for the sense of exclusion are revealed and the imprinted information (i.e. interpretations of events) is restructured from the perspective of a self-aware adult. The second phase involves shuffling off these schemas and programmes (i.e. their reorganisation), where the data that are limiting or make people think of themselves in self-hurting and self-excluding ways are 'deleted'. The third phase consists of implementing new modes of feeling and thinking (i.e. ones that are not constraining and promote growth). This entails using all the available resources in self-awareness, full self-acceptance, care for self and others and readiness for thriving. The discussion of the third stage offers examples of applying elements of various therapies that may usefully support such therapeutic processes. The approach proposed here can be described as psychotherapy which presupposes parallel changes unfolding at the molecular level.

As an advocate of pragmatic psychology of the future, I realise that psychonomy/psychology will soon be one of the most needed and most rapidly developing disciplines. Having access to a considerable amount of thought-provoking hypotheses and studies that provide new knowledge, we can discover the mind and functions of the brain from an entirely different perspective and rely on them in designing new forms of therapy.

Academic textbooks and psychological literature have not taught us about Lamarck's theory. It was dismissed because Darwin's theory claimed the chief position in explaining phenomena in psychology and related disciplines. This is why the contemporary *Homo sapiens* has difficulty imagining a world without hierarchies, divisions, rivalries and consumerism. However, the dissemination of social life and leadership based on natural selection breeds and is bound to continue to engender the sense of exclusion in people. Loneliness and the increasing incidence of mental disorders and degenerative diseases afflict the contemporary 'dying-out' *Homo sapiens* more commonly than ever before. We see numerous people vocally opposing genetic programming, without even realising that they are being programmed memetically all the time. Nevertheless, the two types of information – natural and cultural – contribute to phenotypic changes in people. Environmental informions have access to the genes and set the tone of gene expression (genomics) and evolution (genetics).

The significance of phospholipids, which are among the main components of the brain, the nervous system and all the cell membranes, has been and still is the most ignored theme in psychological-themed and other research. Furnished with new ideas, we can now stand up to scholarly and personal challenges to study and to more accurately describe the interconnections among the body, the mind and the brain. Another challenge for us is to develop carefully designed support programmes for the benefit of individuals and humanity.

Part I

Understanding social exclusion

Chapter 1

Introduction

Most of us have certainly experienced the embarrassing sensation of not fitting in with our own social environment. Experiencing such moments is simply part and parcel of almost every developmental path from childhood to adulthood, and is usually at its most intense in adolescence. Before developing their own autonomous beliefs and independent lifestyles, all people need to first feel that they fit in with their communities, although the strength of this need varies from individual to individual. In this book, I will refer to this feeling of social relatedness as the 'sense of belonging'.

People differ in how closely interrelated with others they want to be and, in fact, are. An individual's expectations toward their group and/or the people for whom they care tend to take shape mostly in the first developmental stage. More precisely, they are formed when human beings begin to realise that, besides their closest caregiver (i.e. the mother, as a rule), there are also other people around and come to find it important to interact with and then engage in various relations with them. The sense of belonging is shaped throughout the period of maturation and, in most people, in adulthood as well. It is predominantly built by ongoing personal experiences and 'tribal' experiences obtained through contact with other people which are confirmed in how well the individual fits in with the group, in how much the individual needs the group and also in how much the group needs that individual. At each developmental level, the person relies on this dynamic exchange to ascertain his/her importance to and use in society—a group which s/he finds important or where s/he forms relations with his/her significant others. These relations include, for example, relations with other family members or with the members of the first significant external group—such as classmates or a peer group. These relationships make up the basis for our future bonds, which paradoxically do not always continue or mirror the initial experiences, but rather represent an entire constellation of a few factors which will be discussed in this book.

Adults differ in the degree to which they want to be interdependent with others. Several people will remain at the stage of close interdependence with others throughout their lifetimes. They will establish very strong bonds with their life partners and with people in various social circles, or they will suffer in various ways if they fail to establish such ties. This is linked to their need to fit in with the community, in which successful role performance, observance of social norms and satisfaction are derived from such conduct. All together, they add up to an approved, even recommended, and safe way of life. In this group, society members benefit from the existing cultural and economic achievements and loyally endorse current social trends and fashions. They form the average, and rather hardworking, middle class who enjoy a middle-to-high financial status. As a rule, they simultaneously perform a few traditional social roles and function in a number of different groups with rules they abide by. They are willing to rely on their roots and family connections and respect the social hierarchy—particularly if it overlaps with their own intuitive perceptions of authority—power and social forces (Marcus and Conner, 2014; Markus and Kityama, 2010).

The remaining smaller part of the population aspires for autonomy and independence (ibid.). They are not afraid to be different, are self-reliant and are sometimes lonely, but actually, even actively seek to be so. This results from their urge to create their own world, to draw new boundaries, to look for new values, to discover and to experiment in various spheres of scholarship and life. They find themselves constantly searching, attempting to assert their relevance and facing up to their environment's responses to the ventures they launch and the solutions, ideas and changes they propose. They are discoverers, pioneers, scholars and researchers, writers, medical and psychological practitioners, passionate teachers and other daring people who work for the sake of change in society and better health of their contemporaries as well as future generations. They function within or outside groups accepting norms and roles while also looking for new approaches. They draw on new concepts and fresh theories that may explain how consciousness works, how individuals function and how people establish relationships; thereby, they welcome collaboration which is underpinned by mutual acceptance and respect. They realise that they are different and perceive their otherness as either facilitating or impeding progress in various situational contexts. Prepared to confront themselves and others, they embrace challenges in order to achieve creative goals.

Another statistically smaller part of society is comprised of anti-dependent individuals and groups whose anti-conformist behaviours stand out against the commonly acknowledged social norms. They form a group that does not want to contribute to the existing community. They neither intend to devote themselves to making the world a better place nor feel an urge to implement creative changes. Basically, they are chiefly inclined to destroy, wreck, oppose or ignore the norms. They either keep to themselves or function within very circumscribed milieus or among people and/or ideas that sustain their anti-conformity and anti-dependence. They function more freely outside groups that cherish norms and roles. They flout traditional ties, challenge authorities and ignore or undermine other people's values, with the opposition being their programmatic mode of being. They are usually people whose adversarial attitudes are driven by egocentric and defensive motives, rather than by prosocial concerns. They are known to take risks in defence of causes they find personally important (Wilczyńska, 2013).

The three groups briefly depicted above are to be found in all societies. Depending on cultural factors, societies in America, Asia and Europe will differ in the size, proportion and diversification of these respective groups. This classification intersects with other measures, explanations and descriptions that will be presented further in this book. It seems to be clear that those two last groups are the most vulnerable to be excluded by others.

My major focus in this study is on people's attempts to meet central human needs. My explorations will revolve around issues such as in what ways, if at all, these needs can be met, how much or how little people need to refer to their lives as fulfilled and of good-enough quality, and what factors motivate people to engage in personal action. The needs I have in mind are connected with the need of belonging. They are the need for security and ease, the need for social recognition and importance and the need of being wanted and loved.

What do people crave most?

People want to be noticed and appreciated—or at least accepted—in their 'tribal groups' (e.g. families, peer groups, schools, etc). Individuals crave to feel part of a group—to fit in in one way or another—even if they are dissimilar from others. I refer to the sense of fit and being part of an idea, a milieu or a group as the 'sense of belonging' (Wilczyńska, Januszek, Bargiel-Matusiewicz, 2015). The endeavours to achieve this by first becoming aware of this urge and then mobilising energy to satisfy it through—for example, communicating this to others—add up to the need of belonging. In a properly developing and healthy society, the needs of individuals are recognised and satisfied. Yet the script of correlation between the need of belonging and the sense of belonging, or the lack thereof, may be entirely different. This is evidenced by the growing incidence of depression across the world. Depression and anxiety are conditions in which one's needs remain either unrecognised or unmet, and individuals do not feel that they belong and do not engage in enjoyable social action (ibid.). When people recognise their needs and they are looking for the reason why they cannot satisfy them, they make the first step toward personal deep development and changes. When people do not see possibilities to discover real causes and try to treat symptoms instead or give up, they enter the path of social exclusion (e.g. they develop psychiatric diseases, isolate themselves, commit suicide, fall into addiction, etc).

In searching for deep motives, my special focus is on childhood, adolescence and prolonged adolescence, because, within those periods, the need of belonging crystallises and is then systematically recognised and satisfied. Departing from Abraham Maslow's hierarchical concept (Maslow, 1954), I believe that this need appears and is met or unmet across all of the three groups identified above. Nevertheless, I believe that there is no moment of saturation in contemporary traumatised societies—meaning that the sense of belonging is like the flame in the fireplace or a bonfire outdoors, affording the sense of existence as long as the (internal) fire is sustained. The sense of belonging is a crucial factor in any individual's personal development and survival.

In later chapters, we will examine various social and individual settings in which the need of belonging surfaces or does not, along with the various desires this need involves, and importantly, the ways in which it can be fulfilled. The individual's future life is fundamentally affected by the situations and systems in which his/her sense of belonging was produced and in which s/he has experienced exclusion. The past experience of exclusion—rejection, ridicule, mockery, neglect, deregulation, hurting, slandering and the like—is conspicuous among the factors that powerfully affect the feeling of belonging.

Social rejection and social exclusion

Hurting and rejection are probably the most painful of all sensations. What I mean here is rejection or exclusion by people whom the individual regards as important and significant (DeWall and Baumeister, 2006). Such conclusions are corroborated by the life histories of children and adults who condoned mobbing, bullying and exploitation, because their fear of losing their family or forfeiting relations with a significant group or person was stronger. However, rejection, once experienced, remains etched in our memory for a long time. Mental/emotional pain is experienced just as physical pain is experienced (Zhong and Leonardelli, 2008). When you scald your hand, you are likely to be cautious for a long time to avoid going through that source of pain again. Exclusion can be experienced both in unforeseen and in expected circumstances. The first instance of exclusion from their closest group may be very surprising to the individual. If s/he could anticipate rejection, s/he would certainly try to prevent it (Gardner, Pickett and Brewer, 2000). I remember a boy who told his classmates about his interests—specifically about the fact that he was collecting My Little Pony toys. The day he divulged this bit of his personal likes to them opened a new and dramatic chapter in his life, as his classmates started to mock him, which continued long into the semester until their teacher had a serious talk with all of the students involved and managed to put an end to it. Another more dramatic example is from a family story when a two-year-old boy was the witness of sexual abuse of his seven-year-old brother.

He could not help his brother because of fear, and his young brain could not provide understanding and solutions. Without any support, he lived in internal loneliness, fear, a sense of guilt, self-isolation and the feeling of social exclusion for many years of his adult life, until he undertook very controversial self-therapy.

Regrettably, effective interventions in those kinds of stories are not always possible.

The personal sense of exclusion is not always linked to the actual fact of being excluded by others. The sense of exclusion may be experienced at many various levels and for many various reasons. Sometimes, self-fulfilling prophecies are at work, and sometimes the feeling of rejection is a product of one's imagination, of self-punishment or of one's fear of anticipated punishments from others. In such cases, the subjectively perceived exclusion escalates in the person's mind, negatively affecting his/her thoughts, emotions and behaviours.

Sometimes a group reacts to this by excluding an individual as a result of total coincidence. Factors in such interplays include the composition of the group—the group leader modelling group behaviour, patterns and stereotypes, or there being no master-teacher capable of perceiving and solving the problem in time, for example by directly intervening or by holding a group meeting.

Some people are more susceptible to exclusion than others and are, thus, from the very beginning, more vulnerable to any symptoms of exclusion which appear in a new group. Similar to the described cases above, their experiences in life or the fact that they find themselves at a difficult developmental stage may make them feel that they do not fit in, especially if they have already experienced being deregulated, overlooked or unnoticed (Wilczyńska, 2016).

People with unstable self-esteem who perceive that they differ from others feel that they are not accepted or liked, even though they do not receive any indication of potential exclusion from the group or at least not initially (Leary and Baumeister, 2000).

Readers may wonder why social exclusion and rejection are some of the major thematic concerns of this book. After all, why should we meticulously analyse the feeling that we tend to try and shake off, preferring not to admit to it?

There are several reasons for this choice of the topic. Firstly, social exclusion is an outcome of various and mainly forgotten experiences in people's lives; hence, exploring which of these experiences affects our life most, in what way it happens and how it can be changed may help us live the rest of this life in a rewarding way. Secondly, multiple research findings have shown that the sense of exclusion is the most dramatic and acute experience for people as social beings. Evolutionally speaking, social exclusion literally entails death. Thirdly, exclusion concerns not only in the past but also future events, as it makes it impossible to plan the future and to live a satisfying life. There are also other reasons that I will discuss further in this book. Briefly, social exclusion involves difficult past experiences, unfolds in the present and affects the future.

Where does exclusion come from?

There are at least three areas where exclusion comes from: these are individual, group/interactional and systemic spheres. The individual dimension is an ensemble of several components and is linked to the person's traits and personal experiences, as well as to the transgenerational transmission in which the person is a vehicle. This constellation of factors affects the person's attitude to his/her social environment and vice versa, generating thoughts, stirring emotions and influencing behaviours.

Transgenerational transmission and personal traits are reflected in, for example, communication within one's family and in the community, as well as in the ways the individual functions. They cover individual, interactional and systemic spheres. Recent discoveries at the intersection of neurochemistry and biophysics have contributed to understanding the human mind by showing how informions (De Meester, 2018) are environmentally and interpersonally received and transmitted, and how they affect the human being and human behaviour. This new promising concept will be discussed in detail in this book's last chapters. It explains, to a considerable degree, why self-care and self-belonging may be a challenge to people, even when their development follows systemic social norms and/or their families are convinced about their proper caring. In such cases, irrespective of other people's actual intentions and attitudes, individuals tend to interpret their position in the community as inferior. They feel they are less important than others and are underappreciated and unhappy.

The power of group dynamic processes

The other area where exclusion is generated is comprised of dynamic group processes that result in the group regarding the individual as odd, even though s/he does not perceive him/herself as different from others in any way (Menzies and Davidson, 2002). Still, the members of the individual's significant group draw lines beyond which people are 'exiled', as otherness and the breaching of traditions or customs are not accepted. While the individual either does not discern differences or does not deem these as reasons for exclusion, group members provide the individual with verbal or nonverbal signals implying that s/he is not wanted or is less desirable than others in the group. The information that the individual is not accepted may also be kept secret (Nitsun, 1996). I know of a team at a workplace where six people shared the same office, but only four of them communicated within a closed group via an internal Internet forum. Exclusion from the forum was particularly cruel, as the two people who did not take part in these chats were ridiculed and censured 'live' and for their physical presence about how they talked, what they looked like and what vocabulary they used. One of the four people who mocked admitted to these practices since he regarded these as fully normal and justified. Of course, it did not take much to make him realise how hurtful and unfair such conduct is for those excluded and ridiculed. Still, without any external supervisor, the four colleagues had practised this type of ostracism for several months.

The interactional area—which encompasses changing conditions resulting from dynamic interactions between the individual and another person, group or ideas—may also produce exclusion. In a complex interplay of adopted group roles, situational factors and systemic aspects (e.g. traumatic events, limited resources, promotion of rivalry, stigmatising and dictatorship), exclusion may take place when access to the available resources is abruptly limited and, at the same time, a conflict erupts within the group (Chudzicka-Czupała, Grabowski and Wilczynska, 2017).

These three areas of influence tend to overlap in various ways and to various degrees. In order to identify the primary reason for an individual sense of exclusion, it is helpful to define in which of these realms the experience of exclusion is specifically rooted. In the following argument, these dimensions will be referred to when discussing support for positive growth and when presenting the ways and examples of growth and inclusion.

The case of Mark

Mark, as a teenager, enjoyed socialising with the group very much, although he was reluctant to speak up when engaged with others in it. When he became a student at a technical secondary school, he became embarrassed when he was supposed to talk about himself aloud or when he had to answer his teachers' questions. When taunted by his classmates, he did not know how to respond to them either.

He felt competent in a few areas and wanted others to recognise that. He was especially bent on making others realise that he knew about botany and was a sailing aficionado. Mark tried to join in such conversations. However, before he made up his mind to say anything, the subject had, as a rule, been dropped, and it did not make much sense to speak then. Occasionally, he managed to offer a remark or two, but, to his surprise, he noticed that almost nobody took notice of that—as if Mark were not there at all. This was particularly painful, not only because he tried speaking more clearly and loudly, but because it took him a lot of time to decide to speak in the first place. He usually voiced his remarks at rather inadequate moments. Subsequently, vicious circle continued: other people were already busy discussing another topic because his comments or questions came too late. This made Mark feel not only unnoticed, but also a misfit. Even when he endeavoured to imitate others and to behave like the rest of the group did, he still had a feeling that people looked at him in a strange way. He noticed that others met together without him after lessons. He also suspected that his classmates communicated on social media, to which he had no access. He was afraid to ask about these conversations and about joining them – as he expected either refusal or mockery. He came to realise that he could not even be a passive witness of conversations, since his schoolmates communicated via mobile gadgets and laptops. Mark felt completely excluded. He did not know what his peers talked about and, worse than that, he did not even know when they talked.

He was extremely sensitive to all signals – be it laughter he heard from individuals or the group or eyewinks. He alertly watched other boys' reactions to estimate his own current position. He sighed with relief when he saw them busy playing games rather than paying attention to him or ridiculing him. He stayed in silence and did not share his sensations with others, because he did not even know what exactly to share and how anybody could respond to him.

Mark's case is only one of many such school stories that could have had a different ending. However, because this phenomenon is difficult to discern by external observers, the severity of its effects—especially on young people whose minds are not firmly formed yet—tends to be grievously underestimated.

Children and teenagers who feel rejected from participating in groups tend to exclude others as well. They do so in a nearer or more remote future, whereby their actions are sometimes even more dramatic and retaliative. Consequently, they turn from victims into perpetrators. They are regressive perpetrators who did not obtain any help when they were being ostracised themselves (Garbarino, 1992, 1999). Tension, anger and often hatred towards their victimiser or victimisers increase and may boil over. Their accumulated anger and regret may be released in either uncontrolled or premeditated ways. If their rejection-related traumas have not been worked through—for example, with the aid of a psychologist—when they start their own families, then they may unknowingly work towards wrecking the relationship with their partners for fear of experiencing rejection anew and having to bear the unimaginable pain of it again.

Mark went into psychotherapy when he was nearing his fourties. He had grown up into a shy man. He had got married and had two children. His marriage had fallen apart after a dozen years or so, but he was still supporting his adult children and his ex-wife financially. He was also helping his brother, nephews and parents. He did not feel at ease in his family, as his brother was jealous of Mark's financial prosperity, and other relatives considered him an oddball. Mark was committed to his self-development in order to be able to enjoy his life. He did not have many friends, and he believed his subordinates and colleagues did not like him. When he turned 47, he developed a range of complaints, including his spine and muscle tone. He was often haunted by anxieties and obsessed with self-critical thoughts, had lost mental flexibility, felt tense all the time and was nervous before any professional meeting. He explained these symptoms to himself as effects of his difficult childhood—when he had felt abandoned to his own resources, with his parents absorbed in their own private matters and work. Mark was also interested in phytotherapy and natural medicine. In one therapy session following a week-long pre-notified absence, he announced that he had taken part in a meeting where psychedelic substances had been used. He had displayed an interest in research on the therapeutic effects of psilocybin even before. In the following sessions, he discussed the experiences of the ceremony he had attended with his therapist. Mark got an insight into his early childhood experiences. The key events included witnessing his older brother being sexually abused. Retrieving those difficult memories proved simpler and less painful than Mark had expected. The traumatic experiences were revealed to be the real reason for his self-stigmatisation, self-isolation, 'guilty' feelings and the sense of being responsible for other people in his life. In the following psychotherapeutic sessions, Mark gradually released himself from the grip of the constraining programmes which had formed in his mind as a young child and had persisted through most of his adulthood. The last stage of Mark's therapy involved reinforcing his new functioning model and supporting his self-soothing part, which was initially aided by the therapist and, on the completion of therapy, was continued by Mark himself.

Mark's case shows that the perceived reasons behind exclusion and the sense of belonging lie far deeper than at the level of conscious observation. Identifying them is thwarted by the programmes and schemas of action which result from them.

Interestingly, the causes of exclusion in adulthood usually do not depend on external circumstances and may only pair up with them. The power of disturbing or limiting schemas and shaking them off later hinge on individuals' personal sensitivity, on the quality of support from the social environment and on situations that these individuals come to experience.

Chapter 2

The roots of social exclusion

A disliked topic

Exclusion is not all people's conversational topic of choice. If you have personally experienced rejection, then the memory of it may continue to make you anxious and remind you of weaknesses, which were, or still are, not accepted by others and, more importantly perhaps, are not acceptable to you either (Corr, 2005). The process of social exclusion is known to often commence from the individual's subjective feeling that s/he is not sufficiently accepted and liked (Leary, Tambor, Terdal and Downs, 1995). Even adults find it difficult to admit when they realise that they themselves are disliked. In most cases, the reluctance to address this topic stems from self-dislike or self-doubts which one only becomes aware of when one embarks on intense self-scrutiny or goes into therapy.

Exclusion, which I examine in-depth in this book, usually originates in childhood or puberty. The fundamental role in identifying its existence or operation is played by the closest people who are important for the individual and his/her development. People scrutinise those around them and examine their own feelings in confrontation with other people, and if they experience dissonance between what they imagine about life and what actually happens in their lives, then they begin to doubt their own value (Baumeister and Leary, 1995). Of course, we might attribute these perceptions to the early bond between children and their caregivers, usually mothers, but this is not always the case. Sometimes, the opposite is actually true, as difficult and even traumatic childhood experiences do not translate into the sense of exclusion in later relationships (Rutter, 1987; Tugade, Fredricson and Barrett, 2004). Conversely, despite quite good bonding with the mother or the closest caregiver at an early stage of the development, the individual believes s/he does not fit in and does not belong.

The cultural context is an important factor in the emergence of the sense of exclusion and belonging. Today, people are reluctant to enter into new relationships or establish new acquaintances. Their unwillingness results less from the current lack of time and rather more from the fear that they will be hurt or not be able to sustain such relations over time in the future. Over the last decade, increasingly more interactions have only been momentary—engaged in fleetingly, and just to talk about one topic in a discussion group or to 'like' another person's statement on a forum.

In the global dimension, our society is becoming increasingly self-aware regarding individual self-improvement efforts. Previous decades predominantly witnessed rivalry, criticism and attempts at development for the sake of an external gratification, such as a better job, the employer's appreciation, etc. Recently, however, the focus of some people's endeavours has been shifting on self-acceptance among others. The situation of the pandemic underlined it clearly. As a parallel development, research findings have been confirming that mindfulness, self-love and self-acceptance, which improve health, focus and stress-coping outcomes, are becoming more popular (Bernardi et al., 2001). Interestingly, people find it difficult to bring these two dimensions together and grasp that they are strictly interdependent. The point is we cannot possibly strip ourselves of others' company and become immersed in meditative solitude outside of the community, even though this is what self-development courses often seek to teach us. The social and cultural settings tend to be interpreted as engendering stressful situations and painful experiences. Some people who are committed to practising mindfulness are in for a bitter disappointment since, in strongly stressful situations, the habits which were inculcated in childhood and adolescence prove more powerful than new neural connections developed through, for example, meditation. When experiencing strong emotions, people offen tend to fall back on old response patterns. This happens because in stress situations we act automatically through activating well-entrenched pathways of old programmes and schemas, because 'stressors and stress reaction' are mainly rooted in an individual emotional story from the past, which eludes one's awareness (Wilczyńska-Kwiatek, Bargiel-Matusiewicz and Łapiński, 2009).

In an effort to understand this process, most people ill-advisedly try even harder to isolate themselves from others and connect to their own selves by, for example, practicing meditative ways of coping with stress and undergoing Compassion Skills Training/Therapy. Rather, they would like to feel comfortable, liked, peaceful and harmonious. The presence of any other human being always makes it necessary to pay attention to, tolerate and accept others, which often seem irreconcilable with showering attention and acceptance on oneself (Simpson and Overall, 2014). More and more people need recognition, understanding and appreciation of their otherness. At the same time, fewer and fewer of them are capable of discerning and recognising the separateness and otherness of another person, since this requires not only special skills—such as empathy and emotional intelligence—but also an effort to perceive each human being as a unique individual. Such efforts are challenging because of personal defence mechanisms, intuitively acquired family and traditional stereotypes and group dynamics, which overshadow personal individualities in school and work settings. When internal codes are activated spontaneously by individuals, other people are viewed through the prism of their unwanted or unconscious features. We call this psychological phenomenon 'projection'.

Today's youth do not cultivate direct contact with one another (Twenge, 2017). Teenagers are less directly socially connected and more isolated. They use psychological support more often than ever in the past.

If not run by an experienced therapist, groups that are set up for the sake of mutual support and sharing experience are seldom visited by people who have experienced exclusion. Exclusion is associated with a very sensitive area of human functioning – a feeling which is extremely evanescent and often ungraspable, even by the person who experiences it. This feeling involves shame and enormous fear, which are felt whenever the person attempts to open up before others and share his/her space (Bartholomew, 1990). How deeply important it is for all of us to belong and to feel relevant at a certain stage in our lives will be shown below on the basis of research findings and the examples from my own 20-year-long psychotherapeutic practice.

At the level of global social discourse and political correctness, countries are challenged to ensure the rights of and to protect discriminated women, exploited workers, LGBT individuals, people of different skin colour and/or religion, socially disadvantaged groups, etc. However, exclusion, as discussed in this book, does not concern any particular community (without any tagging or labelling). Instead, it is understood as an experience of each and every individual. Whatever their group membership or social stigma may be, people who are rejected or whose needs were ignored in childhood continue a similar self-limitation in their adult lives or are subject to being limited by others.

Why do *Homo sapiens* exclude others?

In the evolutionary and social beginning of the world as *Homo sapiens*, we gained an edge in the world of animals, owing to our bigger and most efficient brains. The main purpose for which the human brain developed over thousands of years was to enable humans to effectively cope in various social situations and to manage themselves within the increasingly complex grid of human relationships.

Because it is the brain and, in particular, the brain's specialised faculties that make us stand out against other living creatures, the central nervous system has been especially zealously studied over the last four decades. Referred to as neuroscience, neuropsychology or neurocognitive studies, the disciplines of brain research—which are associated with many new discoveries in psychology—have robustly developed for the last 40 years (Gazzaniga, 2009; Gazzaniga, Ivry and Mangun, 2009). Advanced research has been fostered by the development of functional neuroimaging and the examination of brainwaves. Watching the brain at work, scientists investigate how its operations are linked to mental states. Nearly all studies have so far been informed by the notion that the mind is very intimately associated with the brain. Briefly, it is a common belief that it is in the brain where we should look for the sources and mechanisms of emotions, awareness and memory. As I will argue further in this book, the brain is responsible for and capable of showing us only a part of these complex cognitive-emotional processes.

Brain-focused neurobiological research has found that people use nearly 75% of the cerebral cortex to acquire and expand their general knowledge of the world and, above all, to analyse concrete information about other people and relations with them. Psychological research has shown that the data of the greatest importance to people include those concerning hazards to the continuation of relationships they have with others. By the same token, human beings have been found to actually be oversensitive to potential exclusion from relationships, for example, through being rejected, unseen, ignored or dysregulated (Kerr and Levine, 2008).

Having been committed to psychotherapeutic work for over 25 years now, I have often seen that knowledge about other people or about relationships alone is not enough to competently manage relations with others. Admittedly, people can master emotion management, but this skill is by no means a guarantee of the effective building, sustaining and terminating of relationships. Despite their diagnostic and therapeutic expertise regarding relationships, clinical psychologists and psychotherapists realise that, usually, they have no influence over the emotions they experience. They use those emotions in work with patients, for example, to recognise countertransference.

Emotions, as well as unreflectingly formed stereotypes and prejudices to which they contribute, unfold in the part of the mind which is not fully recognised and conscious. How people behave in particular situations is often determined by intuition or by a specific sense of 'proximity' or 'distance'. This is illustrated by an experiment in which people were assembled in one room; the light was switched off, and, when it was turned on again, the participants were asked to approach a person/people of their choice. Intriguingly, although the people formed pairs or small groups in an intuitive and spontaneous way, it turned out that they had some experiences in common.

In the period of maturation, young people are far more likely to experience feelings of being excluded and to fail to cope with them when in adulthood. Various conditions behind this phenomenon will be discussed in the following chapters of this book. Its ramifications can indeed be dramatic because, as the maturing human nervous system is incapable of fully protecting youngsters, they begin to pose a threat both to themselves—to their integration and security—and to others. When their development starts to stabilise, they can fall back on their 'survival' mechanisms when striving to function in the social world.

Young people often fail to differentiate between what is genuinely relevant to their development now and what is important for their future.

There are traits which help people cope in relationships and understand others and their feelings. The empathetic skills of compassion and mirroring emotions were also of key importance in the past, when close collaboration with the group was a *sine qua non* of individual survival. When living in rather small and isolated groups of 100 to 150 individuals, people certainly found it easier to communicate and to arrive at an agreement than is the case today. In the course of time, interhuman constellations were changing. As societies were developing, human beings and their brains were developing too. At every stage in the development of humankind, there were different frameworks for excluded group members. Those who did not fit in were assigned their place, or rather their non-place, outside of the group. Individuals who failed either to emotionally cope with adjustment or to share emotions felt by others were usually deemed incompatible with the group. In the past, considerable group cohesion fostered certain social and cultural contexts which were far more easily recognisable or more directly sensed than what seems true today. Social exclusion concerned not only the members who differed in appearance or physical capacity, but also those who differed in the ways of 'adjustment'—specifically in their emotional adaptation.

In our times, people's social functioning is far more difficult, because the circumstances of living, though far more comfortable than ever before in many respects, are also less predictable.

The traditional Attachment Theory states that we begin to learn how to be in relationships on the day we are born—first, in our relations with mother and then with the closest kin. The totality of these experiences forms a certain logical gate for the individual, a prism through which s/he will perceive the world later on. However, we also learn as adults who are in relations with other people. This is a lifelong process.

Research has found that young people who self-exclude have acutely experienced exclusion. Intentional exclusion of others is chiefly implemented by teenage girls who deliberately hurt others either by ignoring or by disseminating hostile rumours about them. This also helps them maintain control over the group and make sure that they themselves do not become victims of exclusion again (Benenson, Markovits, Thompson and Wrangham, 2011; Wilczyńska, 2020). The wound of exclusion is usually sore in people's adult lives; it reduces their self-esteem, their experience of pleasure, their empathy for others, their prosocial engagement and, generally, their quality of life with others. Those who have painfully experienced exclusion tend to inadvertently destroy their later bonds and relationships with others, similarly to children from alcohol-affected families who choose partners with a drinking problem in their grown-up lives.

Boys and men differ from women in coping with the risk of exclusion. As a rule, they self-isolate in the world of computer games and pornographic films, through which they strive to satisfy their needs. Without fully realising this, they select virtual scenarios that help them vent off their aggression, divert their minds or calm down. However, as argued by Philip Zimbardo and Nikita Coulombe in *Man Disconnected*, such interactions are not neutral but rather contribute to other personal and social problems (Zimbardo and Coulombe, 2015).

All human beings and all social groups in various parts of our world are oriented to particular information from their environment and secondarily subjected to the impact of the media, films, advertisements and other transmitters. Such an 'influence', which they choose wittingly or unwittingly, is popularly referred to as 'brainwash'. The hermeneutics of media messages has its upsides and downsides. The upsides, such as information about events happening across the world, are largely associated with a deceptive sense of security or an illusion of control.

Video games, television series scripts, song lyrics and literary texts add up to a new wave of invasive and permanent cultural education which can hardly be dodged, because media users believe in the illusory 'freedom' of choice. To stand a chance of acquiring self-knowledge and communing with one's true self, one would basically have to cut all the ties with the world and, in particular, with other people. As aptly summed up by Henry David Thoreau, the author and protagonist of *Walden: or, Life in the Woods*: 'I went to the woods because I wished to live deliberately, to front only the essential facts of life and to see if I could not learn what it had to teach, and not, when I came to die, discover that I had not lived. I did not wish to live what was not life, living is so dear; nor did I wish to practice resignation, unless it was quite necessary'.

Today, computer games, which are played by young people and especially by boys, are supposed to be this separate realm, a modern 'equivalent' of the woods. When playing, one can handle the challenges of nature on one's own or 'situate oneself' in the virtual world of entertainment and rivalry. Narrative video games emulate real-life situations in which the players have an impression of not only 'reading a novel', but also of creating it by making their own decisions. The range of these decisions is nevertheless predetermined by the game designers. However, this makes games even more engrossing, as the situations the users face and the dilemmas they must solve when playing create an illusion of choice and freedom. As such, games can be treated on equal footing with other discursive forms, and their textual worlds are interpreted in ways that their literary counterparts are (Kłosiński, 2017). How the users participate in games and how they play them depends on their hermeneutical competencies, that is, on their knowledge, experience and awareness of social norms. Bringing into the game their personal standards and worldviews, the users rely on them to give a specific shape to the 'non-predesigned' elements, such as the vision of the protagonist whose role they themselves adopt. However, the content they share and absorb, rather than being something new, replicates their beliefs, stereotypes and aspirations in various ways, resembling a conversation in which the same subject is mulled over time and again.

Expectedly, any departure from such a social 'conversation' not only undermines the entrenched world order, but also, primarily perhaps, is iconoclastic and emotionally hits other interlocutors—members of a given community. Alternative and original modes of thinking expose triviality and commonness. Otherness can be punished with exclusion—a defensive or offensive response from the majority or often from the leader of this interdependent majority.

The brain, the heart and the mind

Two worlds coexist and overlap in the lives of contemporary human beings: one of them is the biological and genetic world, and the other is the physical and memetic/cultural world. Humans function in and through a constellation of biologically provided features, but they also modify them on the basis of individually lived experiences.

Science is littered with a plethora of neuro-myths that have obscured or entirely diverted scholarly attention from the essentials. I will first outline my own position and then revisit new approaches in detail in the concluding part of this book. Alongside the call to engage in multidisciplinary research, I will present the principles of human psychophysical nature and discuss the concept which undertakes the challenge of explaining the cellular, molecular, physical and neurochemical mechanisms behind individuals' emotions, feelings and thinking.

Before discussing the core of the matter, we can usefully evoke Paul Martin's biopsychosocial conception (1997). Martin has highlighted that both health and the perception of health depend on the person's mental and emotional condition. Martin aptly concludes that the human mind not only influences the perception of reality, but also that it is possible to change this reality through the system of interrelated chemical and electrical processes: 'The mind can affect our susceptibility to real physical diseases by modifying our behaviour or by directly influencing our immune defences to which it is connected via electrical and chemical pathways' (p. 80). 'The mind-immunity connections have been demonstrated and replicated in so many ways and in so many laboratories that they can no longer be considered even mildly controversial' (p. 116).

Dr Fabien De Meester ventures even further in his analyses and explains how neurochemical and psychophysical processes interact in the human body in people's life environments (i.e. space) across time. The brain, a perfectly trained organ that manages and controls the human organism and human mental efforts, is indeed responsible for biological processes and most of the cognitive ones. However, unconscious emotional processes (a part of the mind) mainly commence in the heart—a hypothesis which will be developed later in this book (De Meester, 2018, 2019).

The experience of the sense of exclusion should be explored not only as a complex concept which subsumes an individual's functioning and coping in the social world, but also holistically, that is, taking into account both physical and mental aspects (i.e. the spiritual and emotional experience of the world, as well as the organisation of cognitive functions) in situations wherein a person loses or lacks the sense of belonging to this world. The most spectacular examples of the exclusion experience include social situations in which people are ignored, ridiculed and rejected, when it is impossible for them to take advantage either of the psychosocial benefits of group membership or of learning from the feelings through which they are going.

People respond to situations of exclusion, therein to ostracism and rejection, by developing significant somatic symptoms. Exclusion is even sometimes called a 'social death'. Anticipated exclusion is a 'kiss of death', as it bears a very palpable risk of its actualisation (Wesselmann and Williams, 2017). Confronted with death or its harbingers, the body incrementally or suddenly stops feeling pain and 'experiences' coldness and alienation without any hope for change and for a return among the living (Zhong and Leonardelli, 2008; DeWall and Baumeister, 2006; Garbarino, 1999). The body dies, or its isolated parts get sick. Excluded people are more likely to die from infectious diseases, cancers, liver disease, accidents, overdoses, heart problems and others (Aldrigde et al., 2018).

Identifying our hidden minds

In recent years, we have been witnessing an increase in the consciousness of and the interest in new theories which account for how the body is related to the mind. Scholars have been particularly preoccupied with the concepts which seek to explain what is referred to as a memory of previous generations. One of them has been proposed by Professor Kerry Ressler, a psychiatrist and neurobiologist at the Emory University School of Medicine in Atlanta, who conducted long-term observations among American inner-city dwellers addicted to drugs or suffering from various neuropsychiatric diseases.

Consistently with other research, his study concluded that there must be a kind of intergenerational transmission. It provided an overview of the main and currently understood types of epigenetic regulation, including DNA methylation (Howie, Rijal and Ressler, 2019) connected with possible reactions to trauma (see Bierer et al., 2020).

In a series of experiments on mice, Ressler showed that emotions—at least the negative ones—which were experienced by one generation could impact the lives of descendants. By exposing the rodents to a pleasant smell and giving them mild electric shocks at the same time, he produced an association between the scent and pain. He repeatedly applied this combination of stimuli until the mice started to respond to the smell which they had initially liked with fear, even when it was no longer accompanied by electroshocks. To the researchers' surprise, the young of these mice reacted to the beloved cherry-like odour with fear, like their parents, looking for a getaway.

An interesting and still not widely known concept has been developed by Fabien de Meester, a biochemist and a philosopher. I have closely watched his work for over ten years and often collaborated with him on various research projects. De Meester's theory convincingly argues that the mind came first and the body only followed later (De Meester, 2019).

Psychophysical and biochemical tests prove that every individual's entire experience is in fact recorded in their body. This record can translate into how the person feels in a given environment, with him/herself, as well as how other people feel with him/her. This rather original and novel proposition put forward by De Meester is grounded on reliable knowledge, analyses and research findings (De Meester, 2018, 2019). Meticulous clinical measurements—for example, SQUID (i.e. the Superconducting Quantum Interference Device) which serves to measure magnetic fields—unambigu-unambiguously confirm that there is a field of magnetic information that stretches up to several metres around every human being.

So far, speculation has been rife as to where exactly and how traumas (especially very early traumas) and other intense experiences are registered in the human body. De Meester's research (2013, 2018) proves that fatty acids of cell membranes bear the inscription of what is known as forgotten memory (RAM/the heart's black box), the processor (CPU/astrocytes in the brain) and the vector of expression (ROM/red blood cells to and from organs/peripheral tissues), which are supposed to ultimately determine human functioning. Unsaturated fatty acids of cell membranes or, more precisely, their double allylic bonds have the capacity to absorb and emit tytes of information (–1, 0, +1) in a fractal way (ibid.). De Meester has shown how fatty acids are instrumental in recording information in the human body. The entire concept appears so evident that it is indeed surprising that nobody figured this out before, even though solving this riddle may help us to understand and to considerably improve people's mental and physical functioning.

Fatty acids, which regulate functions of the mind, are contained in all human cells, similarly to nucleic acids in genes, which determine people's bodily functions (Wilczyńska, 2019). As reported by De Meester, fatty acids are synchronised with brain waves and can express them and affect them.

Some of these lipids were formed first and make up the fixed and rigid structures in the heart. The primary and highly emotionally marked information that is recorded in these works as a selection sieve for other incoming information later in life, allowing only certain aligned data to go through. The details of this process as a biochemical and psychophysical phenomenon are provided in Part III. This psychological mechanism is referred to as a programme or a schema in this book.

EEG records indicate that neuronal networks exhibit characteristic rhythmical activities in various frequency bands. At the neuronal level, this process takes place when the activity of excitatory and inhibitory neurons is synchronised. This neuronal activity depends on chemical and physical processes in every cell and in the entire human body, as well as on people's time-space of existence, including their relations with other living creatures.

According to the proposed concept, the exclusion-oriented mind (i.e. emotions, beliefs) is registered as a substrate that circulates in a person's body based on the biochemical structures and triggers psychophysical processes such as the magnetic field. This substrate is produced by the activity of electrons around unsaturated fatty acids of red blood cells that circulate in the body. One characteristic of fatty acids is that they are capable of carrying chemical and physical information. The body (i.e. the heart and the brain), which is unchangeable in its structure at a given moment, resonates with the physical emission of the Schumann frequency (De Meester, 2019). The heart's electric field is very strong, about 60 times as strong as that generated by the brain, which cooperates with the heart. This resonance is observed as waves in ECG and EEG recordings. The mind issues instructions for the body, due to which the physical information (i.e. mind/electron spins) can interact with the chemical information (i.e. body/genes). As a result, this influences the transcription of genes and, ultimately, people's behaviour (De Meester, 2013, 2018).

De Meester (2013, 2018) has found language codes included in sounds and letters of the English alphabet that correspond to the capacities of respective fatty acids and to the possibilities of their processing. This means that language and thoughts (using words) and emotions (especially their expression) are recorded/coded in the body. They are transferable and readable self-consciously, consciously or unconsciously. How this can happen is described later in this book. For me, the role of fatty acids in psychological processes has been the most illuminating and powerful discovery of the last decade. I am of the opinion that we can finally clarify human mental processes, both those unfolding at the present moment as well as those involving memories. Similarly, at long last, we can uncover the mechanism of the most fascinating, forgotten or transgenerational messages and decipher how they are transmitted, coded, developed and changed.

These analyses and novel concepts require empirical confirmation, which I hope will be provided soon. Given the detailed calculations on which they are based, they are likely to serve several scholars as a strong incentive for further research.

Chapter 3

Psychosocial issues of social exclusion

Special psychological phenomena in our societies

Social exclusion has its social, economic and political connotations. It is worth highlighting this phenomenon in the dimension in which it is identified and treated by nations and communities.

In Europe, the notion of social exclusion first appeared in the 1970s. Back then, it served to capture a new form of poverty and was linked to the practice of conventional social policies (Szarfenberg, 2006). How social exclusion was defined was largely determined by the socioeconomic and political context of a given country. It was unsurprising, as societies whose development was fuelled by utopian socialist ideals demanded the complete equality of people even at the cost of freedom. As the socio-economic transition commenced in Poland in the early 1990s, its social policy made 'combating' and 'removing' social exclusion its major goals. Because Poland's previous system had 'banned' any possibility of joblessness, 'there was work for everybody'. Everybody could have a job, even if that, in fact, meant the rise of what was referred to as 'hidden unemployment'.

Consequently, unemployment and/or homelessness were directly and immediately identified as a pathological or dysfunctional lifestyle. In the 1990s, excluded people tended to be described as 'a social stratum of little significance, which consists of individuals who live parasitic lives, are derailed and breach the rules of law and the norms of social life' (Szymczak, 1992, p. 108).

Social exclusion concerned people whose nonadaptive lifestyles made them irretrievably use up or destroy social and material resources, instead of contributing to the increase of social goods. The socially excluded group was thought to be comprised mostly of homeless and/or unemployed people who did not take the jobs they were offered, even though under socialist Poland, not only jobs were offered, but also accommodations were guaranteed. Such people lived on state-provided benefits. They embodied the anti-dependent attitude, as they illogically and rebelliously opposed the communistic values of 'good and dignity' by choosing their own incomprehensible and 'parasitic' ways of living.

Historically speaking, societies did not practise indiscriminate exclusion. Exclusion concerned, first and foremost, weaker individuals and individuals whose conduct differed from that of others. In recent concepts propounded in various parts of the world, the notion of exclusion has served to depict contemporary forms of social disadvantage (Baumeister et al., 2007; Levitas, 2005; Levitas et al., 2007; Silver, 2006). It has been employed as a useful conceptual framework that helps to operationalise the persistent theme of 'the importance of social structures and belonging in determining human welfare' (Todman et al., 2009, p. 330).

The definitions of social exclusion—as developed by the European Union over the last decade—have prioritised equal opportunity of development and work. They emphasise that the risk of social exclusion, above all, consists of restricting the person's development as a result of his/her incapacity to perform certain social roles and of unequal access to goods and services which are available to others. For this reason, the policy of the European Union member states was, and largely still is, geared to eliminating these differences. Exclusion can concern various age-, status- and health-groups. It can affect both young school dropouts and/or university graduates who cope with difficulties due to the lack of experience and livelihoods or, for that matter, single mothers who raise their children and have jobs at the same time. According to this definition, social exclusion also looms for immigrants who have arrived in a host country without relevant qualifications and/or a sound command of the local language. It may also concern members of sexual minorities and religious groups whose rights are not equal in practice to the rights of the rest of society.

Social exclusion is not a favourite subject either in Europe or in the United States. It triggers a specific agitation, because people are uncertain about to what extent they can safely express their individual beliefs, which are often rooted in stereotypes and traditions, rather than in the projects their communities promote. The young generation—which is referred to as the iGEN—as a rule, professes equality, tolerance and respect for otherness, although they are less than willing to make sacrifices for the sake of these values, as revealed in recent research by Jean Twenge (2017).

The model of situational awareness

An interesting framework for the study of human functioning is provided by the Situational Awareness Theory in which people's behaviours in a given situation are explored as an effect of social forces, systemic or ideological assumptions and the spontaneously unfolding situation. The model of situational awareness was developed by Philip Zimbardo on the basis of his experiences from the Stanford Prison Experiment (1971) and from his work as a court expert on prisoner abuse in Abu Ghraib during the Iraq

War (Zimbardo, 2008). Insisting that the frameworks in which people function are imposed by systems and governments, Zimbardo concluded: 'War is all about old men wanting young men to kill other young men, but we only want them to kill them when they are there; when they come back, we don't want them to become killers. That's why we put men in uniforms'. Zimbardo explained that if the systemic forces—among which he counted poverty, racism and military arrangements (e.g. such as those implemented in Abu Ghraib prison)—were not recognised and changed, individual punishments for deviant and/or harmful acts would never remove the problem of misconduct (Zimbardo, 2007).

The tortures perpetrated by American soldiers at the Abu Ghraib prison in Iraq were a tragic outcome of their purported anonymity, their feeling of not being personally accountable and the military commanders' tacit consent—that is, conditions under which good people have been shown, in a series of experiments, to be prone to do evil things.

Zimbardo argues that people's feelings and behaviours under threat are determined by three groups of factors: individual, situational and systemic. While each of these forces can be separately examined, any sound exploration of a situation must be based on its assessment involving the perspectives of all of the actors involved. The individual brings into a situation his/her unique personal traits, such as expectations, past experiences, religious attitudes, etc. The individual's expectations can produce verbal and nonverbal behaviours that provoke other people to act in given ways (Zimbardo, 2012). The impact of situations hinges not so much on their objective features, but rather on how individuals perceive and interpret the situation at hand and on what meanings they attribute to it. In Zimbardo's framework, the system is an ensemble of rules and norms that are formally or informally instituted, including the legal system and the system of group norms. The influence of the system on people's functioning tends to be difficult to detect, and it can derive from the authority of those in power and/or from group dynamics. The model of situational awareness highlights the relevance of the awareness of the situation as a skill of scrutinising this situation from various perspectives on which the way of handling it largely depends (Zimbardo, 2008).

The model of situational awareness sheds light on the context of perpetrators who exclude but are not necessarily evil by definition; rather, they may simply be more susceptible to influence and are dependent on their environments, which are 'indispensable' for their survival. They need others because they themselves may have suffered in the past, and they use the mechanisms they themselves hated vis-à-vis other people. The model also accounts for the context of those excluded whom the situation of exclusion fits like a glove. People perceive and shape social reality in their minds. Confronted with the risk of social exclusion, individual awareness and situational/systemic awareness differ yet complement each other. Individuals tend to perceive their situation solely from one perspective, and, since they fail to notice any other possible scenario, they do not break the sequence of the developments. Rather, they become even more entrenched both in their own perception of the situation and in the emotions and behaviours that they exhibit in and towards the group or another person. The perpetrator—a group or an individual—is 'blind' to the excluded one and acts in ways believed to be self-defensive. This primary evolutionary mechanism has been preserved and still effectively functions among society members. The failure to perceive the situation from many different perspectives at the same time reduces the coping capacity both of those doing the excluding and of those excluded.

Stigmatisation and the systemic bearing of stigma

Situations in which individuals at risk of social exclusion become targets of stigmatisation or feel stigmatised can be usefully studied in terms of the Labelling Theory. Labelling is an additional aspect of exclusion, which is generated by sociopolitical systems and economies. Labelling Theory derives from the concept of the looking-glass self, which was propounded by Charles H. Cooley, who defined the self as dependent on feedback and opinions obtained from others (Aronson, Wilson and Akert, 1997, p. 250). Cooley argued that one's self-image was produced in interactions between the individual and the environment. As this framework is associated with symbolic interactionism, it tends to be described as an interactionist approach (Kojder, 1980, p. 46). This Labelling Theory is considered to have been inspired by Edwin Lemert, who claimed that deviance arose as a result of socially imposed control.

In 1963, Howard Becker in his book *Outsiders* attributed the genesis of deviance to social groups that institute particular norms and rules. He famously stated that 'deviance is not a quality of the act a person commits, but rather a consequence of the application by others of rules and sanctions to an "offender"' (Becker, 1963, p. 9). On this take, the deviance of a given behaviour is only determined by the social response it induces. If there is no response, then the behaviour is not regarded as deviant even if it objectively breaches the norm. Individuals are known to begin to behave in conformity with others' judgements of them—for example, adopting the labels ascribed to them (e.g. a teenager caught by a teacher smoking a random cigarette and hence deemed to be a violator of social norms begins to flout social norms indeed as a consequence of the very fact of being stigmatised as such). People subjected to labelling may fashion negative self-images, which later affect their overall conduct.

Concepts of labelling state that the socially imposed stigma is usually irrevocable and brands the person throughout her/his lifetime. In his discussion of stigma, Erving Goffman shows who a deviant is in terms of perpetrating the offence. He depicts a stigmatised person as a 'normal deviant'.

Every society has its own ways of classifying its members. What categories of persons are established in a society depends on specific social relations and arrangements. As Goffman views it, 'stigma' means everything that disturbs 'normal' social intercourse. Stigma can be caused by a wide range of factors, including sexual orientation, having a court sentence, occupation (e.g. prostitution) or a lack of income possibilities. Goffman distinguishes three types of stigma (Goffman, 1986, p. 4):

- physical stigma – deformities of the body, bodily ugliness;
- stigma of individual functioning – 'blemishes of individual character' associated with the person's insufficient resolve, surrender to dangerous drives, dishonesty, harmful beliefs, alcoholism, unemployment and/or radical political behaviours; and
- tribal stigma linked to nationality, race or religion, which is handed down from generation to generation.

Stigma is connected to the relationship between the stigmatised subject and his/her environment. The two parties usually limit their mutual contact to the necessary minimum that they both tolerate. As a result, the 'stigmatised' person may feel jealous, envious, angry, suspicious, dejected and confused.

Following Goffman, we could posit that rejection by the peer group may be regarded as a kind of 'stigma', a unique tool by means of which the social hierarchy within a group is to be maintained. We can understand stigma as a part of a moral code which helps to keep people on the right or expected side in their society.

During the Covid-19 pandemic, we have perceived a new kind of stigma. Some people and groups have been and may still be experiencing stigma. Among the groups that are at risk of social exclusion are: people who have travelled (especially from Asia), healthcare professionals and people who have already had the virus. Common ways of exclusion are social avoidance, ostracism, rejection, refusal of housing or employment and physical violence (https://www.cdc.gov/coronavirus/2019-ncov/daily-life-coping/reducing-stigma).

In view of the concepts briefly outlined above, the examination of people's functioning when at risk of exclusion should start from the assumption that the classification of individual behaviour as 'deviant' depends on how others respond to it. In this book, people's ways of coping are explored in terms of the individual's perspective—more specifically, how the individual perceives the interplay of risks, potentials and prospects of successfully handling the situation.

Modern increases in the rates of depression and attempted suicides

Over the last two decades, depression has been spreading across the globe. Worldwide, about 300 million people suffer from depression. Close to one bilion people have different mental disorders. The World Health Organisation forecasts an estimate that by 2030 depression will top morbidity charts (now depression is the second most frequent disease) (https://www.who.int/news-room/fact-sheets/detail/depression).

Depression is also a serious health issue in Poland. According to the official statistics, there are at least 1.8 million depression patients in Poland (WHO Report, 2017). In the age group of 20- to 40-year-olds, 38% suffer from depression. According to Professor Filip Rybakowski of the Adult Psychiatry Clinic, Medical University in Poznan, depression is in fact a far more serious and widespread problem in Poland than suggested by the official statistics, as it afflicts at least 7.5 million Poles.

Women are twice as likely to develop depression as men. Besides, almost 1.5 million Poles suffer from anxiety (ibid.) and thousands of people from other mental disorders. A similar percentage of depression and anxiety is reported in many states around the world. In the Covid-19 pandemic, depression and anxiety are rising dramatically. In April 2020, there was a threefold increase in the prevalence of symptoms of depression in Ethiopia compared to the estimates from before the epidemic. During the pandemic, 47% of Canadian healthcare workers have reported a need for psychological support. In China, healthcare workers have reported very high rates of depression (50%), anxiety (45%) and insomnia (34%) (https://www.who.int/news-room/detail/14-05-2020-substantial-investment-needed-to-avert-mental-health-crisis).

Among these, depression is the major concern of politicians and healthcare services globally since its ramifications for engagement in work life are most severe.

The 2018 report of the NIK (Naczelna Izba Kontroli/Supreme Audit Office) showed that the Polish healthcare system was ineffective in depression treatment services. In the Mazovia Province, one of Poland's major provinces, the waiting time for medical depression consultation was 47 days. In 2020, during the pandemic, many mental health facilities were converted into care facilities for people with Covid-19. Some community services—self-help groups for drug and alcohol dependence—were unable to meet for several months.

Suicide attempt rates have also soared above all-time records. Reports directly state that 'it does not seem possible to reduce all the risk factors in the incidence of depressive disorders' ("Programme Zapobiegania Depresji w Polsce na lata 2016–2020"). Suicide is the second leading cause of death among 15- to 29-year-olds.

Polish research has shown that major risk factors in depression include excessive, long-lasting stress, a quick pace of living, a lack of leisure time, excessive responsibilities, work overload, loneliness and a lack of interaction or shallow interactions with others (e.g. only Internet-based relations). Besides, the risk of depression is increased by biological factors, such as alcohol and substance abuse, sleep deficiency, insufficient rest and inappropriate nutrition (Feliksiak and Omyła-Rudzka, 2018). People who report financial difficulties, poor living conditions, unemployment or inactivity and lack of support from others are also more prone to depression. Additionally, individual predispositions, transgenerational trauma transmissions and traumatic experiences in early childhood are conducive to developing depression.

Depression is also diagnosed in the United States as the most fequent mental disorder that contributes to exclusion from social and family life. The American National Mental Health Institute reports that almost 25% of adult Americans grapple with mental health problems, such as anxiety and depression. According to the analyses of a United States Non-Governmental Organisation, as many as 70–90% of the American population suffering from mental disorders (i.e. people aged 18–69 years old) have quit work (www.nami.org).

Russia is one of the countries with the highest depression rates, as reported by Professor Stanislav Poltorak of the St Petersburg V.M. Bekhterev Psychoneurological Research Institute, and has the highest rate of male suicides in the world. The average suicide rate stood at 26.5 deaths per 100,000 people—therein 48.3 males and 7.5 females—in Russia in 2016. In comparison, the equivalent figure in the corresponding period was 2.7 for the United Arab Emirates and 13.7 for Poland.

Besides depression diagnoses, a new disorder will soon be officially recognised—diagnosing difficulties in job performance. Starting on 1 January 2022, a new World Health Organisation (WHO) classification of diseases will come into force. This classification includes professional burnout, that is, a syndrome comprised of depleted energy or exhaustion, decreased professional effectiveness and negative work-related emotions. Chronic psychosocial stress—which is characteristic of burnout—cripples people's individual and social functioning outcomes, interferes with cognitive capacities and affects the neuroendocrinal systems, eventually leading to evident changes in the anatomy and functions of the brain. The construct of professional burnout was first proposed by Christina Maslach. Currently Professor Emeritus of the University of California in Berkeley and the world's leading burnout researcher, Maslach began to study this new phenomenon in the 1970s. Published in *Human Behaviour* in 1976, her 'Burned-Out' revealed the scope of this phenomenon and its severe consequences for people in the field of work life.

People who are not noticed and recognised at work and perform jobs that are incompatible with them are not only less engaged in their work, but are also more susceptible to diseases. Even if organisms seem to adaptively respond to stress, chronic stress is usually pathogenic. When defence energies are continually activated and squandered, possible effects include muscle atrophy, chronic fatigue and increased susceptibility to metabolic diseases in adulthood, such as diabetes (Sapolsky, 2004, 2010). In the past, unreleased and enhanced muscle tension helped our ancestors flee from danger. However, nowadays, permanently elevated blood pressure and stress-caused metabolic disorders debilitate the human cardiovascular system, gradually causing circulatory diseases and other degenerative disorders.

A classic experiment carried out on rats that were kept in a cage with a running mill found that the lives and health of these animals depended on whether or not they could decide about their activity, rather than on the activity which they actually performed. Specifically, the rats were situated so that one of them could run whenever it felt like doing so, while the other was harnessed to its companion that decided for both of them. Observations concluded that the brain of the former rat—the one that could control its activity—developed new neurons. The latter rat lost some of its neurons because, even though the animal was doing something allegedly useful to its brain (e.g. physical activity), it had no control over its actions (in Carmichael, 2009). The stress involved in task performance also results from the fact that the way in which it is to be performed has been imposed and is incompatible with the person's capacities. In recent years, the concept of the sense of belonging has also been espoused by the psychology of business, and increasingly more companies make arrangements for their employees to work in individual systems of their choice. This increases not only their sense of appreciation and the recognition of their needs, but also their commitment to work.

People with depression have a strong feeling of emotional and social separateness. They do not discern the continuity, the logic and even the point of life. The more they perceive their world as chaotic and disorganised—which, on the other hand, entails freedom and ample options to choose from—the less secure they feel. This entails activating control and alertness, which is obviously not helpful, because they meet demands which were set for them or imprinted in the process of upbringing. The feeling of being unlovable and unworthy in the inner self (i.e. socially excluded) is their own truth.

Given this, prevention is exigent, which means that parents, teachers and therapists must help children and adolescents feel included in oneness – one living human organism sharing the same history, experiences and common ancestors. The focus on the 'We' rather than on the 'I' changes the perspective of thinking of oneself as part of a system—a system that supports all of its members without exception.

Changing the perspective on depression

Depression, which involves a severely reduced experience of emotions (especially the pleasant ones), can actually be associated with a fuller and deeper reception of external stimuli and increased cognitive inquisitiveness. Professor Bettina von Helversen and her four colleagues have shown that people with elevated depression levels make better and more thoroughly thought-through decisions involving cognitive analysis and perseverance (Helversen et al., 2011). In their studies, the depression level in respondents was established by means of questionnaires; one of them was Beck's Depression Scale. The sample was divided into three groups: healthy respondents, respondents with depression and recovering respondents. They were given a simulation computer game task that explored the 'secretary problem' concerning the selection of the best candidate for the job. Each 'candidate's' application was presented separately, and the right selection decision was awarded 'payments'. The assignment made it possible to compare how much the respondents in each of the three groups (healthy, depressive and recovering) approximated the optimal task-performance strategy. In the experiment, the healthy respondents had the lowest scores as they found fewer candidates and gave up on searching earlier. The respondents with depression and those recovering from it were more meticulous in their searches and made decisions that brought them more payments in the game.

Such research findings highlight an extremely important fact. Namely, a person with depression gives information about their own deeper view into situations around. The onset of depression is a clear harbinger of an organism's readiness to engage in cognitive work, which may lead to emotional numbness—indifference—when ignored. The time in which first, non-clinical depression symptoms appear can be considered an effective period for self-development work. This is corroborated by studies that have shown that people's cognitive and insight capacities are enhanced in this period. Besides, the first symptoms are warnings against plunging in helplessness, and, as such, they should be given special emphasis in prevention brochures.

Self-exclusion 2020 and the pandemic of fear

Since the threat of the SARS-Covid-19 infection appeared, and a state of pandemic was proclaimed, fear has been the dominant mental disorder across societies. According to the latest survey carried out by the University of Southern California, about 40% of the population are scared of the pandemic, and more than half of them avoid some or all other people (April, 2020). In 2020 and in comparison to the 2018 NHIS sample, adults in the United States in April 2020 were eight times more likely to fit the criteria for serious mental illness (27.7% vs. 3.4%) and three times more likely to fit criteria for moderate or serious mental illness (70.4% vs. 22.0%) (Twenge, and Joiner, 2020). Basically, almost all people across the world have been pressed to practise social distancing and self-isolation. This drastically changes the World Health Organisation statistics, with the new official data still unavailable as of this moment.

Polish pandemic-time surveys show that what Poles are most scared of is that their loved ones will contract the disease (over 70% of the respondents), and the other causes of fear include the market meltdown and financial crisis, overcrowded hospitals and the impotent healthcare system. Poles are also afraid that the virus will spread too rapidly, because some people do not observe the recommendations and rules in place. Fears are mainly reported by big-city dwellers and by females more frequently than by males. Respondents with lower education levels tend to be less afraid of the coronavirus-related risks than people with secondary and university education.

Psychologists warn that the coronavirus pandemic declared in 2020 may cause a worldwide anxiety epidemic. This particularly concerns certain types of disorders, including obsessive-compulsive disorder (OCD), generalised anxiety disorder (GAD), social anxiety disorder (SAD), agoraphobia, acute stress disorder (ASD) and separation-related anxiety disorder.

Similarly, the pandemic may take a grim toll on the health of depression and paranoia patients. Undoubtedly, it will have a deep impact on the elderly, people who are lonely, care home residents who are remote from their families and all those who cannot be visited on a regular basis (Peisah et al., 2020).

Yet, in all likelihood, the pandemic will particularly gravely affect the youngest generation. Contemporary children have already been labelled a C generation, because the coronavirus pandemic and the conditions of life/survival it produces are bound to be the dominant trauma of their childhood. They are exposed to heightened fear for their own and their loved one's health and life, accumulated stressful and anxiety-laden situations linked to isolation at home, traumas caused by violence from family members, separation from others (especially family and peers), constrained movement and the deprivation of stimuli due to spending several hours a day in front of the computer screen and the impossibility to go outside.

An even larger number of school-based mental health services is needed among the LGBTQ youth. These are likely used by intersectionally marginalised LGBTQ youth, such as racial and ethnic minorities, the homeless, undocumented immigrants and those from backgrounds of low socio-economic status (Golberstein, Wen and Miller, 2020; Peisah et al., 2020).

In years to come, the consequences of pandemic self-exclusion may basically be experienced by everybody, including people who do not report mental problems yet do fear for their future and the future of their families and the world as such. This will certainly be more challenging to people with limited adaptive skills, those who feel helpless in the face of the loss of their previous stability and those who do not experience the sense of community with others (Liem et al., 2020; Zhang, et al., 2020).

The pandemic period increases the feeling of loneliness in young children and adolescents. The lack of contact with other young people, which is necessary for optimal psychosocial development, will change the functioning of the entire generation in the future.

Loneliness versus aloneness

If an individual does not view himself/herself as part of a system, s/he will feel lonely even if surrounded by other people. Loneliness is inseparable from low self-belonging. It is formed as a consequence of the unsatisfied need of belonging when growing up (Raymond and Sheppard, 2018).

In their adult lives, people look for life companions with the belief that they will help them not feel lonely. A lot of women have children because they want to experience unconditional love which is missing in their lives.

Lonely patients visit clinics for consultation and help not because they are ill, but because they feel forlorn. As observed by Robert Putnam (2000) in his book *Bowling Alone* the lack of engagement in relationships destroys communities even if we live within them. People's progressing voluntary withdrawal from communities leaves them confused and lonely. Rates of loneliness during the initial phase of lockdowns due to the Covid-19 crisis were higher. Risk factors for loneliness were young age (e.g. people who are separated or divorced), positive clinical criteria for major depression, greater emotion regulation difficulties and poor quality sleep due to the pandemic (Groarke et al., 2020).

Loneliness is described as an epidemic of today's world. A report of a British governmental committee states that at least nine million adult United Kingdom residents consider themselves to be 'often or always lonely'; this accounts for about 15% of Britons. With a view to combating social isolation haunting United Kingdom citizens, the world's first and, so far, only 'Minister of Loneliness/Parliamentary Undersecretary of State for Sport, Civic Society and Loneliness' was appointed.

The United Kingdom is also one of the first countries to report a particularly high proportion of people who prefer interactions with pets compared to relations with people. As many as 90% of British pet owners regard their pets as family members, with 16% even including pets in the 2017 census. One third (33%) of British pet owners state that they put their pets over their kin, and one in six (15%) hold their pet to be more important than their cousin. Besides this, 12% of Britons say that they love their pets more than their partners. 9% admit to loving their pets above their own children, and 24% give their pets precedence before their friends. According to the statistics for 2018 to 2019, 40% of the United Kingdom's population owns a pet. Over 90% of pet owners in the United Kingdom aver that owning a pet makes them feel happy, and 88% insist that having a pet improves their global quality of life (https://www.statista.com/statistics/308218/leading-ten-pets-ranked-by-household-ownership-in-the-united-kingdom-uk/).

The United States statistics cited by Forbes show that loneliness figures doubled between the 1980s and 2016. In recent years, over 73% of adult Americans felt lonely, and nearly 31% experienced the feeling of loneliness at least once a week. Middle-aged adult people feel lonely during about 38% of the day (Pauly, Lay, Scott and Hoppmann, 2018). Those percentages have increased during the pandemic in 2020, but, at the current stage of writing this book, the details are not known.

As many as one in five United States residents live alone. The most frequently reported reasons for loneliness include shallowness of relationships, reduced social interactions and people's decreasing responsibility for each other. People choose virtual relationships—activity on social media, theme-focused chats and online dating—to give them an illusory sense of belonging in one or another community. However, avoiding direct contact lowers interpersonal skills and may lead to long-lasting social isolation.

Studies report that the sense of loneliness in its most acute form first appears in adolescence and young adulthood (O'Keeffe, 2013). An equally intense feeling of loneliness only reappears in the second half of people's lives. This distribution is due to the fact that, at the middle stage of their lives, people are, as a rule, engrossed in family matters, child-raising and careers, and loneliness is not severely felt. It is only when children leave home and bonds with them loosen or are broken that adults re-engage in introspection. They again confront who they are and what they have faced throughout their lives. That is why it is so important to take preemptive action against the effects of loneliness and isolation in childhood. Professor Julianne Holt-Lunstad calls for introducing social training to schools in order to teach young people how to establish and sustain correct social interactions with their peers. Indeed, teachers and educators should be provided with knowledge and skill necessary to support adolescents in developing the sense of belonging, which entails shifting responsibility onto adults in collaboration with adolescents and children (Holt-Lunstad, 2015).

English-language studies make a distinction between loneliness and aloneness, with the latter denoting the experience of being unaccompanied by other people (Long and Averill, 2003). A person may feel lonely when s/he is alone and also when there are other people around. The sense of loneliness triggers people to look for real attachment and relations with others due to the need of belonging. Researchers explain that a person's attitude to being lonely depends on his/her sensitivity to solitude when there is nobody around (Goossens et al., 2009).

Research findings of Cacioppo, Hawley and Ernst (2006) have shown that loneliness is associated with depression, self-perceived stress level, fear and negative assessments. It is also linked to anxiety, anger, decreased optimism and lowered self-esteem. It does not matter then whether there are other people around or not; the individual may still feel lonely anyway. Some people with a very rich social life, in fact, feel lonely all the time. At the same time, there are people who spend most of their time alone but do not feel lonely, as they live their lives to the fullest and find this meaningful.

Young adults may feel various kinds of loneliness. In terms of the four-factor loneliness model developed by Marcoen and Goossens (1993, in Goossens et al., 2009), the following aspects of loneliness can be identified: peer-related or friendship loneliness, family loneliness, positive attitude to solitude and negative attitude to solitude. The positive attitude to solitude is understood as a desire to be alone or isolated. The negative attitude to solitude means a dislike of being lonely or an inability to remain alone.

The study carried out by Teppers and colleagues (2013) has found that low scores on the acquiescence scale and a strong fear for one's independence are positively correlated with peer-related loneliness and parents-related loneliness (Long and Averill, 2003).

Being alone can produce advantageous outcomes, which are described by Long and Averill as follows:

- freedom, which consists in a free choice of actions and thoughts; since people who are alone make decisions in conformity with their own preferences and without external pressure, they do not have to exert themselves to impress anybody with their choices;
- creativity, which arises from freedom and is understood as an arousal of the imagination; the establishment of links among previously unconnected aspects and the expression of new ideas in ways which are useful and valuable both to ourselves and to others;
- intimacy; and
- spirituality, which is associated with the sense of unity with God, the universe or nature when alone; solitude is an important aspect in multiple religions, as attested by the solitary lives of nuns and monks who devote their lives to meditation, internal contemplation in isolation and prayer.

Research shows that the daily amount of time we spend alone differs across our lifetimes. Students spend about 26% of their day alone; middle-aged people spend between 37% and 39%; elderly and retired people spend about 48%; and the oldest group spends as much as 71% (Burger, 1995; Chui et al., 2014; Larson et al., 1985; Papp, Pendry, Simon, Adam, 2013, in Pauly, Lay, Scott and Hoppmann, 2018). Older people are more vulnerable to negative effects, such as loneliness and social isolation, because they spend most of their time during the day alone (Courtin and Knapp, 2017).

Loneliness does not have to mean social exclusion, but these terms can be equivalent if loneliness determines the state of dependence of one's mood on the presence of other people.

Masculinity, femininity, partnership and marriage

For a long time, researchers argued that marriage was beneficial to females and males in different ways. They stressed that married people and those in partnered relationships were more likely to live longer and be healthier.

It was shown that the health status of married women was 4.8% better than that of unmarried women, and the health status of married men was as much as 27.9% better than that of bachelors. Married women reported lower blood pressure and lower cholesterol. Married men drank less alcohol, smoked less, less frequently developed digestive system diseases, boasted better eyesight, had better blood pressure and sugar levels and slept better. Studies showed that the risk of earlier death was 50% higher for unmarried women than for married women, and for unmarried men, the figure stood at a staggering 250%! Research also suggested that middle-aged unmarried people were 2.5 times more likely than married people to die before old age, and people in relationships, significantly, less frequently died of the ten most common cancer types. Such data invited the conclusion that the very fact of being married protected people against early death and a range of diseases (Stokes, 2016; DePaulo, 2007; Coyne et al., 2001).

Some new light was shed on the reported salutary properties of marriage by findings of a big research study published in 2017. The study was designed to examine the extent to which the marital status of 12,000 respondents born between 1955 and 1984 was related to their health status. By means of refined statistical methods, the study showed that, while the members of the older generations were healthier if married, the effect was significantly weaker among the younger respondents and nonexistent in the sample of young females (Tumin, 2017).

The point is that, over the last decades, the roles of women and men in marriage have changed considerably, as has the function of intimate relationships. In the past, males held gratifying positions both in relationships and in society. This was the case because women did not have jobs but were mostly homemakers and child-raisers. Males went out to hunt, acquired food and provided for their families. Most women had subservient roles for the sake of being married, thus, enjoying a higher social status. Until the end of the 18th century, marriage was mainly considered to be an economic and political institution. The family was a symbol of social stabilisation and economic security. In those times, love was not a precondition of matrimony, and the lack of love was not a reason to terminate the married relationship. Women were expected to be care-providers, to run households and to bring up children, whereas men were supposed to be breadwinners and to help somewhat in domestic chores.

This has changed in recent years, with the greatest shift registered in the position of women. Once economically and socially dependent, deprived of the right of self-determination and barred from individual participation in social life, women have become autonomous individuals who make their own decisions regarding education, vocational career and reproductive plans (Śmieja, 2018). Today, women and men have similar rights and potentials to take care of themselves and their families. They expect their partners to satisfy different needs as compared to before. According to the eminent Belgian psychotherapist Esther Perel (https://www.estherperel.com/), partners in contemporary intimate relationships would like to receive support in their pursuit of self-realisation and happiness. Looking after the home is no longer enough; partners are supposed to help each other in building autonomy, to support each other's personal development, to keep each other company in emotionally challenging moments, to induce passion and to cultivate intimacy.

People in relationships expect their loved ones to be their best friends, passionate lovers, caring parents, resourceful travel companions, independent beings with their own interests, well-paid employees, eloquent socialisers and wonderful interlocutors for long nights together.

When defined in such terms, marriage or partner relationships are bound to bring disappointment rather than satisfaction. Such expectations are simply impossible to meet (Perel, 2006). As a matter of fact, even people who are married or have partners feel lonely. There is an even more interesting phenomenon. If, initially, only one party in the relationship suffers from loneliness, emotional contagion and dissemination of loneliness will soon make the other one feel lonely too. This is indicated by the findings of a study carried out on 1,114 elderly married couples in Ireland. The findings have corroborated the emotional contagion theory by revealing that assessing marriage as a positive quality reduces loneliness, while a negative perception of the quality of the relationship exacerbates the partner's loneliness. The findings have established that one partner's loneliness aggravates the other partner's loneliness (Stokes, 2016; Cacioppo et al., 2009).

At the same time, women have gained independence, have their own careers and are successful in politics and social life. They are eager to engage in pursuits in the public world, live by their own rules and norms and often prefer a one-plus-one family model, where one-plus-one means woman-plus-child. When they cannot find common ground with a man, they do not want to share a life with him or look after the man, especially when they are perfectly capable of earning their own livelihoods and are independent in various spheres of life. Single males work or study, devoting their leisure time to Internet pastimes, such as video games or films, therein pornography, which caters to their curiosity and sexual needs. They construct their own worlds and live in the world without women, unable to establish and to sustain bonds with them (Zimbardo and Coulombe, 2015).

Sometimes people who are in relationships experience mutual hostility. Research shows that when the quality of the relationship is low, the partners are emotionally and physically exhausted; their health deteriorates; and their life expectancy may shrink. Conflicts in the relationship are risk factors in contracting viral infections, developing degenerative diseases and slowing down wound healing processes (e.g. in unhappy relationships, wounds heal 40% slower than in happy couples). Only one in three people who are in unsatisfying relationships survive a cardiac disease diagnosis by more than four years. At the same time, patients who are satisfied with their relationships are three times as likely to survive a heart surgery by 15 years. The strength of these effects is confirmed by quantitative syntheses of research findings from several independent studies which have clearly shown that today partners' health status is correlated with the quality of marriage rather than with the very fact of being married (Robles et al., 2014).

As women and men are hurt in their relations, they are discouraged from commitments. Instead of undertaking reflective work to develop themselves and their relationships, a lot of women and men exhibit escape behaviours.

People observably turn away from themselves and from relationships with the other sex, as they are hurt and fear another event of rejection. One of the most spectacular examples of such escape responses is provided by the male online community of MGTOW (Men Going Their Own Way). Described as misogynist, the movement assembles men who refuse to bond with women and to even participate in society. They believe that women use men for sex, are overwhelmed by 'feminist brainwashing' and want to prove that 'they are right in spite of all'. Followers of the MGTOW philosophy engage in short-term relationships or have sex with prostitutes. Some of them choose to live without sex at all. The point is that they have been hurt by women – in all likelihood by their mothers in the early period of their lives – and this has made them unable to build relationships with other women. They do not seek to further the development of society; rather, they choose to withdraw from society. They prefer withdrawal compared to exposing themselves to another possible rejection. One of the posts on Polish Facebook states: 'MGTOW is a man's life philosophy which is supposed to secure his own mental, physical and material well-being. It aims to make a contemporary man realise that he is not a slave of women. According to MGTOW, a considerable majority of today's women are not worth efforts and sacrifices. The myth of marriage as a coveted goal that a man wants to achieve is just that—a myth—as are the selective "where I choose" equal rights of women'. Posts and comments on this website show that men want to spend their time online as they wish, without anybody interfering with what they do. Some of the users additionally recount how they were hurt in their already terminated marriages or partner relationships.

People seem to be disappointed with relationships or, rather, with the rules which have governed the establishment and functioning of relationships.

As long as modern young women and men fail to understand how they need each other for individual and mutual development, for joy and for pleasure, this gap will only continue to grow. As it extends, the sense of loneliness, inadequacy and lack of love will probably intensify. In fact, rewarding partner relations are possible when people feel happy and acknowledge the differences between women's and men's worlds. This has been shown by a study carried out by Christine Proulx and Linley Snyder-Rivas (2013). Their meta-analysis involving 707 adults found that 60% of Americans reporting the highest satisfaction from marriage considered themselves generally happy in life, while only 10% of the respondents who were not really satisfied with their intimate relationships regarded themselves as happy. Apparently, the interdependence between satisfaction from life and satisfaction in the relationship strengthens over time. There are studies which show that this correlation was twice as strong in 2000 as in 1980.

The models of masculinity, femininity and the partner have, in a sense, collapsed, because they have failed to work. Living in a bad marriage or a bad partnership worsens people's mental and physical condition instead of improving it. Expected to make the dream of felicity and wealth come true, marriage has proven yet another institution and a factor in loneliness and unhappiness. This happens because social patterns resulting from globalised education are unreflectingly copied and reproduced, while the only viable starting point for partnership, love and mutual care is provided by self-knowledge and self-acceptance, undisrupted by limitations and histories of family life.

Binge-watching: belonging to virtual reality

Models are also sought outside. When people have no other source of examples of good relations, partnership or marriage, upbringing and interactions with others, they fall back on what can be found around—for instance, in easily available film productions and in virtual worlds which are crafted to give people a surrogate life in a community of their choice.

Addiction to virtual worlds – such as video games and films – may be an attempt to cope with loneliness and the sense of being outside the system. In the past, people became addicted to television, and this was a gauge of their depression level. Today, addiction to film-watching is more selective and personalised. It is best exemplified in binge-watching, which, in psychology, means the compulsive watching of multi-episode shows (Zimmer, 2013). Inhabiting his/her own space, a person can be immersed in the world of a plot fashioned by other people. People shut themselves off from the external world for hours on end to watch their favourite shows and live the lives of their beloved protagonists. Shows are watched in series comprising several (at least three) episodes of a given season in one sitting (Annalect Primary Research & Insights Group, 2014). Comedy shows (e.g. Friends, Modern Family and Big Bang Theory) and drama television series (Desperate Housewives, ER and Gossip Girl) enjoy less popularity than fantasy shows (e.g. The Game of Thrones, Lucifer and The Vampire Diaries), crime shows (e.g. Dexter, Breaking Bad and Narcos) and thriller shows (Money Heist, Lost and Homeland). These television series are watched alone, with a girlfriend/boyfriend or with family members. By steeping themselves in the world of their aesthetics of choice, binge-watchers enact the principle of pleasure—hedonism. Most of them report that binge-watching makes them feel calm and soothed. They relax though becoming deeply engaged in what they watch. They focus on the problems of the artificial world, committing their minds to it so much that they become distracted from the current matters of real life with its challenges and problems. Binge-watching helps them fill their empty time which they often spend alone (Pittman and Sheehan, 2015).

By following the plot, binge viewers can develop their capacity to understand human behaviour within a given social and artistic framework. They usually seek five benefits: to be informed or educated, to identify with characters in the media environment, to have a good time, to strengthen their social interactions and to shrug off everyday stress (McQuail, 2010). They derive pleasure from immersion in fantasy and from experiencing fun, erotic and sexual scenes (e.g. femininity, masculinity, intimate relations) and episodes of violence or moments of so-called maleness. By watching shows, they can escape from the compulsion of learning and enjoy aesthetic sensations, beautiful views and music. Another motivation is to see the entire season immediately after release, which enables binge viewers to chat and share with others on social media (Pittman and Sheehan, 2015).

Netflix has about 30 million subscribers and is one of the leading streaming media providers and one of the most influential television services in the United States and worldwide (Lehrer, 2014). Similarly to video computer games, film narratives work within a certain hermetic project designed by their developers—television. Importantly, people's attention and thoughts are entirely engrossed by increasingly more complex narrative structures devised and offered by television. Young people devote all their leisure time to watch stories from beginning to end. When Netflix released all the fifteen episodes of the new season of Arrested Development in the summer of 2013, nearly 10% of viewers watched the entire season within 24 hours. Similarly, The House of Cards and Orange Is the New Black were watched episode by episode with no breaks. The skills of the digital generations—that is, generation Y (millennials) and Generation Z (iGen)—are conducive to watching films on laptops and smartphones. In 2013, as many as 63% of United States households used video streaming services and services such as Netflix, Hulu and Amazon Prime (Solsman). As many as 22% of households use Netflix streaming weekly. In Anglophone Canada, about 25% of the residents are registered on Netflix (Matrix, 2014).

Public opinion polls carried out in the United States have shown that binge-watching concerns 67% of television viewers aged between 13 and 49 years old ("MarketCast" 2013, in Pena, 2015). In 2015, 70% practised binge-watching, and 31% regularly watched film shows every week (Deloitte, 2016) more than a few times a week. Binge viewers make up 80% of millennials, 68% of generation X, and 49% of Baby Boomers (Annalect Primary Research & Insights Group, 2014).

Research has shown that 67% of women and 59% of men watch three or more episodes of a show season in one sitting. Additionally, women have been found to be less aware of the risks of binge-watching than men. Men, more often than women, admit that watching shows impinges on their time for work, sleep, exercise, family interactions and meetings with friends (ibid.).

In the United Arab Emirates, binge viewers watch films on big screens, laptops, smartphones and Internet television (Ahmed, 2017). The viewing public's preferred choices are foreign drama shows and Turkish television series. Nearly 50% of respondents do not believe that binge-watching may trigger regret, and only 26% of them state that regret is a consequence of watching without being able to stop. However, as many as 46% of viewers reported that they regretted the time they devoted to watching and felt that they should have been doing something else instead. A lot of people do not control time at all, and they pause in watching a season when they feel sleepy. Gender is not a significant factor in watching rates in the United Arab Emirates. Young people spend more time watching, which is explained by the fact that, after lessons at school, they have no fixed timetables yet. The findings have shown that 84% of respondents watch television shows for at least four hours per session daily (Ahmed, 2017). Most of them tend to watch over the week (68.1%), watch up to four episodes (72%), primarily watch at home (77.7%), watch alone (68.5%) and only a small proportion watch with friends (12.7%) or with family (18.8%) (ibid.).

Studies show that television viewing behaviour and motivations behind it are positively correlated with loneliness and that they are associated with depression and the need for relations. Regrettably, the hypothesis that watching television shows promotes well-being has not been corroborated (Wheeler, 2015). People who practise binge-watching score significantly higher in depressive tendencies than people who do not binge-watch. Additionally, the more episodes binge viewers watch, the higher their depression scores are.

Researchers do not perceive binge-watching as a homogeneous construct. Recent research results show that only the so-called unintentional watching of films is associated with addiction and impulsiveness (Riddle et al., 2017)

Binge television viewing as such can exacerbate the sense of aloneness, emptiness, withdrawal and worsened moods, especially when, after a period of hours-long watching sessions, a season comes to an end. Researchers have also found that having seen all the good and bad moments of the show, viewers may feel emotionally exhausted (Wheeler, 2015). Television series engage people who wish to experience something exceptional (McCracken, 2013) in an interesting and absorbing world which they see as continuous and internally logical as opposed to the real world in which they live.

However, it is exactly the opposite. Film plots are often artificially lengthened, which causes the actors to change in one role. The action often shifts in sudden twists and turns, or the plot is changed due to the addition of the script. It is not uncommon for the personality of one of the characters to change completely. The series only produces an illusion of a more sensible experience of time by temporarily offering different emotions, which is what some viewers need.

Chapter 4

The experience and impact of exclusion

In psychology, social exclusion is defined as an effect of deprivation of one of the most fundamental human needs—specifically, the need of belonging (Baumeister and Leary, 1995; Molden et al., 2009; Bowlby, 1969; Maslow, 1954; Raymond and Sheppard, 2018; Moeller, Seehuus and Peisch, 2020). The person at risk of exclusion unconsciously expects the looming loss of interpersonal relations and has a premonition of impending loneliness or isolation. People at risk of exclusion feel less secure and, as a rule, have no social support network on which to rely in difficult situations in their lives.

The sense of belonging is compromised when the psychological distance between parents and children grows or when emotional interactions within the family are circumscribed without being supplanted by other relations established outside it. Reduced parental control, which may be part of what has come to be known as stress-free upbringing, is one of the factors that can divest children and adolescents of their sense of belonging.

Pressures and influences that reduce people's opportunities for full participation in social life are collectively referred to as disadvantages. Disadvantaging adversely impacts individuals' social self-awareness, involving, for example, deprecating people's talents and competencies, underappreciating their importance or ignoring them. This lowers people's self-worth and self-acceptance, reduces their opportunities for meaningful contribution to the group and worsens social relationships (Moeller, Seehuus and Peisch, 2020).

The mechanism of restoring the sense of belonging is explained as the individual's striving to repair his/her relations and improve his/her well-being. The phenomenon is often framed in terms of the approaching-vs.-avoiding of conflict (Corr, 2005; Hess, Valdman and Knowles, 2018). In the situation of exclusion, the individual makes attempts at rapprochement with the group or significant others. However, such endeavours are assessed by the individual as potentially hazardous and are accompanied by the fear of being rejected again. Attempts at rebuilding the relationship often fail despite considerable efforts that the person invests in this undertaking (Twenge et al., 2007; Twenge, Catenese and Baumeister, 2003).

When facing the risk of social exclusion, individuals are observed to display a temporary increase in social responsiveness and sensitivity to interpersonal feedback (Gardner, Pickett and Brewer, 2000; Gardner et al., 2005; Maner et al., 2007). Frustrated attempts at belonging and the anticipation of exclusion trigger strong distress (Corr, 2005), which can cause an immediate retaliative response or a general increase in hostility and aggression toward the current social environment (Buckley, Winkel and Leary, 2004; Leary, Twenge and Quinlivan, 2006; Twenge et al., 2007; Kirkpatrick, Waugh, Valencia and Webster, 2002; Twenge, Baumeister, Tice and Stucke, 2001). People at risk of exclusion have been observed to exhibit less prosocial behaviour and empathy and to display more emotional indifference and insensitivity to pain/suffering (Dewall and Baumeister, 2006; Corr, 2005; Grey, 1982). They have also reported a lowered threshold of subjectively felt physical pain (MacDonald and Leary, 2005).

Social exclusion is a serious threat to people's physical and mental well-being (Argyle, 1987; Cacioppo, Hawkley and Berntson, 2003; Wilczyńska-Kwiatek and Bargiel-Matusiewicz, 2008). Deprivation of belonging can be directly related not only to worsened mental functioning, but surprisingly also to the debilitation of the immune system (Kielcolt-Glaser et al., 1984).

Separation from emotion

Even though excluded, people, as a rule, do not exhibit overt symptoms, which implies how deeply they have been affected by exclusion. However, their physical and mental/emotional functioning outcomes are known to deteriorate. This happens for two major reasons. Firstly, such people are isolated and rejected—without being aware of this process—and are trapped in this condition without expecting any positive change. They separate from their pain but, at the same time, from feeling others' emotions as well. Secondly, as they do not grasp the reasons for what is going on with them or against them, they often fear loneliness so desperately that they cling to various people at any cost and engage in toxic relationships in which they usually go through another painful failure.

The risk of exclusion disorganises the feeling and understanding of emotions. This contributes to a sudden decrease in self-esteem and self-trust.

The sense of exclusion results in a loss of confidence in oneself and doubts about felt emotions and feelings.

Research has shown that young people who have experienced rejection, as a rule, exclude others in their life. This tactic is intentionally used mainly by girls. Paradoxically, the experience which should help them empathetically understand other people's predicaments stirs them to activate cold responses and pestering behaviours, rather than trying to put themselves in others' place. Such psychological processes aim at self-protection or retaliation, as individual defences are mobilised which promote evasion and suppress responses to others' suffering.

Boys are definitely more likely to react automatically and directly by excluding themselves before anybody else manages to exclude them. They become immersed in the world of the Internet—in computer games or Internet pornography (Zimbardo and Coulombe, 2015).

The weakening of anticipative capacity / the lowering of emotional skills has been documented in a well-known experiment. The participants in the experiment were asked to estimate their own emotional responses to the failure or the victory of their favourite college football team (DeWall and Baumeister, 2006). Interestingly, the participants who had been led to believe that they faced a 'lonely future' reported more neutral emotional responses than the rest of the sample. When they were asked to define the general anticipated level of self-satisfaction, they were altogether unable to correctly estimate their own emotional responses. Paradoxically, they expected greater self-satisfaction in the context of a negative event and lesser gratification in the context of a positive event. The findings of this experiment seriously encourage inferring that, when faced with the risk of social exclusion, people's emotional system stops working normally and causes insensitivity not only to physical pain, but also to an anticipated future emotional event.

Researchers believed that emotional sensitivity versus insensitivity was best measured by self-appraisal of one's own emotional state after obtaining information about their risk of exclusion (Baumeister et al., 2005). However, having legitimate grounds to think that people at risk of losing their sense of belonging were likely to withhold the impact of this information on their emotional state (DeWall and Baumeister, 2006), they decided that it was reliable to register the feelings imagined by the subjects. The results confirmed the researchers' expectations, as people faced with the prospect of a lonely future were found to be emotionally insensitive to the emotional suffering of others.

The decline of empathetic sensitivity in individuals at risk of exclusion was assessed as a reaction of defence against pain in conditions of excessive stimulation. People respond to social exclusion by displaying emotional indifference, which on the one hand, indeed protects them but on the other, actually undercuts their capacity to bond with others. This mechanism also initiates individual defences that result in suppressing reactions to others' suffering and in avoiding information about others' pain. In some situations, they trigger attack and expressions of anger vis-à-vis the victim or curb anger vis-à-vis the perpetrator. The image of an individual at risk of social exclusion which these findings outline portrays a human being who is, in a way, emotionally defective and, moreover, does not realise this.

The psychophysiological experience of the pain of exclusion

Both physical pain and social pain signal impairment in one or another structure which is vital to the human being (Ferris, Jetten, Hornsey and Bastian, 2019). The former concerns a person's physical structure, while the latter is linked to the social structure of an individual's relations. Pain is a regulatory mechanism associated with the reception of external stimuli. When their significant relationship is lost, people render their condition in terms that echo typical descriptors of physical pain. For example, in the aftermath of the breakup of an important relationship, people resort to metaphors of actual pain, such as 'my heart aches', 'these are painful feelings', 'I feel hurt' or 'my heart is broken'. The sense of being devalued by an important partner or a significant group is conveyed in expressions such as 'he cut me to the quick' or 'I got the elbow'.

American researchers MacDonald and Leary (2005) have proposed a theory of social pain as an explanation of individuals' responses to social exclusion. They argue that the interrelatedness of physical and emotional pain goes far beyond such verbal metaphors. Advanced brain imaging methods show that both social pain and physical pain work through physiological processes that are engineered by the same regions of the brain. The experience of pain consists of two components: pain sensation and pain affect. The former signals that tissue is being damaged, while the other is synonymous with unpleasant feelings which are paired with pain sensation and comprise emotions related to its later consequences. Because pain affect is independent of pain sensation, painful feelings can be experienced even if there is no tissue damage.

The partial overlap of physical and social pain is evolutionally functional, as it alerts individuals to the fact that their belonging is at risk. The affective component of pain signals the potential threat, activates a strong stress-response and motivates people to undertake action in order to reduce the harmful stimulation or to put it to an end by initiating the mechanisms of flight, fight or freeze (Berkowitz, 1993). While social pain is considered to be a subcategory of emotional pain, the two notions tend to be used interchangeably (Thornhill and Thornhill, 1989).

When a person has difficulty functioning within the group, s/he grows afraid that s/he will be rejected. When s/he refuses to admit to these difficult emotions, s/he may feel heightened physical pain, for example, in the throat, or exhibit voice-related problems. Unarticulated words 'get stuck in the throat' and become a symptom of an already existing risk of exclusion. People under severe stress are also known to suffer from increased muscle tension in the neck and the nape.

Social pain, unexpressed emotions and unworked-through situations result in palpable disorders of various body parts (Scaer, 2014).

Social pain also appears under the conditions of what is known as 'relational devaluation', wherein self-esteem vis-à-vis the partner or partners in a relationship is lower than expected. This situation is both painful and taxing to individuals. Research has found that, in such circumstances, people tend to distance themselves from those who may be the source of rejection or hurt. If a relationship is identified as at risk, people seek help or try to establish another relationship (Leary and Springer, 2001). Another common reaction is not to undertake any action except attempting to isolate oneself from the hurtful environment as much as possible. When the environment changes and the person begins to experience it as supportive, recovery starts.

A recent study carried out by United Kingdom-based Professor Paul Gilbert and colleagues (Gilbert and Choden, 2014) has revealed that mindful compassion practised towards oneself may help people reassess their situation and their relations with others. Gilbert, whom I have known since 2014, argues that pain and suffering (Hind.: *dukkha*) can be overcome through proper mental practice and training. By learning compassion, people may better understand their emotions, live in the moment and feel deep bonding with others.

People who can find neither their own place among others nor a way to experience belonging respond to social exclusion with emotional indifference in order to shield themselves against suffering (Eisenberger, 2008; Macdonald and Leary, 2005).

Reduction of prosocial behaviours

Social exclusion undercuts people's motivation to engage in prosocial behaviour. Most people at risk of exclusion do not take advantage of possibilities to make new friends or to garner others' fondness through displaying prosocial conduct. Produced as a result of exclusion, emotional numbness reduces individuals' empathetic compassion and their understanding of others' needs or suffering. Based on the same mechanism, people who are being excluded tend to protect themselves, for their prior experiences make them all the more insecure about or distrustful of the intentions of their social milieu (Twenge et al., 2007).

Prosocial behaviours mainly depend on how far the individual feels part of the community in which everybody similarly needs help, support or love and then actually receives it. Prosocial behaviours are found to be strongly correlated with social acceptance. Children and adolescents from families that ensure stable support behave in more caring ways and exhibit more prosocial behaviours than children from families that do not offer support (Cochran and Bo, 1989). Children who are insufficiently supported by adults tend to interpret other people's ambiguous behaviours as more rejecting and aggressive and to perceive the world as more hostile (Weerdmeester and Lange, 2019; Twenge et al., 2007).

Findings show that the decrease in prosocial behaviours of excluded people was not associated either with their self-esteem or with their sex. The effects were found to be very strong and clearly indicated that participants in control groups helped others, while most people at risk of social exclusion did not exhibit prosocial behaviours (Twenge et al., 2007). The position adopted by people at risk of exclusion involved a rather cautious attitude towards others—despite their interest in re-engagement in relations—and waiting for contact from others in order to avoid being potentially hurt again.

Self-destructive and aggressive behaviours

It has been over 20 years since Roy Baumeister and Mark Leary (1995) published their theory about the need of belonging, meticulously investigating the causes and effects of the unsatisfied need of belonging. Emotional indifference, atrophy of prosocial feelings, increased anger and aggressive behaviours represent only a handful of possible responses to the threat of social exclusion (Kornienko, Ha and Dishon, 2020; Buckley, Winkel and Leary, 2004; Leary, Twenge and Quintivan, 2006).

The early 21st century was fraught with tectonic social, technological, economic and political changes, which went hand in hand with new social movements dedicated to tolerance. Research findings show that while the young generation declared openness to otherness, they did not stand up heroically in its defence. They only knew that they were expected to profess tolerance. At the same time, more and more young people report mental health complaints (Twenge, 2017). Mental hospitals and the offices of clinical psychologists are inundated with a soaring wave of young patients who report a range of addictions—the Internet, dieting, physical effort, psychoactive substances, etc.

On a scale yet unprecedented in Poland, children and adolescents seek psychological support; tellingly, almost 25% of children have used or are using psychological or psychiatric help. Worldwide statistics show that one in five adults are being treated for depression. The World Health Organisation, in fact, anticipated this increase a few years ago. Currently, ailments related to impaired mental health are the second most frequent cause of incapacity to work in the world, following cardiovascular diseases.

The growing rate of suicides and attempted suicides among young people, school shootings in which students are killed or injured and the loss of control over addictive behaviours have all become very serious concerns for many societies (Newman, 2004). The greatest need reported by people is the need of belonging, security, stable jobs and positive relationships within a small and welcoming group.

The exclusion of vulnerable/weaker individuals from disadvantaged families and backgrounds may indeed breed tragic effects. We still notice in society that a sizeable group of people experience violence, abuse and abandonment in an early period of their lives.

At the end of the 1990s, James Garbarino, a UNESCO expert dedicated to the problems of 'lost boys', conducted interviews with young people who had perpetrated serious crimes. Garbarino described the phenomenon he called 'insulation' in teenagers from poor and conflicted backgrounds as the response of numbness resulting from humiliation, rejection and emotional neglect experienced in their childhood. A series of experiments has since confirmed that adults who are excluded from relationships respond with emotional numbness, lowered empathy and also increased aggression towards others (Garbarino, 1990, 1999).

Even a cursory examination of causes behind many tragic incidents involving juveniles shows that most of these young people felt excluded to the point of not even being able to imagine ever re-engaging with their group. On many occasions when I analysed people and patients who felt excluded, ridiculed and unwanted, I noticed that, instead of seeking help, they undertook deleterious actions that only aggravated their problems. I have often wondered why they do not approach a psychologist, a teacher or a parent for help and why they do not try and change something in their environment in positive ways

The scrutiny of the most dramatic cases implies that people who felt rejected in the past 'coped' with exclusion by opting for the worst strategies both for themselves and for others. For example, instead of seeking help and support, they chose to 'retaliate'. They avenged on others their past, present and anticipated hurts. Seeking help was never an item in their catalogue of coping strategies.

I have always felt surprised at how little was, as a rule, done to curb aggression caused by harm people had experienced. In many countries, legal regulations, rather than psychological solutions, are put in place to prevent aggression which arises from the pain of exclusion. While restricted access to weapons will not alleviate the pain of exclusion, the strategy may reduce the number of human tragedies in the world. Several dramas related to school shootings may not have happened if the potential perpetrators had been contacted in time. I often wondered how it was possible, in the first place, that young people attended a school and were 'seen' by their parents and the school staff on a daily basis, yet nobody could either perceive their pain or properly respond to their suffering or their need for hostile retaliation.

In a 2012 school shooting in Newton, Massachusetts, United States of America, 26 people, 20 of whom were children, were killed, sending a shock wave throughout the United States and the entire world. The barely 20-year-old killer, Adam Lanza, was an intelligent and well-read boy but was also a 'loner who never had friends and whose chief hobby was playing violent computer games'.[1] One day, his inner rage erupted as he stormed into a primary school and fired 100 shots at innocent young students. Having committed this shocking deed, he took his own life.

Examination of the personalities of school shooting perpetrators implies that they share basic characteristics: they have no relations with their peers, and they feel that they are misfits. The attackers are usually lonely and alienated school youngsters—outsiders who are poor at handling peer relations, believe they do not fit in with others or feel underappreciated and disliked. In the United States, where over one-third of the world's school shootings take place, preventive solutions are in place to protect the potential victims by training the school staff and students to escape efficiently. The American army has produced a set of explanatory and training films called School Shooting Simulators (e.g. https://youtu.be/0BMo2Ulm4PQ), which help teachers, children, the police and school guards learn what to do when the school is attacked. The same technology was earlier used to train soldiers to cope in wartime situations. However, in war, it is clear who the enemy is and usually where they are located. In contrast, school shootings are rare, unpredictable events, so preparation for them is typically unproductive. In the United States of America in 2019, there have been more than 249 mass shootings (https://www.politifact.com/article/2019/aug/05/viral-tweet-about-mass-shootings-country-it-needs-/).

Admittedly, school shootings are an extreme example, but they conspicuously indicate the extreme relevance of some mental processes that push people to commit such violent deeds. Studies of perpetrators' minds show that only 5% of them are or were afflicted with mental diseases.

The risk of social exclusion of young people characteristically locates the individual both in the space of existing social threats and also in individual conditions and experiences which are related to the need and sense of belonging.

Social exclusion not only contributes to the deterioration of the individual's mental health and well-being but can also exacerbate any propensity for engagement in criminal activity (Levitas et al., 2007; Gore and Figuereido, 2003). The famous developmental psychologist Alfred Adler (1879–1937) already emphasised that 'the honest psychologist cannot shut his eyes to the social conditions which prevent the child from becoming a part of the community and from feeling at home in the world, and which allow him to grow up as though he lived in an enemy country' (in Ansbacher and Ansbacher, 1956, p. 454; Todman, et al., 2009, p. 330). The current studies of social exclusion partly rely on Adler's insight, and the sense of belonging lies at the core of the contemporary discourse on exclusion (Baumeister, DeWall, Ciarocco and Twenge, 2005; Twenge et al., 2007).

Fear of loneliness in the future

Individuals who anticipate being socially excluded are unable to imagine how they themselves could influence their own future. They tend to 'protect' their resources so as not to be hurt again. This makes therapeutic work very difficult. In fact, many people carry an injury that they have hidden from others. They are less prosocial and more aggressive (active aggression and passive aggression) within the family, in work teams or in society. In order to examine how social exclusion is related to angry or aggressive behaviours, a series of experiments on exclusion from the group were carried out (Twenge et al., 2001). The subjects were told that they were likely to be lonely for most of their adult lives, as opposed to others who had important and enduring relationships 'announced' to them. Besides this, the participants in the research sample were given information about either exclusion (i.e. they were told that nobody had picked them as partners for a collaboration-based assignment) or inclusion (i.e. they were told that all the other participants had picked them for the collaborative task). Two control groups were formed (one including 'unlucky people' and the other comprised of the participants who were given no feedback). The participants' aggressive and angry behaviours were observed, wherein the frequency of unfounded negative assessments of others or exposing them to unpleasant sounds was recorded. The findings showed that social rejection was associated with a greater likelihood of aggressive treatment of others by excluded people as compared to the remaining participants. Rejected individuals evaluated others (e.g. job interviewees) more harshly and more often exposed others to unpleasant sounds. Aggressive behaviours targeted people who were not the source of rejection. It was also noted that aggression was not transferred onto people who treated the participants in a friendly way.

Although the participants manifested aggressive behaviour in social situations, no changes in their mood were registered by the PANAS scale (Ibid.). A study on a sample of 186 children aged between 11 and 14 years old has shown that the regulation of emotions is mediated by the cognitive assessment of events. A negative cognitive assessment of the situation or catastrophising it (i.e. exaggerating its adverse consequences for the individual) increased negative emotions in adolescents. When the assessment of the event was positive or strategies of distancing or not thinking of the situation as a threat to inclusion were activated, positive and neutral emotions were noted (Reijntjes, Dekovic, Vermande and Telch, 2008). For their part, Cassidy, Parke, Butskovsky and Braungart (1992) have found that rejected children are perceived by their peers as more prone to anger in conflict situations.

The United States Surgeon General's Report on youth violence (qtd. in Twenge et al., 2007) demonstrated that social exclusion, operationalised as 'weak social bonds', was the strongest predictor of violence among teenagers; its strength of effect surpassed that of gang membership, poverty and drug addiction! Besides this, it has been shown that early rejection causes an increase in aggressiveness (Buckley, Winkel and Leary, 2004; Leary, Twenge and Quinlivan, 2006; Twenge et al., 2007; Kirkpatrick, Waugh, Valencia and Webster, 2002; Twenge, Baumeister, Tice and Stucke, 2001), low school achievement, reduction of prosocial behaviours, self-destructive surrender to drugs (Twenge, 2002; Twenge et al., 2007; Wilczyńska-Kwiatek, 2009) and other signs of relinquishing self-control (Baumeister et al., 2007). Garbarino (1990) has found that many perpetrators of serious crimes are young people who feel rejected by family members, peers and society in general. Direct evidence that deprivation of belonging thwarts social-emotional adaptation has been presented by DeLongis, Folkman and Lazarus (1988).

Developmental psychologists have proved that aggressive children and adolescents are more likely to be rejected by others, have fewer friends and obtain less acceptance from peers (Coie, Dodge and Kupersmidt, 1990; Newcomb, Bukowski and Pattee, 1993).

Mental and physical desensitisation processes

Exclusion thwarts the expression of emotions and causes people to react in ostensibly neutral or emotionally indifferent ways (Argyle, 1987; Myers, 1992; Kiecolt-Glaser et al., 1984).

A series of laboratory experiments have been carried out in which the participants were exposed to the risk of social exclusion (i.e. they had a future without close relations with others 'predicted' to them). The results of the measurements of emotional states in people faced with the risk of exclusion did not differ from the scores of control groups (DeWall, Baumeister, 2006; Baumeister, Twenge and Nuss, 2002; Twenge, Catanese and Baumeister, 2002). The researchers concluded that social exclusion increased emotional suffering, but its implications for the emotional state were not registered. It was discovered that people at risk of exclusion responded with indifference. Waning engagement and lowering cognitive functions were also observed (Buckley, Winkel and Leary, 2004).

In seeking the cause of this inconsistency, a possible mechanism activated by people in response to the threat was explained. To account for this phenomenon, DeWall and Baumeister (2006) theorised that the risk of social exclusion disturbed the person's functioning by making them emotionally numb. The destructive effects of emotional numbness were observed in laboratory studies. People who had experienced exclusion displayed a lowered capacity for empathetic compassion and for intellectual effort, while their behaviours were more aggressive, more antisocial and less prosocial (Baumeister, 2011).

In response to the risk of exclusion, people tend to fall into the state of cognitive deconstruction. This state is typical in people in what is known as a pre-suicidal situation. It is characterised by emotional numbness, a changed perception of time, increased brooding on pointlessness, an avoidance of focusing on the self and general inertia (Baumeister, 1990).

Excluded people exhibit such symptoms by way of self-protection. Emotional numbness has a defensive function, as it helps individuals distance themselves from pain or suffering (Twenge, Catanese and Baumeister, 2003). In literature, this symptom is described not only as a short-term escape behaviour but also as a behaviour specific to serious psychopathologies (Stanik, 2012).

Emotional indifference is linked to insensitivity to physical pain. The mechanism of this interrelatedness is based on the evolutionary model of reacting to social and physical pain (Herman and Panskepp, 1978; Eisenberger, Lieberman and Williams, 2003). Studies have shown that even brief isolation of rats from other members of this species results in reduced sensitivity to physical pain or even in a complete inability to feel pain (i.e. analgesia) (Kehoe and Blass, 1986; Naranjo and Fuentes, 1985, qtd. in DeWall and Baumeister, 2006).

The sense of social exclusion is associated with sensations and changes in the field of attention, disturbed bodily functions, decreased vigour and heart rate variability (HRV) and possibly increased negative affects (Schwerdtfeger and Friedrich-Mai, 2009).

Decreased experience of pain

DeWall and Baumeister (2006) also carried out studies to test the hypothesis that the experimental subjects at risk of social exclusion would have elevated pain thresholds as compared with socially accepted people. Subsequent research was designed to find out whether insensitivity to physical pain was associated with emotional insensitivity.

In the experiment, the feeling of being at risk of social exclusion was induced by telling some participants that psychologists 'predicted'—on the basis of self-report questionnaires—that they would live a lonely life in the future, while other participants were told that psychologists 'anticipated' them to establish several enduring and significant relationships. In fact, the questionnaire administered to the subjects was the Eysenck Personality Questionnaire measuring extraversion and introversion (Eysenck and Eysenck, 1975), which served to disguise the aim of the study. Two research groups and two control groups were randomly sampled. One of the control groups did not receive any information sealing their feature, while the other was informed about misfortunes possibly awaiting them later in life. The 'bad luck' component was introduced to exclude the possibility of associating the effects of social exclusion simply with any unpleasant future anticipations. The assumption was that the 'lonely future' sample would display both higher pain thresholds and higher pain tolerance (De Wall and Baumeister, 2006). The samples only included non-smoking and right-handed participants, because smoking had been reported to reduce pain and left limbs to be more sensitive to pain (Kanarek and Carrington, 2004, qtd. in DeWall and Baumeister, 2006). Prior to the study, the participants were supposed to abide by a dietary and medication regimen. Subsequently, the Brief Mood Introspection Scale was applied to measure the state of mood (Mayer and Gaschke, qtd. in Dewall and Baumeister, 2006), and a pressure algometer was used to measure pain response parameters—the pain threshold and pain tolerance.

The experimental results showed that the participants at risk of social exclusion exhibited significantly higher pain thresholds and also elevated pain tolerance, as compared with the remaining subjects. The effect was estimated as strong (Cohen, 1977). The Mood Scale scores did not reveal any significant emotional differences among the groups. The experiment confirmed the hypothesis that when faced with a threat to meeting their need of belonging, people become less sensitive to physical pain.

The sensation of physical cold

People who experience exclusion perceive the temperature as lower than that reported by others. This was concluded by Chen-Bo Zhong and Geoffrey J Leonardelli, who in their study entitled 'Cold and Lonely: Does Social Exclusion Literally Feel Cold?' describe the research project which showed that experiencing social exclusion increased the sensation of coldness. In fact, people are popularly known to unwittingly rely on the terminology of warmth and chill when describing their experiences. Unfriendly interactions and/or people who keep themselves at a distance are depicted as 'frigid', 'cold', 'with an icy look', etc., while friendly ones are portrayed as 'warm' or 'hot'. Experimental research has shown that people indeed literally feel cold and prefer hot meals in situations where they experience social exclusion (Zhong and Leonardelli, 2008).

In their overview of studies, Philips and Gatchel (2000) show that extroverts exhibit both higher pain thresholds and higher pain tolerance. For their part, introverts tend to conceal their pain even if they suffer a great deal. Besides this, it has been reported that chronic pain makes suffering people more introverted, more timid and more inclined to avoid social situations. Social experiences are, thus, associated with people's physical and somatic sensations (Barsalou, 1999). The specific feelings of both pain and cold may be a characteristic and probably inseparable element of the experience of social exclusion.

Notes

1 http://www.polityka.pl/swiat/analizy/1533781,1,26-ofiar-strzelaniny-w-connecticut.read#ixzz2IEJw9JnY

Part II

Experiences of exclusion

Chapter 5

How young people cope with stress

Studies carried out in recent years have shown that only moderate stress experienced at early developmental stages may have a protective function against the destructive impact of stressors in later life. Such conclusions are corroborated, for example, by the findings of research on how stress experienced in the prenatal period and at a young age affects children. These data suggest that moderate stress at early stages of individual development makes people resistant to the negative effects of stress in adult life (cf. Carmichael, 2009). Stress itself is not bad for people. If it is not long-lasting and it can be controlled and is predictable, then stress can actually increase immunity (Martin, 1997).

Stress and strain versus coping

In the broad field of stress research, the very notion of stress is understood in multiple ways. Stress is defined as an external stimulus or an external event with particular properties (i.e. a difficult situation) or as human inner emotional reactions (e.g. fear, anxiety, anger, hostility, etc.) which are experienced when faced with a particular event, and as related physiological and biochemical states which exceed the baseline activation level. Stress is also depicted as a relation between external factors and personal traits, involving a disturbance or an impending disturbance in the balance between demands posed by the environment or resulting from one's own standards and one's possibilities of meeting these demands (Wilczynska, 2013).

For the sake of clarity, in my analysis of psychophysiological conditions and consequences of responses to stressors, I distinguish between stress and strain. Stress corresponds to the mental state which is also referred to as mind stress or mental pressure, while strain represents body strain or physiological tension. Such a notional distinction helps us recognise reactions to stressors on both the psychological and the physiological levels.

Strain, which literally means 'tension', is identified by monitoring physiological changes or departures from the standard norms established for a given sex and age group. Strain can be experienced as mental pressure or stress which is physiologically expressed as a vegetative contraction or tonus associated with a response to mental challenges. It can also be triggered by unsatisfied and frustrated physiological needs. For example, malnutrition may induce reactions identical to stress-response in children. Raised blood pressure, lowered heartbeat frequency, disturbed hormone levels and the like serve as objective symptoms of changes or of the risk of changes (Maddi, 1999; Halberg et al., 2003; Sapolsky, 2004). Mental stress, followed by physiological stress, causes the person to implement action aimed at restoring the regular psychophysiological state.

Neuropsychological and neurochemical studies carried out in the last two decades (Crawford, Bazinet and Sinclair, 2009; Fontani, Corradeshi and Felici, 2005) have found that susceptibility to degenerative diseases, including those that are stress-related, is associated with component ratios in the biochemical composition of human cells. A survey of research findings suggests that nutrition has played a considerable role in making the human body less resistant to degenerative diseases over the last centuries (De Meester, 2009; Wilczyńska-Kwiatek, De Meester, Singh and Łapiński, 2010). The transformations observed in human emotional and cognitive functioning are associated with the changes in the composition of cells and with the depletion of the body's protective neurochemical resources (Wilczyńska, 2019).

Strain is the body's automatic response to stressors, but it also takes place as a result of implementing particular coping strategies in reaction to stress and everyday challenges (Wilczyńska and De Meester, 2011). Coping, which is focused on problem-solving, can reflect responses specific to people with the Type A behaviour pattern. Implementing actions that are characterised by excessive alertness and responsibility under acute time pressure increases the risk of cardiovascular disease, digestive system diseases and rheumatic disease. While the focus on emotional sensations may alleviate unpleasant feelings or suffering, it may also increase the sense of helplessness. The emotions we experience may variously affect the intensity of self-perceived stress and strain, depending on the meanings that we ascribe to these emotions and our attitudes toward them.

How responses to stress unfold is also regulated by chronobiological rhythms, which are linked to fluctuations in the functioning of the body (e.g. the secretion of hormones) across the day, the month and other timeframes. The connections between people's psychosocial functioning and the functions of their cardiac system were studied by the American psychologist and physiologist Walter Cannon (1970) nearly 100 years ago. Paul Obrist (1976) has explained the heart rate variability based on the theory of active or passive engagement in coping with stress. The theory holds that active coping increases the heart contraction rate together with systolic blood pressure. Passive coping, on the other hand, lowers the cardiac parameters.

Meditation may help people repair stress-caused damage and foster the activation of the brain regions which are responsible for learning and happiness. Results underline the unique and important role that dispositional mindfulness plays in regulating rejection fears and in supporting more constructive behaviours (Dixon and Overall, 2016). Besides this, meditation helps regulate the variability of cardiovascular functions (see also Bernardi et al., 2001). According to the data from the Centre of Mindfulness in Medicine, Health Care, and Society, the University of Massachusetts Medical School, the capacity to retain mental stability and calm displayed by Buddhist monks is of biological, rather than of mystical, character.

The practice of mindfulness is positively reflected in the improvement of focus on the task at hand. This has been demonstrated by the outcomes of at least a six-month-long systematic individual study/training in a sample of traders (Górecka, 2019). EEG tests which were administered while the subjects were practising meditation techniques and concentration showed that, as early as after only a few months, their frontal cortex had indeed enlarged, and their quantity of alpha waves linked to concentration had increased. The examination of changes in other brainwaves also implied that favourable changes had taken place. At the same time, however, QEEG monitoring of brain operations in a sample of males performing very stressful tasks that involved decision-making showed that, in strong stress situations, the participants copied their previous habits. Even those participants who had very good outcomes in mindfulness and concentration training did not employ those resources when under strong stress. This implies that the prior and more deeply entrenched habit (i.e. schema of response) is likely to have a primacy effect. In this situation, it seems that, in the following step, it would make sense to devise a strategy of changing or exploring a new way of experiencing to replace the old habit (i.e. schema/programmes) with a new response.

The rebuilding of relationships may involve what is known as reparative stress, which is associated with the individual's active endeavours to reconnect with the group despite anticipating another potential failure (Corr, 2005). The heart and the circulatory system are particularly sensitive to situations of behavioural uncertainty. A new task situation or a new socio-cognitive challenge that involves uncertainty causes the activity of the heart to increase and then to gradually decrease (Carroll, Turner and Hellawell, 1986). By monitoring the cardiovascular variability, we can obtain an insight into most human mental, cognitive and emotional motivational processes (Corr, 2005; Sosnowski, 2002).

The greatest increase in the activity of the heart was observed when people engaged in demanding cognitive tasks on a higher level than easy or impossible assignments (Allen and Crowell, 1989). Several authors have analysed this finding in relation to coping with stress, while others have concluded that it is rather linked to the kind of task to be performed (Sosen, Van der Molen, Jennings and van Beek, 2000).

As early as in the 1960s (i.e. long before Jon Kabat-Zinn developed his concept of mindfulness), John Lacey proposed the concept of 'intake-rejection of environment'. He found that when the person's attention was drawn to elements of the environment, such as music or other perception tasks, the heartbeat tended to decelerate. Furthermore and in the other way round, when the person's attention was diverted from external stimuli which could act as distractors, the heartbeat accelerated (Lacey, 1967). Schwartz and Higgins (1971) have shown that heartbeat speed increases when people imagine performing a particular activity (e.g. running). Research findings indicate that individuals' mental states and their relations with the environment also depend on the neurochemical and psychophysiological aspects of their functioning.

When children, teens or adults are forced to exceed their abilities—for example, when they are expected to perform a task when they are too tired or when activities go beyond their strength—this is a form of deregulation that leads to stress. It is exclusion in the form of ignoring the needs of a person, forcing the organism and suppressing individuality and integrity.

People are also known to activate the stress-response for psychological reasons, that is, when they actually face no objective threat to their health and lives. The chronic experience of stress is typical of 'socially advanced species', where solely psychological stimuli—such as anticipated reactions of others or the potential course and imagined consequences of events—are major stressors. The stress-response is adaptive if stressors appear in actual reality. Still, when the threat is exclusively a product of the person's mind—as when s/he is afraid to meet a deadline or believes that his/her work has not garnered enough appreciation—the mobilisation of the costly stress-response is ungrounded. Psychological stressors include current experiences (e.g. public speaking) and experiences which are remote in time and space (e.g. war on another continent, a rumination on one's death, fear of virus infection, fear of the future, fear of rejection, etc.) (Sapolsky, 2004, 2010). The above stress reactions may be connected with intense traumatic stress in childhood. Early life adversity (ELA) may affect permanent disturbances in brain-body signalling. These disturbances contribute to emotional dysregulation and physical symptoms in adulthood (Schaan et al., 2019).

Growing up as discovering oneself among others

In my research below, I look into how adolescents cope with stress caused by exclusion, including being rejected, ignored, ridiculed, etc. There are two reasons why adolescence is an optimal timeframe for identifying and studying the experience of exclusion. First, in this specific period, people mature and begin to perceive the value and importance of a wider community outside the family, therein of school and the peer group. This is also when individuals come to make a truly weighty choice for the first time in their lives, sometimes, even without fully realising it. Specifically, youngsters choose whether to abide by their family or their first socialisation group and to discover the external social world with their assistance, if not together with them, or whether to part with the family in order to later return to them when they have developed a tolerable understanding of the social world, become versed in its rules and gained its recognition. These are complicated and emotionally-fraught processes whose major aim is to grasp what one means, who one is and what place one holds in the social world. Only once having established this can one acquire a notion of one's own identity and of who one is in a general sense. This process is the first harbinger of the path on which individuals will embark on their quest for self-discovery and self-formation. While such developments typically unfold throughout adolescence, it is in adulthood that many people also strive—fully consciously this time—to live in conformity with the truth about themselves and about the world of which they are part, with this truth being different for every individual. Such efforts can be accompanied by ongoing self-improvement, in which people feel integrated with and responsible for the world.

In puberty, social developmental processes are concurrent with psychophysiological processes that promote or hamper socialisation in ways that are new to individuals. As a result of physical and biological changes, youngsters' interest in other human beings shifts from the closest caregiver to other people in school-based, peer and cultural communities. These transformations can be confounding, because even though young people come to phenotypically resemble their ancestors, the shapes that their body parts take come as a surprise to them, and they have no way of knowing when their biological development ends or reaches an advanced stage. All these shifts are entangled with individuals' expectations which have been moulded by their families and cultures. This is evinced by fashions and fads that determine a young person's attractiveness or even acceptance in the group at a certain stage of adolescence.

This is where the period of individual transformation begins during which the person will decide or express his/her will to continue in close interdependence with the group, to become relatively independent of it or to linger suspended in counterdependence. Throughout this process, the individual is subject to the operations of a powerful cluster of forces. They include, first and foremost, conscious or unconscious needs and aspirations, defence mechanisms, remembered or forgotten early experiences, transgenerational and multigenerational family transmissions and individual genetic (epigenetic) predispositions.

Depending on these memetic and genetic codes and transmissions, the transformation may be either stormy or barely noticeable to the individual. The feeling of being part of one's significant group is the most important criterion of success and failure. Since 'being' is perceived as satisfactorily continuable in the future, this criterion is tantamount to the sense of belonging. All situations which carry the risk of losing belonging trigger efforts aimed at restoring or stabilising the status quo. All situations and episodes in a young person's life which expose him/her to rejection, ridicule or disregard entail his/her body's strong stress-response and the implementation of coping strategies (Eck, Schoel and Greifeneder, 2016).

After chronic stress in childhood, long-term changes in affects may occur in adolescence and adulthood. They may be a diagnostic criterion for diagnoses such as post-traumatic stress disorder and personality change after a catastrophic experience. Researchers suggest that supporting children to adequately integrate their traumatic experience into their biographic memory is substantial to buffer the effect of childhood trauma on negative emotionality. It seems crucial to help children and adolescents who experienced early childhood trauma to increase consciousness of their stress-induced bodily and emotional changes over time. It is important to differentiate emotional and cardiac signals from bodily signals/changes. This may help them to perceive and better regulate their emotions (Schaan et al., 2019).

Analysis of stress behaviours

The literature catalogues an array of ways in which youngsters cope with stress, depending on their volition and engagement in the coping process. Bruce E Compas, Jennifer K Connor-Smith and colleagues (2001) have described young people's coping as an aspect of a broader category of self-regulation processes. They define coping as 'conscious volitional efforts to regulate emotion, cognition, behaviour, physiology and the environment in response to stressful events or circumstances' (p. 89). Regulation processes depend on the level of the individual's biological, emotional, cognitive and social development. Thus, a young person's first response to exclusion could involve conscious efforts to regulate feelings, thoughts and conduct, only later to be followed by the mobilisation of available resources for coping. Regulation processes include a wide range of responses, such as initiating, terminating or delaying a change or modifying the content and/or form or modulating the intensity of thoughts, emotions and behaviour, as well as physiological reactions and orienting/re-orienting thoughts and behaviour towards a new aim.

Individuals' respective development levels determine what resources are available to them and limit the coping responses which they can use.

Consequently, adolescents' coping-related behaviours are divided into voluntary versus involuntary, and into engagement coping, in which the stressor is approached, versus disengagement coping, in which the stressor is pushed away.

Controlled coping strategies appear as the nervous system matures in middle childhood. The initial strategies involve behaviours geared to mitigate negative emotions, withdrawal from dangerous situations and obtaining support and relief from others. Children use material objects, such as cuddly toys and pillows, to increase their sense of security and calm.

In early and middle childhood as metacognition and language skills develop, more complex strategies are used in order to assuage negative emotions, and engagement in problem-solving appears. These include restructuring problem situations, forming cognitive representations of the absent caregiver, relying on inner speech to calm negative emotions and devising new solutions to problems. In late childhood and in adolescence, even more diversified and flexible coping methods appear (Compas et al., 2001).

Engagement coping encompasses responses oriented toward exerting influence on the stressor or on the thoughts and emotions linked to the stressor. Such responses include behaviours aimed at obtaining support from others or focusing on solving the problem at hand. For example, when a group member notices that s/he is ignored by others and his/her ideas are not taken into consideration, s/he will design strategies for new ideas or new ways of communicating them and focus on implementing those. Disengagement coping involves reactions of avoiding the stressor or the thoughts and emotions related to it. They are comprised of all cognitive and emotional behaviours and processes that are geared to denying, withdrawing and diverting attention from the stressor. Jennifer K Connor-Smith and Bruce E Compas (2000) divide control processes into primary control engagement coping, which consists in problem-solving and is reflected in emotional expression and emotion modulation, and secondary control engagement coping, which entails cognitive restructuring and is expressed in positive thinking, acceptance and redirecting of attention

Disengagement coping responses include wishful thinking and denial (Connor-Smith et al., 2000).

With volition as a criterion, adolescents' reactions to stress can be divided into involuntary responses and volitional coping efforts. The former refers to all reactions of the body to stress, whatever the degree of control or consciousness of these reactions are. Sometimes, these are the first responses that the individual realised were taken notice of by others (e.g. horseplay, extreme behaviours, 'a classroom clown's' tomfoolery, etc.). The latter encompasses voluntary coping, volitional efforts and conscious control of outcomes—for example, actions focused on problem-solving or soliciting others' support, as mentioned above.

Functions of coping with social exclusion

Coping in the situation of exclusion aims to maintain, enhance or change the sense of personal control over the environment and/or over one's own reactions.

Among strategies of coping with exclusion, **basic coping strategies** concern efforts oriented toward influencing objective events or environmental conditions or toward the direct regulation of one's own emotions. They are, thus, attempts to affect others, including trying to stir their interest or to impress them in order to have their attention at least for a short amount of time. The regulation of emotions refers to any effort aimed at commanding one's feelings—for example, sadness, despair and helplessness—or at venting emotion, such as anger. It also involves shifting attention away from the stressor and finding an outlet for the mounting tension, for instance, through physical effort.

Advanced strategies for coping with social exclusion comprise two types of strategies: adaptation and change. Adaptation strategies involve all methods of coping through the individual's best possible adjustment to the existing environmental conditions. The individual endeavours to figure out the environment, its needs and rules, which requires a kind of acceptance or cognitive and, consequently, emotional restructuring. Such responses include both active coping (i.e. decision-making, direct problem solving, seeking others' understanding) and social support (i.e. soliciting emotional support or support in problem-solving).

The change strategy is a set of efforts focused on cognitive restructuring, which is geared to exploring and understanding one's own needs and those of the environment, as well as devising a plan of investment in positive changes and self-development. It is accompanied by emotional changes and attempts to understand oneself and others.

The vacuum strategy means not undertaking coping attempts as a result of the perceived lack of coping possibilities, the perceived lack of effects or a failure to see any way out of the situation. In my view, this strategy also comprises attempts at avoiding situations in which exclusion can happen or recur.

The counterstrategy refers to boycotting the endorsed ways of coping, engaging in oppositional and destructive actions or seeking socially unaccepted forms of support and help.

What do adolescents get stressed about?

Issues and stressors which are most frequently cited by children and adolescents include problems at school, domestic problems (e.g. parents and relations between them) and peer relations (e.g. friends, initial romantic relationships, etc.).

Boys more often report school- and education-related stressors, while girls report interpersonal difficulties. Irrespective of gender, adolescents most commonly cite school requirements and social expectations, fear of success, initiation of friendships and conflicts with peers (Ribner, 2005). This stands in contrast with the primary predictors of strong stress in adults, such as 'daily hassles', which are qualitatively different from interpersonal and school problems reported by youngsters (Lazarus and De Longis, 1983). Major adult stressors are reported by them as associated with financial problems, household maintenance and childrearing responsibilities.

Younger children are more likely to rely on problem-focused solutions. The use of emotion-focused strategies increases with age and the level of development. Such strategies emerge in late childhood, and its application increases until late adolescence. Emotion-focused strategies are especially useful in situations where individuals have no influence on what is going on but must participate in it nonetheless (e.g. destructive family relations) or where they assess action as ineffective. The incidence of emotion-focused coping increases as children grow and develop in later years (Frydenberg and Lewis, 2000).

Children who lithely 'switch' between these two coping modes and use them flexibly are described as more competent socially. As children grow, they switch between the two strategies with increasing flexibility, particularly in situations when this is more adaptive (Pincus an Friedman, 2004).

Children who often use emotion-focused coping in response to situations that are difficult to control are perceived as better socially adapted (Pincus and Friedman, 2004). When it is possible to control the stressor, children and adolescents more often rely on problem-focused coping. Research has shown that when adolescents and children used problem-focused strategies in controllable interpersonal situations, they exhibited fewer behavioural-emotional issues. At the same time, emotion-focused coping initiated in corresponding situations was positively correlated with emotional problems (Compas et al., 1998). Social exclusion counts as what is referred to as a high-risk situation in which the individual's situation may deteriorate if the devised coping strategy fails to produce expected outcomes. To avoid pain is a natural human tendency, and rejection by the individual's significant others breeds emotional pain which is identical to physical pain. Emotional pain tends to be called mental or social pain.

Girls are more likely than boys to fall back on nonadaptive strategies of coping with stress, such as tension reduction, ignoring the problem or self-blame. Boys tend to seek to decompose strain (e.g. by engaging in physical exercises and playing video games), but they also often ignore problems and do not reveal their feelings. As a rule, they do not admit that they cannot see how they can cope. Girls more often than boys own up to the fact that they have no strategy of coping with problems (cf. Frydenberg and Lewis, 2000).

As adolescents grow up, they increasingly often use productive strategies. The most conspicuous shift in adolescents' coping has been observed between 14 and 16 years of age; the repertoire expands, and the number of both productive and non-productive coping strategies increases. This suggests that this period may be associated with young people's reflection on coping styles and on the effectiveness of the strategies they use. Starting at about 14 years of age, youngsters more than ever rely on the strategies of seeking social support and reducing tension. Thereby, as compared with boys, girls tend to use increasingly more dysfunctional strategies (Frydenberg and Lewis, 2000). This finding is consistent with the studies showing that girls in middle adolescence have lower self-worth than boys. This result is explained by citing girls' considerable sensitivity to cultural, therein medial, messages which highlight the ideal image of the woman.

At around 16 years of age, young people more often engage in social activity and look for spiritual support, physical recreation and professional help. The older adolescents grow, the more prone they are to self-blame and to reducing tension by alcohol consumption or overeating. Older adolescents are also less inclined to work hard and to seek professional support.

Children and adolescents usually do not remember strong stress experiences and traumatic events from early childhood. Their potential for resilience may be undercut if trauma was severe or repeated. At later developmental stages, their ways of coping with stress result from the resources which have remained available in the aftermath of such very early traumas. Psychologists seek to establish how productive and unproductive coping strategies that adolescents use are, without correlating them with their family situations, environments in which they have been growing up and other experiences that activate particular response schemas. However, it is imperative to study such correlations. It is also imperative to engage children who fail to cope with stress or cope with it unproductively in such therapeutic relationships that will help retrieve the layers of memory which are still relatively accessible before they are pushed even deeper down under the mass of defence responses to the world and to themselves.

Adolescents' ways of coping with the stress of exclusion

Frydenberg and Lewis (1993) have compiled a list of 18 strategies used by adolescents to cope—the Adolescent Coping Scale—and classified them under three major coping styles. The authors identify the following three styles of coping:

1. Solving the Problem, defined as productive coping through applying various ways to solve the problem at hand;

2. Non-Productive Coping, described as an inability to cope or as avoidance of coping; and
3. Reference to Others, depicted as approaching others for help, using support of other people or joining organisations

These three styles are comprised of various combinations of behaviour strategies, specifically:

1. Solving the Problem encompasses eight strategies oriented toward problem-solving, whereby the individual retains an optimistic attitude and a sense of freedom in social relations with others.

   These strategies are: seeking social support, focusing on solving the problem at hand, sports recreation (e.g. practising a sport, cultivating health and fitness), finding a relaxing entertainment or hobby (e.g. listening to music, reading, drawing), investing in close friends, striving to feel that one belongs (e.g. caring about relations and improving rapport with others), goal-achievement through hard work and goal aspiration (e.g. ambition), and focusing on the positives.
2. Non-Productive Coping is comprised of eight strategies associated with avoidance or incapacity of coping.

   These strategies include worrying, striving to belong (i.e. worrying about what others think), wishful thinking, not coping (i.e. not perceiving coping possibilities, inability to share the problem and developing psychosomatic symptoms), ignoring the problem, tension reduction (e.g. through drinking and smoking), keeping to oneself and self-blame.
3. Reference to Others is composed of four strategies and is characterised by appealing to others (e.g. peers, professionals, God/deities) for help and/or support.

   These strategies include seeking social support, seeking spiritual support, seeking professional help and implementing social actions (Frydenberg and Lewis, 2000).

Coping strategies in situations of exclusion:

1. SEEK SOCIAL SUPPORT – the strategy is reflected in looking for people who can offer support and in talking about one's problem. For example, when children who feel excluded approach a trusted person who can help them solve the problem or offer support. 'I will look for a trusted adult and tell them about my problem: they are laughing at me at school'.
2. FOCUS ON SOLVING THE PROBLEM – the strategy concerns concrete solutions. When being rejected, ridiculed and excluded in other ways, the person may explore the problem, identify his/

her behaviours which are negatively marked by the group and consider changing them. As described above, exclusion is often a means that the group uses to maintain control and to eliminate destructive and undesirable behaviours. 'I will identify the problem, find a solution, test it in a safe setting and apply it in my group'.

3. WORK HARD AND ACHIEVE – the strategy is characterised by individuals' dedication, ambitious plans and, above all, motivation to gain social approval through succeeding in a field of his/her choice; it may involve rivalry or attempts to prove one's worth. 'I will work hard to achieve, to be the best in this field, and I will be noticed'.
4. WORRY – the strategy typically involves ruminating and fear-tinted thoughts. People are anxious about the future in general, especially about their happiness in the future—a sensation which paralyses them. 'I am not important and I do not fit in; maybe I do not belong in here; the future may be difficult or there may be no future whatsoever'.
5. INVEST IN CLOSE FRIENDS – the strategy in which one copes through entering a relationship with a person or people in a similar situation, promoting mutual support or spending time together. 'I will find an ally and establish a relationship with another person'.
6. BELONG – the strategy generally represents taking care of relationships with other people and specifically the concern whether others consider the individual a member of the group. It may be a symptom of foresight, excessive courtesy and conformity in relationships in order to belong, or it may involve pursuits to be part of the group in any available way (e.g. as an emotional leader or as a mascot). 'I constantly build relations with others and will be part of the group in order to avoid exclusion'.
7. DO WISHFUL THINKING – this kind of thinking is based on the faith that everything is or will be alright and on the expectations of favourable outcomes. 'It is difficult now, but things will turn around and it will be better.'
8. DO SOCIAL ACTION – this strategy consists in telling others about the problem and soliciting help/support through complaints or launching social actions in support of excluded people. 'Let us start an initiative supporting people who experience exclusion'.
9. REDUCE TENSION – this strategy involves attempts to feel better through reducing tension, such as binge-watching, playing video games and using tension-lowering substances (e.g. alcohol).

'I'll spend all my free time playing video games, or I will have a pint and I will be less stressed out'.

10. NOT COPE – it represents a lack of strategy and reflects the individual's inability to cope with the problem, often involving the emergence of psychosomatic symptoms. 'There is no possibility to cope'.
11. IGNORE THE PROBLEM – this strategy is characterised by a conscious denial of the problem and by resignation, which is combined with accepting that there is no way to handle the problem. 'There is no problem whatsoever; I do not need others, and I have no need to be with others'.
12. DO SELF-BLAME – this strategy implies that the person believes that s/he is the cause of problems and often entails acceptance. 'I know that I am no good at being and living with others; I am an oddball, and nobody can possibly take it, but it is my responsibility, and I accept it'.
13. KEEP TO SELF – this strategy is characterised by withdrawal and concealment of the individual's problems from others, which is often accompanied by shame at being excluded. 'Nobody needs to know what is going on; I will not tell anybody; I am alone and will be alone in it'.
14. SEEK SPIRITUAL SUPPORT – this strategy reflects prayer and involves faith in having divine protection or the help of a spiritual guide. 'I believe that things will change; I pray for my situation to change'.
15. FOCUS ON THE POSITIVE – this strategy is characterised by an optimistic outlook on the current situation. It involves perceiving the upsides of the events and regarding oneself as a lucky person. 'Apparently, it was meant to be, and I am lucky that this is how it has panned out; I only have more time for myself if I do not spend it with others'.
16. SEEK PROFESSIONAL HELP – this strategy entails using the help of a counselling professional. 'I will consult a psychologist or a coach to help me find out what to do'.
17. SEEK RELAXING DIVERSIONS – this strategy consists in indulging in a relaxing pastime or hobby, such as painting, dancing or meditation. 'I will listen to my favourite music and relax'.
18. DO PHYSICAL RECREATION – this strategy includes various sports and physical exercises. 'I will shape up, train my body and improve my fitness'.

The 18 types of coping behaviours, which are referred to as strategies, are combined in various arrangements into three broader groups called coping styles.

The results of a study carried out on a sample of youngsters aged from 11 to 17 years old have shown a high correlation between helpful strategies and non-productive strategies. It is not easy to interpret this finding, since the use of productive coping strategies, as a rule, makes the dysfunctional ones redundant and, consequently, people discard them. Nevertheless, adolescents apply non-productive coping strategies when the productive ones fail for one reason or another. Non-productive strategies appear in stressful situations, such as previous and repeated social exclusion.

Likewise, so far, research has not provided any data which makes it possible to predict how adolescents cope when faced with the risk of social exclusion. In this context, to describe the relationship between adolescents' coping ways and factors in social exclusion is an urgent and practically relevant endeavour/venture. Given this, the following sections of this book present my original research study and its findings, which foreground the individual perspective and the mobilisation of a comprehensive range of mental processes and individual characteristics.

Strategies of positive change

As individuals' awareness of existing in the world develops, coping strategies that are based on expanding their possibilities by crossing the previous frameworks of social perception are becoming increasingly important. Effective strategies of positive growth in the 'change strategies' category are: the strategy of augmenting the individual's emotional and cognitive system and the strategy of enhancing the capacities of group members, therein social perception, improved empathetic understanding, heightened compassion and readiness to engage in non-standard actions. The former strategy concerns the increase in mindfulness, self-development, the expansion of positive thinking and self-soothing. Research confirms that mindfulness and compassion are factors in enlarging brain structures within the cerebral cortex. Emphatically, however, it is vital to develop 'new solutions' that can replace the 'old habits' of thinking and destructive emotions. Automatically kicking in stressful situations, the old habits cause dysregulation and obscure the possibility of using newly built cerebral structures for coping. Actually, when people face exclusion, instead of exhibiting their newly-trained and desirable resources of self-compassion, they fall back on lower-order defence mechanisms rooted in the brain areas which are strongly linked to the limbic system rather than to the neocortex. When a panic fear of exclusion arises, there is neither time nor space for initiating any of the constructive strategies of coping with the consequences of the stressful situation, as described in the previous chapter. As fear prevails, people habitually resort to primitive responses of attack (e.g. aggression), escape (e.g. alcohol and substance abuse) or freezing (i.e. the vaccum strategy) (Wilczynska, Januszek and Bargiel-Matusiewicz, 2015). The strategies which were described above as proposed by scholars only offer a second chance of coping when the exclusion-related event has already happened. The other developmental strategy involves, for example, fostering and developing empathy, stimulating the social imagination and initiating reflective actions. The technique of enhancing non-evaluative mindful attention may help adolescents better understand their internal states. However, as automatic responses to stressful situations are generally more available to individuals, communities similarly rely on automatic 'habits' of reactions which are underpinned by primitive mechanisms of survival and competition. The former is particularly strong when the risk of exclusion appears in the group (Schaan et al., 2019).

People's commitment to developing strategies that foster and reinforce empathy and prosocial behaviour is sometimes viewed as a heroic feat, because it requires intentional reflection and imagination—that is, empathetic crossing beyond the rigorously delimited 'secure' and usually informal group norms. Besides this, such acts also take courage to manifest a divergent viewpoint or an alternative approach in the group for the sake of protecting and supporting another human being. In fact, this is one way of supporting individuals at risk of self-exclusion or social exclusion.

There is not a single, invariably useful and universal coping strategy. Changing somebody's mind is not easy because of deeply imprinted information/programmes from their past.

Recent psychological research reports that therapy of adults suffering from loneliness, anxiety and depression focuses on reducing causes by using combined therapeutic strategies. Targeted psychotherapy which employs substances affecting states of consciousness helps reach deep layers of memory and releases emotions accumulated since childhood and related to difficult family histories.

Chapter 6

Teenagers at risk of social exclusion

The issues related to the risk of exclusion are mainly discussed in the context of implementing effective prosocial policies and preventing social exclusion. In literature, two broad approaches to this problem are prevalent. One of them relies on sociological theories, such as theories of social inequality and social stratification and/or theoretical explorations of poverty and deprivation (Silver, 2006; Levitas, 2005; Szarfenberg, 2005a). The other approach, which is more affiliated with the psychological take on individuals' experiences of and coping with difficult situations, depicts social exclusion in terms of the conditions and consequences of rejection, the frustration of the need of belonging and the sense of belonging (Baumeister and Leary, 1995; Hagerty et al., 1992; Wilczyńska, 2013).

Psychologists who advocate this approach focus on studying the consequences of exclusion of individuals in experimental conditions. In controlled, laboratory settings, they conduct observations to examine how the risk of social exclusion affects the psychophysiological (Herman and Panskep, 1978; Eisenberg, Lieberman and Williams, 2003), behavioural-cognitive (Twenge, Baumeister, Tice and Stucke, 2001; Twenge et al., 2007) and emotional (De Wall and Baumeister, 2006; Twenge, Catanese and Baumeister, 2003) changes in people's functioning.

They research and look for new ways of supporting group members who are excluded or at risk of exclusion, thereby devising programmes for reducing differences, social stereotypes and prejudices.

Nevertheless, when surveying the existing research findings, one can easily notice that there is no single, integrated framework for exploring psychological and situational factors in young people's behaviour when faced with social exclusion, one of the greatest contemporary threats. The psychological dimension of adolescents' functioning when at risk of social exclusion has not been comprehensively discussed in the literature yet.

In designing the studies discussed here, the underlying assumption was that the problem issues can at least partly be explained by investigating how individuals experience and cope with difficult and/or stressful situations. The existing research findings concerning stress have not conclusively.

As social distancing and segregation are growing, increasingly more young people feel socially excluded. Furthermore, although most young people (Twenge, 2017) believe that they should express tolerant attitudes and that minorities or aliens should be protected, they fail to stand up in defence of these values when they find themselves under threat. Young people fear that their future is bound up with the prospect of loneliness. Today, a lot of young people tend to curb their contact with others, including sexual contact, already when growing up. Major communication models, with virtual communication as the prevalent one, pull people apart and do not protect them against cyberhate and bullying, which shifts from school settings and into individuals' private lives. However, the behaviours initiated by children and adolescents in various situations involving the risk of exclusion have not been systematically studied yet. Rather, the most spectacular manifestations of adolescents' sense of rejection, such as school shootings and suicides, occasionally make it to the press headlines and primetime news programmes.

Reports based on the statistics of the Polish Ministry of Health offer surprising and worrying data. Specifically, the number of children and adolescents who use interventions from mental health specialists is growing at a staggering pace in Poland, with one in five young people having already consulted a psychologist or a psychiatrist or being in regular therapy. According to reports, adolescents and children in the United States and Poland alike do not believe that they are attractive, that the future will be good or that life even makes sense.[1]

Discussing the risk of social exclusion and solving problems related to it are among the most pertinent social challenges today, because young people's future and the future of their communities hinge on how strong and supported youngsters feel now. Individuals will develop autonomously and invest positively in others and in the future generations provided that they live in a good-enough community that makes sure they feel that they belong (i.e. that while growing up, they feel like a fitting and appreciated part of their community).

While the problem of social exclusion calls for urgent study, researching social exclusion is plagued by several limitations. On one hand, such research shows an important social issue, yet on the other hand, it is fraught with a risk of stigmatising individuals, social groups and entire communities while examining this phenomenon.

Selecting research methods produces doubts, as some of them may expose the subjects to the experience of rejection anew. As already observed, the findings of experimental research into social exclusion have importantly contributed to social psychology, but the participation of children and adolescents in such studies is not recommended due to ethical considerations.

Studies carried out in natural conditions seem to be both scientifically advantageous and practically valuable. The risk of stigmatisation and of experimentally induced exclusion is minimised. This approach requires a special caution in choosing research instruments and wariness of potential confounders.

Under the conditions of 'a natural social experiment', research opportunities expand, and the findings are more readily translatable into psychological practice.

The aim and the implementation of the research project

The study aimed to identify the conditions of adolescents' coping in various situations involving the risk of social exclusion.

The survey of the literature does not facilitate positing any hypotheses in this respect, because the relevant studies are scarce, and their findings predominantly concern the outcomes of adults in experimental laboratory conditions. Additionally, the findings about human functioning when at risk of social exclusion tend to be contradictory to a degree, as outlined above. Given this, the research problem was formulated in an open-ended fashion in order to explore the issue comprehensively. The central research intent was 'to depict how adolescents cope in situations involving the risk of social exclusion', that is, in the context of multiple situational and psychological conditions.

The risk of social exclusion was defined as a subjectively perceived set of factors and life circumstances (situational conditions) combined with the related individual personal characteristics (psychological conditions, i.e. the person's own resources and features) that are associated with adolescents' functioning, especially with their coping. Youths at risk of social exclusion have limited opportunities for performing social roles and participating in mainstream social life.

This definition emphasises individuals' self-perceptions of their own traits, the characteristics of the situation as well as the manner of functioning or coping in the situation of exclusion. The constrained participation in mainstream social life and the reduced possibility of coping or lowered social-role performance are understood, above all, as limited participation in the existing formal and informal social groups within and outside the school which are accessible to others (to the majority) and in which individuals can feel that they are appreciated and that they fit in (Hagerty, Williams, Coyne and Early, 1996). This condition is also fulfilled when individuals join minority groups, but at the same time, they do not feel that they belong and do not feel valued in the groups which are commonly accessible to others.

Possible predictors of social exclusion, with the sense of belonging serving as its indicator, include factors related to particular risks (their types and intensity, e.g. school- and family-related risks), as well as the individual's self-perceived need of belonging.

One indicator of the risk of social exclusion is the lowered sense of belonging and a related ensemble of other symptoms, such as reduced self-esteem, raised levels of anger and aggression, changed mood, limited empathetic compassion and the thwarting of prosocial behaviours (DeWall, Anderson and Bushman, 2011; Twenge, Baumeister, Tice and Stucke, 2001; Twenge et al., 2007; Connor-Smith et al., 2000). Such a constellation of characteristics may impair the individual's capacity of coping with stress and solving problems through contact with others, expression of his/her feelings, seeking support and active pursuits. In other words, this can produce the risk of social exclusion as a result of abstaining/disengagement from activities, especially from those based on interactions with others (Baumeister and Leary, 1995). These variables, together with the reasons behind their selection, are described in the subchapter devoted to the space of variables. The image of their interdependencies is rendered in the confirmatory theoretical model.

The study was carried out in two stages, with the data handled in a distinct way in each of them:

I In the first stage, the data were introduced into the research model in the quantitative way for the entire sample.
II In the second stage, the variables were introduced into the model in the qualitative way for the subsamples identified in terms of the kind of social exclusion risk.

Why the two-stage data analysis was used is explained in the section that describes the processing of the generated data (Wilczynska, 2013).

The nature of the studied variables

The research design was predominantly based on exploratory analyses.

In the first stage, the confirmatory theoretical model was analysed, and an exploratory analysis was subsequently performed. Two categories of exogenous variables were defined:

1 Risk of social exclusion (three risk factors in social exclusion)
2 Need of belonging

The other variables were introduced into the model as endogenous variables.

In the second stage, the intercorrelations among the variables were analysed separately for each risk group, and their relevance to the mobilisation of coping strategies was investigated. This examination was based on exploratory analyses and an agglomerative analysis. In this way, psychological profiles were generated for each risk group, depending on their respective configurations of situational factors and personal conditions. The need of belonging was defined as an exogenous variable.

The risk of social exclusion

The existing studies on adolescents' functioning when at risk of social exclusion conspicuously fail to take into account the perspective of the individual at risk. Research problems are mainly informed by assessments from external observers who examine selected aspects of adolescents' coping in situations which are regarded as excluding or as producing the risk of social exclusion. Prior studies have often included sizeable samples of adolescents, but individual case studies have only been illustrative or not numerous enough to generalise their findings onto populations.

In this research study, the risk of social exclusion is comprehended as the current configuration of adolescent-perceived problematic factors and circumstances in life which preclude meeting the need of belonging and achieving the sense of belonging, which affects individuals' functioning in their environment, hampers their performance of some social roles and limits their participation in their significant fields of social life.

In the study, the risk of social exclusion was measured by means of a purpose-developed questionnaire called the Social Exclusion Risk Scale (SERS; Polish: *Skala Zagrożenia Wykluczeniem Społecznym/SZWS*). The questionnaire measures factors in three different categories of the risk of social exclusion; specifically:

- family-related risks,
- school-related risks, and
- personal risks.

Risk factors in social exclusion are associated with adolescents' functioning and, consequently, with particular ways of coping. Across these factors, the risk is variously linked to the application of active coping strategies, emotion-focused strategies and the seeking of social support. It must also be taken into account that the risk produced by certain factors makes individuals withdraw from coping, rather than engaging in coping (cf. Weisz Mccabe and Denning, 1994; Connor-Smith et al., 2000). Some similar results have been obtained in studies on rejection, where individuals at risk avoided focusing on emotions, did not seek social support and, indeed, viewed with hostility the people whom they could approach for help, responding with aggression and withdrawal from prosocial behaviours (Twenge et al., 2007; Twenge, Baumeister, Tice and Stucke, 2001). Individuals have also been observed to exhibit 'encapsulation' as their first response to social exclusion (Garbarino, 1999).

In these three categories, risk factors in social exclusion are diversely associated with adolescents' coping.

Below, I discuss the variables and personal characteristics that were taken into account in this study, as suggested by the review of literature and the research findings chiefly reported by American scholars.

The need to belong

The need of belonging is regarded as a precursor or an antecedent of the sense of belonging. It is defined as the person's potential, energy and striving for meaningful involvement and as a resource that can be shared or complementary (Hagerty et al., 1992, p. 174). The need of belonging concerns the individual's desire to meaningfully engage in relationships, to be appreciated and to fit in with others through an identifiable potential for complementarity (i.e. the perceived shared or complementary characteristics).

The need of belonging, or the need for relatedness, is associated with people's propensity to establish relations with others, to care about them and to be in a community. This need is particularly pronounced in adolescence when the peer group is an important point of reference for a young person who is looking for authority figures outside the family and among people of comparable age or other significant adults (Deci and Ryan, 1991).

An increased motivation for engagement and an increased need for compatibility with others, alignment with others and involvement in meaningful activities typify a heightened need of belonging. Individuals feel at risk of exclusion when their need of belonging is not met and when they do not achieve the sense of belonging despite their desire for involvement (Newman, 2004).

The need of belonging in people at risk of social exclusion tends to be less revealed than in people who face no such risk (Twenge, Catanse and Baumeister, 2003; Baumeister, Brewer, Tice and Twenge, 2007; Baumeister and Leary, 1995). Young people are known to withdraw from relationships and minimise their expectations towards others out of fear that they will be rejected again (Garbarino, 1999). The need of belonging serves as a mental motivation to solicit others' attention and to communicate one's need to be an integral part of the group. The manifestation of this need should help individuals satisfy it and, thus, to increase their sense of belonging.

The sense of belonging

The sense of belonging denotes both the experience of being appreciated, needed, respected and considered important by others and the experience of fitting in or the sense of compatibility with other people, groups, organisations and/or environments. Belonging is the opposite of exclusion and is a unique concept that is distinct from other constructs, such as loneliness, alienation or soliciting social support, which are discussed in the literature (Baumeister and Leary, 1995; Hagerty and Patusky, 1995). People who feel that they belong may experience loneliness as a result of separation or parting. The sense of belonging is the necessary condition for a youngster to establish his/her place within the group, in the sense of his/her special position associated with his/her exceptionality and uniqueness. If this condition is not met to the indispensable minimum degree, the person starts feeling irrelevant, unneeded, unwanted and, as such, standing no chance of living a happy life and especially of having a successful relationship with another person. People who feel they belong are less depressive and have better social functioning outcomes (Napoli, Marsiglia and Kulis, 2003; Hagerty et al., 1992, 1996).

A low sense of belonging can be an indicator of the sense of social exclusion. The level of belonging is usually correlated with the urge to express the need of belonging. The less effort and commitment the person invests in seeking possibilities of joining in, fitting in and being appreciated, the lesser sense of belonging s/he tends to exhibit. The two variables are in fact reciprocally associated, for the individual who strongly believes that s/he stands little chance of social inclusion may altogether give up on efforts to belong. Most people who experienced a tolerably balanced upbringing and development find externalising the need of belonging a natural thing. People who faced adverse responses from their environment early in life tend to learn how to express their needs later in life.

People who become personally involved in a system or an environment feel that they are an integral part of this system or this environment (Hagerty and Patusky, 1995, p. 173). In this study, the sense of belonging is approached as a psychological equivalent of being 'socially included'.

Experiential and strategic emotional intelligence

Emotional intelligence and related socio-emotional competencies represent one of the important predictors of success and coping. The capacity to understand oneself, to self-regulate and to aptly read one's own and others' emotional states makes it easier for people to cope with difficulties and to marshal their strength for effort (Goleman, 1997). In fact, emotional intelligence enables people to navigate the complexities of social relations and to recognise their need of belonging.

Research confirms that emotional intelligence is a factor in school achievements and vocational success (Schutte et al., 1998), as well as highlighting the relevance of emotional intelligence to individuals' mental well-being, satisfaction from the quality of interpersonal relationships and general contentment with life (Salovey, Mayer and Caruso, 2004).

Studies of the 'emotional numbness' syndrome, which is characteristic of excluded people, report reduced empathy and increased difficulty in understanding one's own and others' feelings. This is explained, among others, as self-doubt and the loss of confidence in one's own capacity to understand and to successfully cope in such a situation (Twenge, Catanese and Baumeister, 2003).

If we know about the individual's potentials and possible deficits in emotional intelligence, we can better understand his/her possible difficulties and failures in interactions with others. Emotional intelligence is comprised of two specific faculties: experiential emotional intelligence and strategic emotional intelligence. The former is grounded on empathy, that is, on understanding and endorsing other people's feelings, accepting one's own feelings and expressing them in action. The latter concerns controlling and understanding one's own feelings, directing their flow and revealing them in deliberately selected circumstances. In adolescents at risk of social exclusion, these two indicators of emotional intelligence can be expected to be mutually independent. This means that experiential emotional intelligence is linked to the sense of belonging and the expression of the need of belonging, while strategic emotional intelligence, which is associated with greater control over emotional states, is connected to self-esteem, attitude to the self and the way of thinking about oneself (Rosenberg, 1965).

Emotional intelligence reflects the individual's potential to cope in situations involving relations with other people. Its manifestations in the forms of experiential and strategic emotional intelligence may provide feedback in the situations of coping with the risk of exclusion, with empathy on one hand and understanding and controlling emotions on the other both playing an important adaptive role.

Mood and positive emotions

In recent years, psychologists have become particularly interested in coping through the regulation of emotions. Coping through the command of emotions involves experiencing and expressing feelings. Susan Folkman and Judith Tedlie Moskowitz (2004) have identified three ways of coping which generate positive affective outcomes: a positive secondary appraisal, i.e. a cognitive strategy which consists in identifying advantages of stressful events; goal-orientation through setting realistic priorities, adaptive recasting of goals and stimulating goal-oriented coping; and ascribing positive meanings to common, everyday events.

Mood is defined as an affective experience of moderate duration which encompasses three dimensions of core affect: tense arousal, energetic arousal and hedonistic tone (Matthews, Jones and Chamberlain, 1990).

Research has found that prolonged or acute exclusion leads to temporary mood impairments or even to depression, which is followed by the restoration of mental balance (Warr, 2004). Depressive symptoms in adolescents can be triggered by both genetic factors and changes in brain biochemistry, as well as by psychological and situational factors, such as adults' destructive behaviours, family conflicts, love disappointments or the loss of a loved one or a close relationship.[2]

Experimental findings concerning exclusion have shown that the mood of people at risk of exclusion ostensibly does not differ from the mood of people who face no such risk (Twenge et al., 2007). In fact, quite an opposite effect has been described, as people who have experienced a serious risk of exclusion report positive moods or the so-called self-regulation of mood takes place, which is characteristic for people who display higher self-esteem and low depression levels due to an unrecognised increase of positive emotions (DeWall, Anderson and Bushman, 2011). This may indicate the activation of an automatic self-rescue mechanism, which is also explained by recourse to the concept of cognitive dissonance. In order to continue to function, the individual who has high self-esteem 'diminishes' the significance of events or of people. Mood appears to be an important variable that can help establish how people at risk of exclusion regulate their emotions.

As research findings in this respect are inconclusive, it was assumed that the sense of belonging would be associated with positive mood in adolescence, high hedonistic tone.

Self-esteem

Self-esteem is still in the focus of several researchers, because finding out how people think of themselves and what their attitudes to the self are helps understand how they function socially and how they experience and receive reality. High self-esteem is the belief that one is 'good enough' and valuable as a human being. Low self-esteem means being dissatisfied with oneself and not accepting the self (Rosenberg, 1965).

Self-evaluation can be described as a state which reflects the likelihood of social exclusion and of the sense of belonging (Leary, 2004). As such, it is a possible response to social approval or disapproval that the individual is experiencing at a given moment.

People with high self-esteem perceive themselves as more attractive socially, but they are more likely to become angry and undertake risky behaviours when their self-esteem is jeopardised (Baumeister et al., 2003). They have more trust in themselves, a greater need for achievement and a lower need for social support (Dzwonkowska, Lachowicz-Tabaczek and Łaguna, 2008). High self-evaluation is associated with experiencing positive emotions. DeWall and colleagues (2011) have shown that people with low depression levels and high self-esteem respond to social exclusion with increased positive emotions.

Therefore, self-evaluation is involved in acceptance or rejection. The frustrated need of belonging can show in reduced self-esteem and, thus, stir the conviction that one is not accepted enough or valuable as a human being.

The individual's attitude to the self can incline him/her to activate particular ways of coping. Thus, the self-assessment variable seems to be an indicator not only of the acceptance level, but also of the implemented behaviours.

Anger expression

Anger and aggression are among the most frequently cited manifestations of the feeling of social exclusion and are the opposite of productive coping. Anger is an emotional response whose expression is as a rule negatively perceived by society. Externally directed anger can speak to frustration or to attempts at controlling the environment; however, to 'repel' others can also be one of its functions. Children and adolescents who exhibit aggressive behaviours are less accepted and less liked by their peers.

Frustration-triggered anger enhances the inclination for aggressive behaviours (Berkowitz, 1989). The incidence of actual aggressive responses is determined by the intensity of anger and the strength of signal stimuli in a given situation. The intensity of experienced anger depends on the acuteness of physiological arousal generated by aversive events and on the way in which the individual explains and assesses arousal (Zillmann, 1979).

Expression of anger may be associated not only with hostile or aggressive behaviours, but also with socially accepted reactions. It is observed that the stronger the tendency to reveal externally directed anger, the greater the inclination for aggressive behaviours (e.g. physical or verbal assaults), negativism and irritability. At the same time, internally directed anger corresponds to controlling, suppressing, clarifying and naming anger responses, rather than venting them on others.

As the risk of social exclusion increases, externally directed anger tends to exacerbate. Restricted available options, space or equipment trigger aggression. The classic experiment carried out by Barker, Dembo and Lewin (1941) already showed that children whose access to toys within their reach was constrained responded far more destructively and aggressively as compared with children who did not know that there were toys to be used in the first place. Angry and aggressive behaviours can also result from the desire to restore control; for example, an aggressive response is better than no response at all (Leary, Twenge and Quinivan, 2006). It is also a way of improving mood or expressing revenge or punishment for one's deeds (Twenge, Baumeister, Tice and Stucke, 2001).

Anger can be an automatic response to the risk of social exclusion when the individual does not see any other way of coping with the situation.

The sense of being rejected breeds aggression which can be suppressed by the individual if s/he perceives other people as a source of future acceptance.

The exploration of the anger variable in terms of its direction and intensity helps explain why adolescents initiate or, for that matter, do not initiate certain coping strategies.

Coping in difficult and stressful situations

Coping with exclusion, and especially adolescents' coping in difficult and stressful situations, encompasses three major ways of coping: active coping oriented towards solving the problem, focusing on emotions and seeking social support.

The relationship between adolescents' ways of coping and the risk of social exclusion has not been investigated enough. The studies on coping with stress carried out among teenagers have not established conclusively which coping strategies are most preferred or most frequently chosen. It turns out that adolescents simultaneously use the strategies which are geared to problem-solving and avoidance strategies. However, it has been shown that reliance on multiple strategies, that is, a certain flexibility in applying them, is associated with individuals' better mental adaptation and greater social competencies in difficult situations (Pincus and Friedman, 2004). Frydenberg and Lewis (1999, 2000, 2002) have found that young people tend to apply productive and non-productive techniques at the same time, and that it is impossible to identify the dominant way of coping especially for the age group between 14 and 16 years of age.

Adolescents are known to activate nonproductive and even entirely destructive ways of coping when faced with rejection (Leary et al., 2001). Behaviour in the situation of exclusion is linked to the state known as cognitive deconstruction, which resembles people's 'pre-suicidal' functioning. It is manifested, for example, in emotional indifference, intensified musing on pointlessness, avoidance of self-awareness and general lethargy (Twenge, Catanes and Baumeister, 2003). Adolescents at risk of social exclusion can be expected to engage in unforesightful and nonproductive coping activities or to abstain from action altogether.

School shootings and suicides, the number of which increases every year among adolescents, are among the most dramatic responses and reactions to exclusion.

Coping with stress depends not only on individually perceived features of the situation, but also on the configuration of personal properties or psychological characteristics. Understanding the factors which condition launching particular ways of coping may help design and implement preventive interventions that are geared, for example, toward strengthening the resources of adolescents.

Description of our study of Polish youths

The study of the sense of belonging in young people was carried out on a sample of 643 young Poles. The younger subsample (below 16 years of age, $n = 332$) was additionally assessed in terms of the risk of social exclusion. In the first stage of the study, the average age of the respondents was

$M = 20.73$. The total sample included students of lower and upper secondary schools and university freshmen.

For the study that focused on exclusion risk factors identified in the social environment, a sample of youngsters were recruited from a number of randomly chosen public lower secondary schools. The average age was $M = 15.72$. Three hundred and eighteen fully eligible sets of research results were collected. Young people whose personality structures are fragile and unrounded are most vulnerable to being hurt. At the same time, the period of maturation and defining social roles is the stage in human life when the experience of exclusion is easy to come by and happens more frequently than in adult life. The sense of belonging is one of the main dimensions which determine the status of a young person in the group. Teenagers usually rebel in their families when these families are a tolerably solid basis for them. Stable and strong parents or parent are a guarantee that limits will be set and the family will not fall apart. It is one of the reasons why, as my observations suggest, in 'weakened' families (e.g. ones where a single mother raises her children alone not by choice, but because things have panned out this way), teenagers don't want to burden others with additional troubles. Similarly, in families in which members suffer from serious mental or physical disorders, young people's cases of rebellions are usually mild. This is because, when youngsters rebel, they in fact do not want to 'destroy' their family. Separation and individuation as a way to construct themselves as stronger and separate individuals are possible only when the family provides a quite stable basis for further optimal development. When young people feel as important and appreciated members of the family system, their sense of belonging improves their prospects of developing into autonomous and independent people. To accomplish this, they must feel that there is an important group in their lives where they feel seen, wanted and loved (Siegel and Bryson, 2020). If they cannot find support in their family, they tend to seek it outside the family. For the purposes of this study, I assumed that it is the sense of belonging that determines how a person's traits are shaped and used. Besides the sense and the need of belonging, I also examined mood, the ways in which teenagers cope with emotions, especially with anger, and the variations in their self-esteem. Additionally, I examined whether ways of coping with stress change as the sense of being at risk of social exclusion changes.

Psychological tools

A set of standardised psychological tools with well-tested and satisfying psychometric properties were selected for the study. The risk of social exclusion was measured by means of an original questionnaire including the most frequently cited risk factors in worldwide research. The survey initially contained 60 items, which were later cut down to 26 items representing 13 different factor groups related to real social exclusion. It was discovered that it was impossible to gradate the factors 'from the strongest to the weakest predictor of future exclusion'. It was likewise impossible to ascribe any defined relevance to respective categories. The competent judges concluded that each of the risks could independently be an equally strong predictor of future exclusion.

The need of belonging and the sense of belonging were measured by means of the SOBI tool, an adapted version of the Sense of Belonging Instrument (SOBI) developed by Bonnie Hagerty and colleagues (1992, 1995), who kindly made it available for the purposes of the Polish study (Wilczynska, 2013).

The belonging measure consists of two subscales, each containing a different number of statements/items. Nearly 20 of the items represent the psychological component of the sense of belonging (the SPP-P scale), and several items describe the antecedents of the sense of belonging which represent specific motives for seeking recognition and becoming part of the group (the SPP-A scale).

Self-awareness of undertaking actions in order to increase the sense of belonging or the need to belong is an equally important component of the sense of belonging. This is supposed to be exemplified by the scale which measures antecedents, that is, motives and efforts to acquire the sense of belonging in the Polish version of the tool.

Examples of items in the SPP-P scale which identifies the Sense of Belonging include:

1 Basically, I am not certain whether I fit in with my friends.
2 I feel like a stranger in most situations.
3 I would like to make a change in my environment, but I feel that what I have got to offer will not be appreciated.
4 Generally, I do not feel I am part of the social mainstream.
5 I am not appreciated, and I am not important to my friends.
6 If I died tomorrow, very few people would come to my funeral.

Examples of items in the SPP-A scale which identifies the Need of Belonging are:

1 It matters a lot to me to fit in with others around me.
2 I want to be part of what is going on around me.
3 I can make myself fit in with others.
4 I want to feel that I really belong.

The reliability values (Cronbach's α) obtained for the measures are high: 0.95 for the SPP-P scale and 0.84 for the SPP-A scale.

Experiential emotional intelligence and strategic emotional intelligence were measured by means of a questionnaire based on Salovey and Mayer's theoretical model (Mayer and Salovey, 1997, qtd. in Jaworowska and Matczak, 2005). The instrument was developed by Polish researchers and consists of 94 items which are used to calculate the overall score and separate scores for the two respective varieties of intelligence, experiential and strategic, each of which is comprised of two subscales. The score for experiential emotional intelligence is derived from the subscale of acceptance and employment of one's own emotions in action (AKC) and the subscale of empathy, i.e. understanding and recognising other people's emotions (EMP). The experiential component of emotional intelligence subsumes receptivity to one's own and others' emotions, easy reading of emotions and respecting and accepting them.

The score for strategic emotional intelligence consists of scores in the subscale of control, therein cognitive control, over one's own emotions (KON) and the subscale of understanding and recognition of one's own emotions (ROZ). As this implies, strategic emotional intelligence concerns relating to one's own emotions. This component of emotional intelligence underpins the sorting out and differentiation of emotions, naming them, realising where they come from, directing them and revealing them in a controlled way. The values of correlations between the subscales of the two different intelligence types are small or even negative (Jaworowska and Matczak, 2005). The reliability of the overall PKIE[3] score is very high, with Cronbach's α reaching or exceeding 0.90 for all groups.

People's moods can be measured in various ways. Hedonistic tone was depicted by means of the UWIST Mood Adjective Checklist developed by Gerald Matthews, A Graham Chamberlain and Dylan M Jones (Goryńska, 2005). It was concluded that self-description through adjectives was direct and convincing. A person can identify his/her mood as serene, dejected, worried, happy, glad or sad. It is important and relevant to measure mood in situations which are identified as threatening to inclusion or as excluding, because sadness, dejection and depressive mood are known to reciprocally limit people's capacity to cope with the situation of exclusion. People are also known to react in the opposite way, i.e. by defensive denial and an upsurge of positive emotions, as an automatic and unconscious self-regulatory response to exclusion (DeWall, Anderson and Bushman, 2011).

Self-esteem was examined by using the Rosenberg Self-Esteem Scale (1989). The scale measures global self-esteem, which is framed as a one-dimensional construct. It has been effectively used to study self-esteem in children and adolescents. It is short with only ten statements and, at the same time, has high reliability as Cronbach's α oscillates between 0.81 and 0.83, depending on the age of the subjects. The Scale serves to measure what is known as 'explicit' self-esteem, which is understood as an individual's positive or negative attitude to the 'self'.[4]

It was concluded that the scale examined the level of self-esteem, which was closely associated with people's coping in the situation of social exclusion risk. The Polish version of the Rosenberg Self-Esteem Scale developed by Irena Dzwonkowska, Kinga Lachowicz-Tabaczek and Mariola Łaguna (2008) is a tool whose theoretical validity has been amply confirmed.

Pre-diagnostics of circulatory diseases in children have been addressed in relatively few studies so far. However, the regulation of anger is inseparable from the proneness to such diseases in later life. To measure anger control in teenagers in the study, we used a questionnaire which is strongly correlated with the factors of the Buss-Durke questionnaire and with the Spielberg Questionnaire and is appropriate for studying children from 11 years of age onwards. The instrument was developed by Nina Ogińska-Bulik and Zygfryd Juczyński (2001) in response to the need to measure various behaviours associated with anger expression in children and adolescents. The stronger teenagers' tendency to reveal external anger is, the more they are likely to use aggression, display negativism and be generally irritable. Internally directed anger, which is subject to conscious control reactions, restrains external expressions of anger. Further in this book, the abbreviated terms 'internal anger' and 'external anger' will also be used in this context. Cronbach's α ranges between 0.73 and 0.83 for externally directed anger, and from 0.67 to 0.84 for internally directed anger, depending on the age of the subjects.

Coping with stress was measured by means of the 'Jak sobie radzisz' (literally: 'How do you cope?' and 'How are you doing') (JSR) scale developed by Z Juczyński and N Ogińska-Bulik (2009), who drew on Lazarus and Folkman's transactional theory of coping with stress. The questionnaire was devised in order to study coping in children from 11 years of age onwards within three strategies: Active Coping, Focusing on Emotions and Seeking Social Support.

Research design and statistical procedures

In the analysis below, the main statistical tool was provided by Structural Equation Modelling (SEM), specifically by its variety referred to as Path Analysis (PA) which exclusively takes into account pointer variables without latent variables. Only the first model was fully confirmatory. The remaining models used parameters that were previously exploratively established and/or were modified on the basis of modification indices (MI) and reduced by removing insignificant paths ($p \geq 0.05$).

Each model was assessed on the basis of fit statistics. In the initial versions of SEM (Jöreskog and Sörbom, 1984), the basic fit index was derived from the result of the χ^2 test as a measure of the model's exact fit or from the χ^2/df ratio. Today, these measures are considered to be strongly dependent on the sample size, the number of variables, the number of free parametres and the deviation from the standard distribution of the studied variables; additionally, the assessment of the fit includes other indicators. The statistics which are most frequently applied to describe the model fit include CFI (>0.95), RMSEA (<0.05), TLI/NNFI (>0.95) and NFI (>0.95) (Bentler, 1990; Browne and Cudeck, 1993; Hu and Bentler, 1998, 1999). Besides the χ^2 test, two indices were selected for the purposes of this study, namely CFI and RMSEA, which are regarded as the most stable ones, because they are independent of the number of parameters and of the sample size.

Results uncover four different youth groups

The analysis was carried out in two stages, and the results were divided into two groups of models. Before conducting SEM, agglomeration analysis was performed for the scale of social exclusion risk (SZWS/SSER). Specifically, it was two-step clustering which included 13 dichotomised SZWS/SSER categories (with two items per category, 26 items render 13 categories). This analysis proceeded in two stages. First, the criterion of the BIC cluster number was used to identify two clusters. One of them was made up of people who reported a very low degree of social exclusion risk (i.e. almost all 'no' answers), and the other was comprised of people who gave varied answers to the scale's questions. Subsequently, the latter cluster was subjected to cluster analysis. This procedure made it possible to divide the group at risk of social exclusion into three clusters, each of which was characterised by a different configuration of risk categories. In this way, one 'no risk' group and three 'at risk' groups were identified, according to the division below:

1 'No risk' group – the Socially Included.
2 'At risk' group with family problems – the Invisible Kids.
3 'At risk' group with learning and peer problems – the Rejected, Frozen and Needy.
4 'At risk' group with substance abuse and learning problems – the 'Unneedy' Loiters.

For each cluster with good fit indices, a separate model was constructed. The interrelations among variables within the respective models are discussed below.

Path analysis aimed to establish what coping conditions are and what strategies are applied by young people in the 'at risk' groups as listed above. The model included the need of belonging as an exogenous variable. This stage ended with obtaining a relatively good set of fit statistics.

In the model, I assumed that the need of belonging would precede the sense of belonging and lead to achieving it. I also assumed that adolescents' ways of coping would depend on social exclusion risk factors, particularly, on individual and family-related risks, as well as on mood, self-esteem and strategic emotional intelligence. This model was submitted to exploratory analysis on the basis of MI values and removing statistically insignificant parametres. The obtained model yielded quite surprising results. It was found that the need of belonging, even if it was expressed, did not lead to achieving the sense of belonging, especially in the group at risk of family exclusion. Self-esteem was found to depend on the sense of exclusion. Given this, the second stage of model exploration was launched.

A decision was made to carry out further analyses in which model 2.0 was treated as the starting point for developing separate models for each of the four cluster groups.

The ultimate versions which were obtained in this procedure had good fit statistics, which allowed drawing conclusions about interdependences among the studied variables.

The socially included: the feeling of relevance and belonging

Significant correlations among the variables yielded a vivid psychological profile of the 'no risk' adolescent group. Unfortunately, this group only accounted for one-fourth of the entire sample.

The sense of belonging takes the central position in the model for adolescents who feel that they are important and belong. The sense of belonging is associated with the largest number of direct and indirect significant paths with other variables, that is, psychological characteristics. Furthermore, it is the sense-of-belonging variable that reaches the highest level in the adolescents from this cluster group as compared with other clusters.

The most important characteristic that sets apart the 'no risk' people form people 'at risk of exclusion' is a direct relationship between the need of belonging and the sense of belonging. This finding unambiguously shows that these adolescents express their needs related to belonging and that they are satisfied, which is represented in a stronger sense of belonging. These correlations are evident and directional, with the vector from the need of belonging to belonging.

This is only the beginning of the advantages rendered by this relationship. The level of belonging directly influences adolescents' self-esteem. It is a strong directional relationship. Besides this, the sense of belonging impacts the 'thwarting' of externally directed anger and controls anger so as to make it expressible in ways that benefit the individual and his/her relations with others.

Furthermore, the sense of belonging influences the level of experiential emotional intelligence. It is a powerful resource in young people which helps them recognise emotions, feel empathy, accept their own and other people's emotions and express emotions in action. This resource optimises mobilisational functions, supports development and fosters adequate self-knowledge. It also promotes effective coping in social situations. The adolescents in the 'belonging' group are eager to activate and use various coping strategies in stressful and/or difficult situations. The higher the level of experiential emotional intelligence, the greater the willingness to use others' support and cope (Figure 6.1).

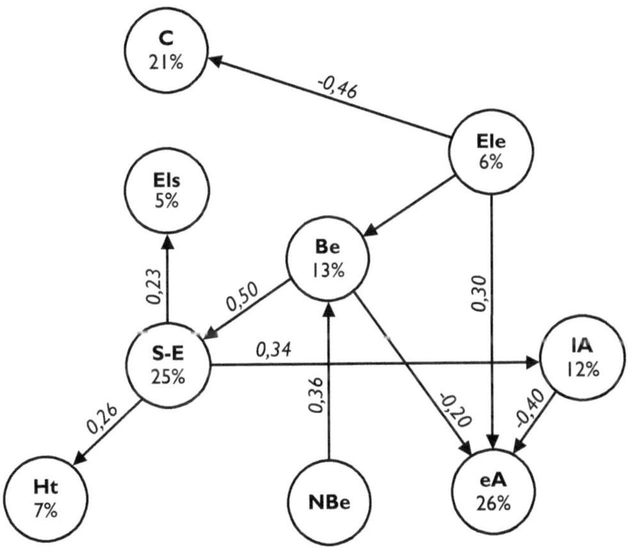

Legend:
Be – The Sense of Belonging
NBe – The Need for Belonging
Ele – Experiential Emotional Intelligence
Els – Strategic Emotional Intelligence
S-E – Self-Esteem
Ht – HedonisticTone
eA – External Anger
iA – Internal Anger
C – Coping

Figure 6.1 The Socially Included.

Self-esteem also plays an important role. As a way of self-perception and self-evaluation, it is, to a significant degree, associated with the feeling that one belongs, the sense of belonging and the need of belonging. In this adolescent group, self-esteem is linked to strategic emotional intelligence and to increased mood outcomes. This means that people with high self-esteem have also a lot of knowledge about how emotions are controlled and how these can be used in social situations. Besides this, self-esteem is also positively correlated with anger control. The higher self-esteem people have, the easier they manage unwanted feelings or reforge them into beneficial emotions.

Characteristically and specifically, psychological characteristics in the profile of people who feel that they belong are associated with each other and mutually correlated. It is as if the feeling that one belongs not only contributed to a better self-perception, expression of emotions or coping in stressful situations, but also increased people's self-awareness of their characteristics and the possibilities of using them in development. The 'no-risk' group (cluster) was the only one in which the sense of belonging ensued from the need to belong.

The invisible kids

The research findings obtained from the model of family-caused exclusion risk are exceptional. The model stands out among all the three models for the 'at risk' subsample by displaying high-value paths between the variables, which means that there are strong directional correlations between the respective characteristics of the respondents. This is also the only of the models under discussion in which a clear indirect effect can be observed.[5]

The psychological profile of respondents in this group is, in a way, atypical because, although all of them report a strong need of belonging, no correlations whatsoever have been found between their need of belonging and their sense of belonging. This finding unambiguously shows that even if the need of belonging is acknowledged and reported, it is not necessarily satisfied.

The study also found a high percentage of explained variance for externally directed anger, which increases as the need of belonging grows, as well as independently as the sense of belonging drops, (a negative correlation).

The established relationship between the need of belonging and anger shows that the need of belonging which is expressed but not met manifests in an increase of externally directed anger in adolescents. This conclusion can be inferred from the following interdependence: the more a young person needs to belong but this need is not satisfied, the more angry s/he becomes and demonstrates this angers vis-à-vis the external environment. We can imagine several families that consult psychologists and psychotherapists because their child displays aggression or self-aggression. If the expression of anger is impossible in a given family system, other symptoms emerge.

A few years ago, a married couple with an 11-year-old son named Julius came to see me. Julius had, for quite a while (about nine months) displayed strange symptoms of an obsessive-compulsive nature. When at home, the boy cried and loudly protested, including screaming, whenever his father produced any hygienic or natural noises, such as nail clipping, hiccupping, yawning, etc. The parents were worried by the fact that Julius heard those sounds even while being in another room and hysterically responded to them. Putting his hands over his ears, he would scream, 'Oh, stop that, stop, I can't take it any longer. I'm in pain! My head and ears are hurting!' The family complained that they had visited several specialists, but none of them was able to help with their son's untypical reactions. He had been in dedicated therapy of obsessive-compulsive disorders and in individual, personalised therapy. My basic principle is always to obtain a clear picture of the family system before starting therapy; I learn how each member functions in it and find out how they functioned before the symptoms appeared. What was going on in Julius's family did not differ in any particular point from the ways in which most Polish families functioned. Specifically, both parents had full-time jobs, and the boy's mother additionally took care of the household and meals. At this time, Julius's father could work extra hours in order to make sure that the family lived comfortably, and the children did not lack anything. In the evenings, the parents spent their time watching television to relax, while Julius was preparing for another day at school.

As early as during their first visit, I found out that the life comfort of their children (Julius had a five-year-old brother) was the top priority for the parents. The parents believed that they took good care of their children and that family was always at the top of their hierarchy of values. However, the mother's love was paradoxical because she was constantly tired from balancing her job and house chores for her family, while the father's love was paradoxical because, in order to make the children's lives 'better', he had taken an extra afternoon job. As both parents were fatigued every day, they were unable to devote quality time to their children. Julius's father's way to 'relax' often involved having a beer in the evening.

Our conversation revealed that Julius's father had taken his extra job for a couple of hours daily about ten months before. It became obvious that this ostensibly 'minor' change of the previous day schedule made Julius miss the time he had spent before with his father cycling or playing football. His father failed to notice that he no longer spent quality time with his son. When asked to recall the last time they had played football together, he found it hard to believe that it had been on Christmas the year before. When we drew up a new time schedule with Julius and his parents, his symptoms receded after a mere few days. Julius and his parents agreed that they would together go on outings on Sunday afternoons and that every Wednesday afternoon, the boy would spend two hours with his father alone.

I remember working with this family with a lot of fond memories because, indeed, the family really loved and respected each other very much. I met Julius and his parents separately, or we all met together, and, whenever we did, almost every family member had tears of tenderness and love in their eyes. They came to understand how much they meant to one another and how important every moment of being together and talking was to make each family member feel important and included. For Julius, who was still a young boy then, the time he spent with his father and parents was invaluable.

In the case recounted above, the mechanism of dependence is very vivid. Julius deeply wanted to feel that he belonged. The more he felt the need of belonging, the less he felt that he actually belonged and that he was part of his significant system and, consequently, the more anger he expressed. He did it in a way that was possible for him and his family (i.e. he used his father's natural behaviour to vent his own anger with him).

Among children and adolescents at risk of exclusion in the family are also members of families who quarrel or become separated because of a parent going abroad or those in which the child's caregivers are embroiled in a conflict.

For this group, a very interesting finding was obtained which confirmed the interdependence between the need of belonging and experiential emotional intelligence. It means that people who recognise their need of being part of the family group are, at the same time, people who are well-versed in the sphere of feelings and emotions: they recognise their own and others' emotions, are empathetic and experience an entire palette of feelings. As such, they much more acutely experience what is going on in their families. They are individuals who not only easily recognise others' feelings, but also tend to be particularly receptive to them. Besides this, they realise which emotions are important for them. The co-feeling of emotions is expressed in action, which was represented in the correlation between experiential emotional intelligence and the use of coping strategies. It is as if people who experienced hurdles and pain in their own situation or in their family situation were more empathetic. Likewise, they are far more sensitive to painful situations in which they or other family members are involved; in such circumstances, they are eager to use coping strategies that involve expressing emotions or seeking social support (cf. Nordgren, Banas and MacDonald, 2011). Consequently, they may become 'family heroes' by standing up for themselves or in defence of a family member (Figure 6.2).

In this model, coping is explained by 30% of variance, which is the highest proportion for this variable in the studied groups. The initiation of strategies of coping with stress is affected by self-esteem, but this association is negative. This indicates that the lower a teenager's self-esteem is

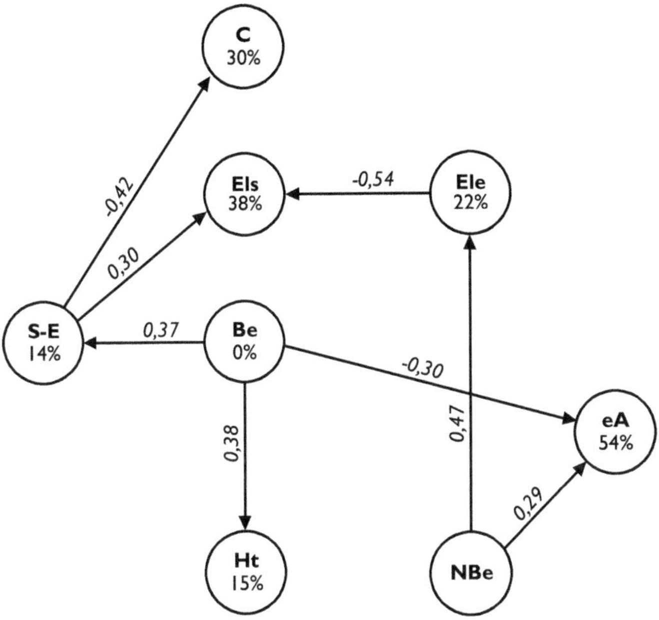

Legend:
Be – The Sense of Belonging
NBe – The Need for Belonging
Ele – Experiential Emotional Intelligence
Els – Strategic Emotional Intelligence
S-E – Self-Esteem
Ht – HedonisticTone
eA – External Anger
C – Coping

Figure 6.2 The Invisible Kids.

the more likely s/he is to use coping strategies, understood as a set of approaches focused on emotions, aimed at solving the problem actively and involving reliance on social support. The reverse dependence shows that teenagers whose self-esteem is high do not want to use the 'help' of others, parents or teachers. It is highly probable that they lack trust and do not believe that such help is indeed possible. This suggests that family problems and family conflicts do not produce the foundation of trust on which adolescents with high self-esteem could rely. Rather, they tend to rely on themselves and their own sensations, as high self-esteem is associated with the capacity to understand and control emotions, which can be used by young people in various situations. Their strategic emotional intelligence helps them view problems as if from outside. At the same time, low self-esteem levels are linked to lower levels of understanding and controlling emotions. The perception of one's self-esteem as high goes hand in hand with the self-perception as a person equipped with considerable social skills, able to control emotions and capable of initiating new relationships (Twenge, 2007).

In the family risk group, strategic emotional intelligence is strongly negatively correlated with experiential emotional intelligence, which means that people who accept their spontaneous emotions and others' emotions are unable to control, understand and steer them at the same time (-0.54). The strong negative association between experiential emotional intelligence and strategic emotional intelligence indicates a disjunction between spontaneous emotional expression and empathy on one hand and emotional control on the other.

In this group, self-esteem depends on the sense of belonging which can be achieved in various ways, therein outside the family system. When a person experiences belonging or the sense of belonging, his/her self-esteem increases, and, at the same time, this interdependence of properties enables him/her to learn what emotions consist of and how they can be managed. The findings also show that the experienced sense of belonging is not only associated with high self-esteem but also contributes to positive mood in people.

This picture portrays two forms of human functioning. One of them is based on articulating one's needs, perceiving deficits and experiencing the situation emotionally. The other model of functioning is based on the belief that one belongs, on higher self-esteem and the capacity to control emotions. In the group at risk of family exclusion, the former model is vivid and makes a clear imprint on family members. Anger and bitterness are dominant emotions. The manifested but not met need of belonging breeds frustration and expressions of external anger and prompts spontaneous and uncontrolled emotional expressions. When a person's need of belonging is not satisfied, his/her possibilities shrink; s/he becomes more irritable; s/he finds it difficult to understand and control his/her emotions; s/he cannot use them to his/her own advantage; s/he has low self-esteem and deeply craves others' help.

In the other case (i.e. when the family offers the sense of belonging), the person's self-esteem is bolstered, the skills of understanding and controlling emotions grow and positive mood and the sense of calm increase.

These findings and conclusions show that the sense of belonging plays a crucial role in the lives of young people. The sense of belonging is a perfect, and probably the only, 'springboard' for a smooth transition into another, independent stage of identity development and maturation. All the data indicate that the experience of belonging enables the individual to further develop and to muster the courage for independent, conscious and autonomous actions. If the sense of belonging is satisfactory, it contributes to the person's capacity to use his/her many other resources, such as emotional intelligence, anger regulation, mood increase and coping skills. All this augments the person's prospects of development, increased autonomy, independent, self-reliant functioning in adult life and the establishment of mature relationships with other people based on mutual respect and acceptance of otherness.

The rejected, frozen and needy

Peer exclusion is felt like an extremely painful experience with which a teenage person is hardly able to cope or hardly imagines being able to cope. This can be inferred from statistically corroborated evidence. Specifically, the study carried out on a cluster group of adolescents experiencing peer exclusion has found a complete lack of correlations impacting individual coping. Among all the studied variables/characteristics of the respondents, coping remained beyond the possibilities available to the individual in the situation of exclusion. Importantly, no denial or repression of coping was noted, which happens when the individual insists that s/he does not need support or other ways of coping. In this case, the results obtained mean that the psychological aspects of the person's functioning are not associated with any potential strategies of coping with exclusion by peers.

To illustrate this better, try to imagine that you find yourself in a group of teenage girls during recess at school and that you are ignored. You try to approach them and join the conversation, but nobody takes any notice of you, as if you were invisible and inaudible. You feel that there is an enormous distance between you and them, an abyss, in fact. Others either pretend that they do not see that you are there or do not hear what you say, because they really do not see and do not hear you.

Another illustration is provided by the common story of a boy, a typical 'classroom clown', who is a laughing stock for others and is never included in what his peers do. Others consider him an 'oddball', and nobody can find common ground with him. His way of thinking and behaving may indeed differ from how others think and behave. The 'odder' his behaviour is becoming, the more bent he is on inventing ways to make people 'notice him'; unfortunately, his endeavours are all thoroughly misguided. He tries clowning around and telling all kinds of crazy stuff, which, regrettably, is not funny to anybody. One can easily guess that this is not appreciated by the group and that the boy is avoided as others have no idea what to expect of him.

As shown by research, in such cases people do not even consider any way which could effectively include them into the group. Some adolescent girls practice exclusionary behaviours fully consciously and intentionally. Such exclusionary practices undertaken by girls typically include ignoring a person, 'failing to perceive' her or disseminating rumours behind her back. This happens either in real life or on the Internet, on various forums, or as official comments on Facebook and other social media, e.g. Instagram. The person who is being excluded in this way has basically no chance to cope with it, first, because the manipulation takes place through channels which are inaccessible to her, and second, because, even if a confrontation with the perpetrator is possible, she deliberately engages in exclusionary practices and usually has no intention of giving up easily. The power of the group that sides with the excluding ones may be overwhelming, since negative authorities are capable of exerting an enormous influence on the group. Coping with this kind of power may simply be unimaginable or impossible for the excluded person. Exclusion is an ostensibly invisible tactic. Neither parents nor teachers perceive it. Sometimes, the entire group only 'notice' such a practice when they have its mechanism directly and explicitly shown to them by a psychologist or an educator. Those excluded believe that it is impossible to find social support from others or to share their emotions with them, including the potential perpetrator.

The situation is all the more complicated as exclusion drastically diminishes self-esteem; consequently, the excluded person does not believe s/he even deserves to be defended. S/he may even be convinced that s/he is different, odd and socially 'disabled'. Besides this, the perpetrator or the excluding person usually experienced exclusion early in his/her life, and excluding others is his/her 'strategy' of coping with his/her own past exclusion and other anxieties. What people who have ever experienced social exclusion fear most is that this may happen again to them.

As long as a person feels that s/he is important in one group or another, his/her self-esteem remains tolerably high. Self-esteem is very strongly dependent on the extent to which the person feels that s/he belongs.

Research findings have also shown that manifesting one's need of belonging is perceived by the environment as in fact being more 'cool' than secretly coping with not having this need met. Unfortunately, young people who are uncertain which strategies are effective are afraid that their messages will be ignored and, consequently, tend to give up on attempts to join the group as they dread being hurt again. We can imagine that teaching teenagers how to express their needs in assertive and socially effective ways and preparing the group for understanding such situations would be enough to help young people shake off the experience of social exclusion.

The results of this study show that the expression of the need of belonging is associated with higher self-esteem, similarly to the experience of belonging, which is also connected to higher self-esteem. However, in the group of people at risk of exclusion by peers, no event has been found to corroborate the link between these two processes. This implies that people who experience peer exclusion do not undertake any effective attempts to join in.

Their strategy involves watching what is going on in the group, and, in particular, focusing on the extent to which they are included or treated with indifference. The analysis of the model implies that individuals become 'frozen', and, besides observing what is going on with their self-esteem, they do not initiate any other action. In the face of exclusion risk, this sociometer automatically starts working, whereby it performs adaptive and informative functions, helping identify the potential risk of social exclusion (Leary et al., 1995). Self-esteem mirrors the generalised sense of self-worth in relations with others and the sociometric position within the group on the basis of the identified sense of belonging and the expressed need of belonging (cf. Leary, 2004).

Nevertheless, the observation of the 'temperature' of the environment does not amount to action. How then do adolescents who feel that they are rejected by their peers function? Do they not engage in any action whatsoever?

The model also exhibits the impact of the sense of belonging on strategic emotional intelligence and the influence of the need of belonging on experiential emotional intelligence. These findings again indicate that expressing the need of belonging is associated with a strong experience of one's own and others' emotions.

In this model, like in the previous one, both kinds of emotional intelligence are strongly negatively correlated. This means that people who experience a lack of belonging may feel this situation very acutely, yet without revealing such feelings. They may feel aggrieved and hurt, and, in extreme cases, they may harbour a desire for revenge.

Tellingly, the perpetrators of school shootings are known to have experienced the sustained sense of being rejected, disliked or overlooked, without ever activating any coping strategies (either those oriented to venting negative emotions or those focused on securing social support) and rather choosing to behave in ostensibly indifferent ways (Verlinden, Hersen and Thomas, 2000; Leary et al., 2001; Twenge et al., 2002). This configuration of interdependencies indicates that people who grapple with school and peer problems in a group freeze their behavioural activity which is oriented to implementing or not implementing coping strategies, while they activate the internal system of monitoring the risk or exclusion. Children who have learning or relationship-related problems often experience such states. By way of illustration, I present the example of Jacob, an adult man who told me about his life and about his emotions when he felt he was excluded by his peers (Figure 6.3).

Jacob was dyslectic and had considerable difficulties learning, remembering information and reproducing information since birth. At school, he lagged behind other students. The teacher offered his students knowledge in an accumulated and theoretical manner. He gave assignments on a portion of the material, quizzed his students about it during the lesson and then proceeded to present another theme. Jacob was never able to

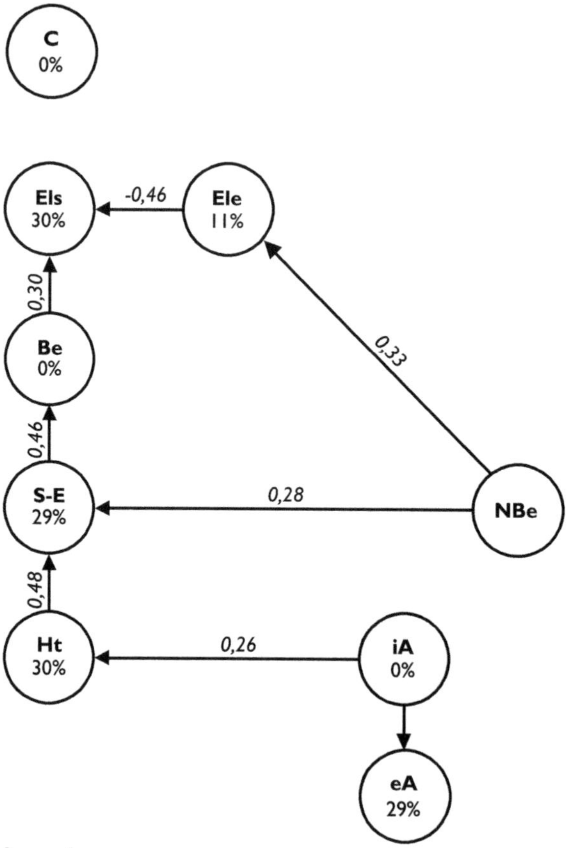

Legend:

Be – The Sense of Belonging
NBe – The Need for Belonging
Ele – Experiential Emotional Intelligence
Els – Strategic Emotional Intelligence
S-E – Self-Esteem
Ht – HedonisticTone
eA – External Anger
iA – Internal Anger
C – Coping

Figure 6.3 The Rejected, Frozen and Needy.

reproduce the knowledge which he had mastered at home with an enormous effort of several-hour-long toilsome rote learning. Although at home he flawlessly repeated whatever he had memorised, at school, he was stressed out by being asked questions in front of his classmates, who often burst out laughing at his 'funny' mistakes. He was not able to keep up with the class and with the pace at which the teacher presented new knowledge. As a result, he spent long hours at school and then long hours studying at home as well, while his classmates had free time and could play football outside. This made him more and more distant from his classmates. Even if he tried to play football with them, it would turn out that his lack of motor coordination skills made playing team sports difficult for him.

Jacob had caring parents, who devoted a lot of time to him and patiently helped him study and memorise his school material. Jacob had his parents' support, love and assertion that whatever happened they loved him and appreciated his efforts. However, he often suffered among his classmates. Although he craved his peers' respect and acknowledgement as a member of the group, this hardly ever happened.

Jacob basically focused only on the present and on how to make his mark and be noticed and wanted by the group.

The more rejected he felt, the more he tried to ingratiate himself with the group. However, he did not know how he could join the group or in what situations the group would include him in their pursuits. He dreamt of being important and appreciated by others, especially because he had a lot to offer to others: he had a big heart; he was eager to help others; he was physically fit, strong and athletic.

The boy's levels of stress and anxiety soared every day when he went to school. However, he could not reveal that to the group. On the contrary, he pretended that everything was all right and that others' conduct did not hurt him.

In reality, Jacob saw no future for himself. What could it possibly be like, after all? He did not like his self-image, but, at the same time, he had no idea how to change it. There was nobody around who could help him. He was afraid to approach teachers for fear of being labelled a 'snitch', and he did not want to make his parent worried. In front of his peers, he pretended that everything was ok. Yet his stress level was so high every day that it affected the boy's entire body, his body was tense and his pupils were nearly always so dilated that Jacob's light blue eyes seemed to be black.

For Jacob, the best way was to 'survive somehow' and try not to undertake any action in order not to expose himself to others' hurtful remarks.

The unneedy loiterers

The picture of correlations for the fourth 'at risk' group of adolescents is surprising, because it basically boils down to associations among three strongly correlated paths. This group describe themselves in terms of 'substance abuse and problems at school'. The characteristic features of their functioning are school absenteeism and meeting in small groups who drink alcohol, smoke cigarettes and use substances. The sense of belonging,

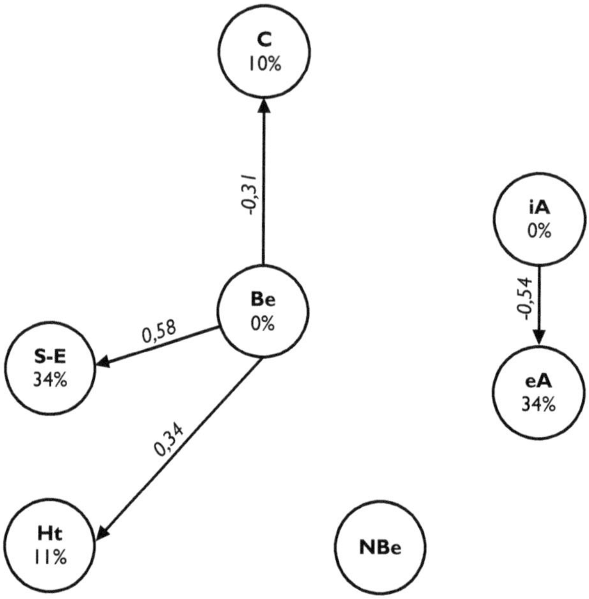

Legend:
Be – The Sense of Belonging
NBe – The Need for Belonging
S-E – Self-Esteem
Ht – HedonisticTone
eA – External Anger
iA – Internal Anger
C – Coping

Figure 6.4 The 'Unneedy' Loiters.

which takes a central position in this group, is achieved by participating in a minority group of 'substance abusers', which, at the same time, increases their self-esteem and improves their mood.

The psychological profile of the group at risk due to 'learning problems and substance abuse' is thus specific in quite a different way than the model of the 'no risk' group. The former is depleted in terms of psychological assets that its members have at their disposal.

The specificity of the model is vividly brought into relief by the relegation of the need of belonging beyond the scope of consciously recognised needs. The need of belonging is isolated from other variables here, and it indeed may have been 'frozen' or minimised in the face of the anticipated exclusion risk. The 'freezing' of the need of belonging is understood as 'indifference', a disinterest in pursuing both 'belonging' and 'not belonging'. This can be interpreted as a symptom of emotional numbness, which is characterised by limited recognition of the need of belonging, among other aspects. We could conclude that the mechanism of endeavouring to be appreciated and important, which is risky and too 'costly' for the individual, has not been activated or remains unrevealed (cf. also Hagerty at al., 1996). People who experienced traumas and exclusion at an early stage of their development initiate so-called 'thick skin' as their way to survive, so they do not feel painful emotions and keep them at bay. This is a strategy of coping and survival, which is developed when children are exposed to scenes of aggression or traumas. The repeated character of painful experiences makes them 'immune' to hurt, compassion and the need of belonging; they prematurely 'grow up' and become insensitive to their own and others' pain.

Substance abuse is considered to be one of the defence mechanisms. A famous experiment on rats carried out by Bruce Alexander in 1985 showed that alcohol and poisonous substances are used to prevent social pain, to muffle it or to experience an illusory euphoria triggered by chemical substances rather than relationships.

Correlations between the sense of belonging on one hand and self-esteem and positive mood on the other may imply that the Unneedy Loiters experience belonging within their own minority group, which abides by its own norms and rules that differ from those endorsed by most of society. The Unneedy Loiters are reluctant to use support from their wider social community, do not reveal their emotions and dismiss socially accepted ways of coping. There is a high probability that despite being socially excluded in a way (they find themselves outside the social mainstream), they do not feel excluded. This result can be explained on the basis of Nicholas Emler's Theory of Reputation Management (1995, 2014), which is also applicable to marginalised adolescents. Social exclusion usually does not mean exclusion for 'excluded' people. Research has shown that they may experience the sense of belonging and even attractiveness in their minority/marginalised groups. In Emler's study, more delinquent adolescents had more friendly relationships and were more popular in their groups than the less delinquent ones. The former also enjoyed more intimate and more satisfying relationships with family members and had a lot of close friends (Emler and Reicher, 1995).

Socially excluded people may boast top positions (e.g. that of a leader) in their minority subgroups. Results of a team study (Estévez et al., 2014) imply that adolescents who are aggressive and at the same time popular have multiple friends who admire, respect and like them. Correlations among the variables in the author's original study appear to confirm this finding. The limited number of intercorrelated variables and a high correlation between the sense of belonging and elevated self-esteem suggest satisfaction from belonging to this group.

The dearth of correlations among other variables may also indicate that the respondents were wary to reveal information about themselves, or that they represented a considerable degree of emotional numbness. While this serves a specific function of blocking access to difficult emotions associated with traumatic experiences from previous periods of life, including sadness, despair, regret and (suppressed) anger, it may also curb the possibilities of using one's own empathetic co-feeling and self-care. A case presented in Chapter 7 shows in some detail how numbness sets in, what role substances play in this and what therapy is possible for such individuals.

Notes

1 http://www.polityka.pl/spoleczenstwo/artykuly/1530421,1,nastolatki-w-glebokiej-depresji-dlaczego.read; http://zdrowie.dziennik.pl/dziecko/artykuly/425760,dziecko-z-de-presja-jak-pomoc-dziecku-z-depresja.html.
2 http://zdrowie.dziennik.pl/dziecko/artykuly/425760,dziecko-z-de-presja-jak-pomoc-dziecku-z-depresja.html.
3 PKIE stands for the Popular Emotional Intelligence Questionnaire.
4 Explicit self-esteem should be distinguished from 'latent' self-esteem which is revealed automatically and spontaneously.
5 In this model, all paths clearly surpass the threshold of 0.25. The highest values are again found for the intercorrelation between anger variables (A) and emotional intelligence (EI) (respectively 0.54 and -0.60). Strategic emotional intelligence (EIs) is influenced by experiential emotional intelligence (EIe) and also by self-esteem (S-E: 0.30) and, indirectly (via experiential emotional intelligence) by the need of belonging (NBe). This resuls in a high EV = 38%. Similar interdependencies can be seen for external anger (eA), where besides the 'traditional' impact of internal anger (iA), effects of the sense of belonging (Be) (-0.31) and of the need of belonging (NBe) (0,29) are found. Consequently, it is not surprising that, in this model, EV for this variable stands as high as at 54%. Also for coping (C), the proportion of the explained variance is highest in this model (30%), which results above all from the effects that experiential emotional intelligence (EIe) (0.34) and self-esteem (S-E) (-0.42) have on this variable.The remaining paths concern the impact of the sense of belonging (Be) on self-esteem (S-E) (0.35) and mood/hedonistic tone (Ht).

Chapter 7

The orphan

Notes from a psychodynamic therapy

Magda, a student of a vocational high school, lived at a children's home (CH) in a small town. She was referred to a psychologist at the local mental health outpatient clinic by her housemother for two reasons: it was difficult to establish any rapport with her, and she had undertaken suicide attempts. The girl first started therapy at the mental health outpatient clinic eight months after she had come to live at the home; she was 17 at the time. The therapy consisted of consultations with a psychiatrist with a CH care worker present. It was difficult to make contact with the patient, and her housemother reported that she had not responded to questions or attempts at communication, had drunk alcohol a few times and had attempted suicide; there had also been weeks of impaired mood when she would refuse to eat. The staff were worried about her, and her life was in danger due to her starving herself and drinking lethal quantities of alcohol within a day for a few times a week.

She was diagnosed with adolescent depressive disorders by the psychiatrist and was put on Asentra; she also had psychotherapy recommended to her. Still, Magda did not feel like seeing a psychologist and directly announced that she would not use psychological help. In the period, the patient's mood periodically dropped and improved; she systematically cut herself and kept away from others, and she did not initiate any contact with her peers, while others kept away from her.

Paramedics were called a few times to the CH to intervene when Magda undertook a suicide attempt or indulged in dangerous self-harm. On such occasions, she was given tranquilisers and sometimes even taken to hospital. Before her last referral to the clinic, she had spent two weeks in the hospital, where her life was at risk after another suicide attempt. The CH staff found it difficult to find out why the girl was behaving this way, because they could not communicate with her. They feared that her suicide attempts would have a tragic ending and insisted that she consult a psychologist.

Consultation

When Magda turned 18, the CH care workers told her to start therapy as they were terrified by her conduct and were afraid that, someday, they would come to her rescue too late and find her dead. They found a recommended mental health outpatient clinic and made an appointment with a recommended psychodynamic practitioner within the programme funded by the National Health Fund. I was this therapist.

When I met Magda for the first time, she made no contact, either verbal or nonverbal, and she avoided eye contact. Both her arms were covered in old and new scars. She sat down at the edge of the couch, stooping and looking distrustful. When I asked her a question, she would answer in monosyllables, short sentences or nonverbal responses, usually laughing out briefly as if she found the situation amusing. Alternatively, she did not respond at all, shrugging her shoulders and staring into the window. She never ventured to ask any questions, except when she requested a 'note confirming that she had seen a therapist because she needed one to show to the director of the children's home and be left alone'.

During that first meeting, Magda showed that her motivation to seek help was external as she insisted that the decision had been made by the director of the CH and said that, 'The director of the children's home told me to come here'. Such a verbalisation of 'coercion' was by no means conducive to establishing a therapeutic bond. However, to establish a bond with Magda was an expedient and justified thing to do, given that her life was in immediate danger. It was obvious that helping the girl on the basis of the external motive she had cited was impossible. I considered various options of solving this problem. One option was to respect the patient's declared decision to continue her isolation and her disinterest in obtaining help, but I rejected it due to the evident hazard to her life. Another option involved trying to establish an alliance and contact with her in the framework of psychodynamic therapy. Yet another option was to refer the patient to a behavioural-cognitive practitioner. The option of further referrals was rejected because it was imperative to start intervention immediately, while the only other directly available therapies were private and the CH could not fund private services. As the local market of psychotherapeutic services was very constrained, and the patient had already unsuccessfully gone through many psychological and psychiatric interventions, I was inclined to endeavour to keep her in therapy, especially that, despite her protestations, Magda had in fact eventually voluntarily decided to see psychologists after several months of refusing this.

The girl's information sheet indicated that she had been isolating herself since her arrival at the CH, if not longer. During the conversation, the girl, with considerable difficulty, revealed that she had often seen school psychologists in childhood. She also mentioned a few 'unpleasant' visits at the local mental health outpatient clinic, which always ended up with her terminating all contact. The patient did not understand why she had been made to fill in tests and make drawings. She did not like the way the psychologists had worked by focusing on conducting an interview either, and as a result, she 'did not believe' such help would be effective.

The girl behaved in a deprecating, rough and superficial way. To start a conversation with her was tedious work, and even once started, the conversation was interrupted by her long silences. She would often sarcastically laugh in response to the therapist's question or comment. I imagined her previous contact with psychologists, feeling firsthand the power of the negative countertransference triggered by the patient.

Before Magda made her decision to start individual work, I tried to verbalise my acceptance, especially of the feelings and needs that she was demonstrating and of the reluctance she was displaying. Magda expressed her interest in further meetings 'on her own terms'.

Importantly, because of the impeded contact with the patient, the therapy was supervised from the moment of preliminary consultations on. In particular, countertransference required detailed discussion. Being constantly in touch with the supervisor, I could discuss and analyse the material as I was collecting it during my sessions with Magda.

Collecting data

The patient did not offer any information about herself. Her defensive attitude and deprecating conduct made the meetings difficult both for the patient and for the therapist. As a therapist, I could basically work exclusively with the information I elicited through the questions I asked, which were usually closed questions. I could also consult the data in her medical record.

The patient consented to the contract and made her voluntary decision to start individual work when she had the principles of psychodynamic therapy explained in detail to her and when the possibility of using this therapeutic form had been shown to her. We made a short-term contract covering the period of the school year. We agreed that, during therapy, Magda would not make another attempt on her life.

The establishment of contact and the contract with the patient was preceded by a consultative interview. Before coming to see the therapist, the patient had no contact with her family. Ever since her arrival at the CH, she had not been visited by anybody. She had neither casual friends nor a close girlfriend. She had not formed any closer relationship with any of her three roommates at the CH. She did not have a boyfriend. She was a student at a vocational high school; she stated that she 'liked maths, but did not like Polish, and had problems with history'. For a few months before being placed at the CH, she had lived with her father, his partner and their daughter. She did not know why she had found herself at the CH and, since arriving there, she had not inquired about her family's whereabouts. Her family did not visit her. She reported headaches at least once a week, and every night she had difficulty falling asleep until late at night, or she woke up at dawn. She refused to talk about the scars on her arms. This was the only information elicited from her based on the therapist's concrete questions during the first three meetings.

After the two first meetings, the patient received a note certifying her participation in the consultation, but she decided to remain in therapy for the entire coming year. She did not answer questions either about her expectations or about her problem. She claimed that there was no problem she wanted to discuss and that she did not wish to have any family-related issues addressed. She wanted 'others to feel better with her'. She agreed to meetings and the contract based on her reported wish that 'others should find it easier to live with her'.

The data concerning the patient's life history were collected during consultations, and the gaps were gradually being filled during therapy. At the early stages of the intervention, I also built on the fragmentary data the clinic had obtained from the CH when the patient had first reported at the clinic over one year earlier.

Admittedly, some of the data came from foreign sources (i.e. information from the housemother, the hospital and court experts), yet as verbal contact with the girl was hampered, these data served as the hypothetical basic source of historical information at the first stage of the intervention and were verified in further therapeutic work by the therapist and the patient.

The information supplied by the housemother implied that the patient had revealed no personal details to the CH staff and had not established any close contacts there for two years. She sometimes wrote letters to the housemother, which was the only way in which she communicated with her caregivers. The girl had been taken from school and to the CH all of a sudden, she was 17 at the time, and brought directly to the facility. The initiative to take the girl away from her parents had, in all probability, come from the neighbours, who were witnesses of her father's violence and aggression against her. Hearing the girl's terrifying screams from behind the wall, they feared that she was being hurt and called the police. At that time, Magda was in the custody of her father and his partner. Before that, she had been in 'the care' of her alcohol-addicted mother. Based on how the girl responded to television shows about homeless and hungry children, the CH staff inferred that she had been no stranger to sleeping with her mother on staircases and looking for food in waste containers.

The court files and court experts' opinions indicated that, as a minor, the girl underwent a court examination in connection to the lawsuit against her father who had been accused of domestic violence against her and the family. Nevertheless, the patient did not give evidence, did not agree to be examined by a psychologist and, in the experts' opinion, was 'tense, inhibited and displayed no motivation to take part in psychological examination; no contact could be made with her, and she did not even answer neutral questions. An attempt to use the Wechsler scale to test her mental development failed because, having answered merely a few questions, she refused to perform further assignments'. The experts' examination only confirmed the therapist's own observations that the girl had 'limited vocabulary, low verbalisation skills and a tendency to avoid speaking of her parents, the other sex and her own needs'. Analysing the body of the available data, it was impossible to identify the sources of the girl's emotional disorders. Experts claimed that it could only be inferred that one of the main factors which negatively affected her development included an adverse atmosphere within the family, her parents' unstable relationship, trauma related to scenes of violence, the lack of stability in life and sometimes even homelessness, her mother's abuse of alcohol and periodic neglect of the young girl. The girl reported that she 'had been abused by her grandfather a long time ago, but as nobody had reported it to the competent agencies, the problem remained unsolved'. The experts suggested that the girl was probably vulnerable to secondary victimisation and possible abuse from her father, observing that 'it cannot be ruled out that she was sexually abused by her father. One factor that makes this hypothesis likely is the characteristic structure of the family: the mother's weak position and her incapacity to protect the child, the father's authoritarian attitude and his use of physical and mental violence in relation to his sexual partners and both parents' disinterest in the girl's needs'.

The documents quoted above served as an additional source of information at the stage of consultations for therapy and were never used directly during the therapy sessions. These only provided additional insight into the events in which the girl had been involved. The patient herself never mentioned her experiences, and when asked by the therapist 'what she did not want to talk about here', she answered, about the family. All the above information had been collected during the patient's and the CH care worker's prior meetings with a psychiatrist. I had access to the data from the court documents because they were included in the medical records, but I never cited these passages to the patient. I asked the patient whether she wanted to have a look at all or any part of the documentation. She was not interested. The entirety of the intervention and all the data available to the clinic were made confidential, of which the patient was informed at the first meeting. This description does not contain any clues which could compromise the patient's identity.

Identifying the focal theme

The analysis of the data elicited from the patient, her attitude and the facts from her life which she confirmed suggested that the focal theme that came to the foreground in her case was comprised of losses, therein the past, present and anticipated losses of her significant others and of her self-image components. With any other data missing, it could only be posited that serious damage to her self-structure was probably early, permanent and prolonged in time. Inferably, due to the deficit of the environment's accepting response to Magda's existence, she had a lowered sense of self-worth and vitality. In all likelihood, she had been entirely deprived of repeated healthy experiences of participation in an adult caregiver's peaceful life. Presumably, the tendency of self-rejection and self-blame had become the central and, at the same time, a vulnerable aspect of her structure of the self.

Such conclusions seemed to be substantiated by the 'compiled' life story of the patient. The girl had gone through multiple traumas in her life, an alcoholic mother who abandoned her, an abusive and aggressive father, highly probable incestuous sexual abuse, the loss of loved ones and the lack of their interest and balancing on the verge of life and death through self-harm and suicide attempts. The fact that, for over two years, the patient had no contact with the family confirms that she did not experience care and understanding in the family of origin. Her needs and expectations were not reflected, neither satisfied nor noticed. Relationships with her kin had not furnished her with a sense of security, and contact with them had put her health and, in all likelihood, even her life in jeopardy (extreme conditions of living, searching for food in waste containers, sleeping on staircases); alternately, this contact was abruptly broken, without any opportunity for the patient to have a say in decision-making as in interrupted contact with her father's daughter and family.

During the meetings, the patient displayed depressive and self-deprecating attitudes. She perceived and presented herself as an insignificant, useless and inferior person who was to blame for the situation in which she found herself. This was expressed in her remarks, such as 'others do not like me', 'it is tough for others to be with me', or 'I am stupid'. She withdrew from contact because, on one hand, she presumably had no constructive models of functioning in relations and, on the other, she perceived herself as inferior and inadequate and transferred this perceptual pattern onto others. She functioned in a similar way in her relationship with the therapist, deprecating and testing my 'resistance'. In all probability, she also functioned in the same manner in contact with others. Simultaneously, she came across as very sensitive and vulnerable, as suggested by her earlier episodic contact with psychologists, from which she had withdrawn if feeling hurt, not understood or dissatisfied with the rapport. She had built a rigid defence structure that was supposed to protect her against close relationships. She either retreated from or did not enter any relations for fear of being rejected and hurt.

Sigmund Freud described resistance as a patient's unconscious defence and an activity that prevents the revealing of inner truth. Later, psychoanalysts also talked of resistance to refer to an activity that is meant to hide something within oneself or to strong impulses that preserve habits and entrenched patterns that function either to protect the individual or to make him/her feel s/he is protected. In its structure, resistance is a mechanism that ensures unchangeability and stability. If defence mechanisms beneficially worked in the past, or if a person feels that they did, such behaviours tend to be repeated later, which is an obstacle to emotional development. This was how the patient functioned: sometimes she made an impression of being disconnected from the world and from her own emotions so as not to feel hurt the way people do when others reject them or completely ignore them while making life decisions for them, ones on which experience has taught them that they have no influence whatsoever.

Throughout her life, the patient had presumably engaged in a series of nonadaptive interactions and roles that she had unconsciously assimilated as her own pattern, stripping herself of any expectations of her own or meeting self-destructive expectations which she had probably attributed to others in relation to herself. She had internalised and activated against herself a range of destructive actions, such as self-deprecation, self-attack, self-harm, self-assault and self-starvation. Self-harm and suicide attempts could have been expressions of the difficulty she had in coping with her emotions, self-guilt, anger and self-aggression.

The self-image she presented to others in external-directed conscious and unconscious behaviours portrayed her as a person distanced from and independent of emotions, having a lowered self-esteem, unable to live up to her tasks and not believing in herself. Her conscious and unconscious beliefs about others made her form certain expectations as to others' reactions to her, which involved the sense of alienation, loneliness and being misunderstood by others. She treated others as those who rejected and did not accept her.

The patient took notice of difficulties she had in communicating with others; she would repeat that she was no good with words and 'why should I speak if that is unimportant after all'. However, when establishing the contract, she reported that she needed contact with others, which kindled some hope for attempts to change. She was clearly uncomfortable about the way she performed in social relationships: having difficulty in verbal communication, she deprecated herself claiming that she had nothing to say that others would want to listen to. She oscillated between curiosity about being in any kind of relationship and an immense fear of being rejected and hurt. At the same time, she felt unworthy and empty, which made her believe that life was pointless and painful, an attitude that propelled her to indulge in self-destructive and self-aggressive actions.

The psychodynamic aspects suggested by the patient's life story, her self-structures and functioning called for a long-term intervention based on the patient's conscious identification of her problem. However, the circumstances of Magda's appearance at the clinic implied that the only plan that could be proposed to her at that moment was short-term therapy, which could possibly be extended while in progress.

Establishing the contract in the relationship with the patient

The patient decided to start therapy with an aim of examining her relations with others so as to derive more satisfaction from them, 'so that others feel better with her' and also so that she should feel better with others.

In deciding how to work with the patient, I considered

> – her symptoms: problems with forming relations with others, which she noticed, reported and wanted to have addressed in therapy and which were the only motive that mobilised her to start and possibly continue therapeutic meetings. The patient stated that she did not want to touch upon her family and life history in therapy. She also reported specific symptoms - including sleeplessness and headaches. The patient was ready to start working exclusively at the level of these symptoms.

The psychodynamic component could only be implemented indirectly (i.e. through the initial proposal of a time-restricted contract). The upsides of the contract included a possibility to establish a clear framework comprised of a defined approach, the duration of therapy and the number of meetings so as to produce stable reliance. The safe and clearly defined framework of contact with me made therapy more intelligible, predictable and, thus, secure to Magda, especially in the context of her previous experiences with psychologists, as during and after sessions with them, she had not known why she was in therapy, how long it would last and what rules governed the meetings. As a result, she was dissatisfied and dropped all of them. Because her previous relations with therapists had never had any recognisable structure, in this case, the tiniest details of the course of the intervention were established so as to develop a positive, collaboration-underpinned relation with the therapist.

It was obvious that Magda was in need of long-term therapy promoting efforts to modify the defectively shaped defence structures, which arose in response to the experiences and problems that had appeared when developing early object relations and were reinforced by pathological relations and experiences in later years.

Observable in the patient were a serious underdevelopment of the ego, disturbed object relations and the deficit of the self; as such, in a long run, therapy should primarily aim at building, strengthening and consolidating the patient's inner structure. Achieving self-understanding and relative self-acceptance combined with identifying her own needs would help the patient function more safely and effectively in her social environment.

However, the contract was established for a short term; it covered one school year, from the end of September until June, envisaged one visit weekly on a fixed day and, in keeping with the patient's wishes, aimed at examining her social relations in order to improve them. I explained to her the rule of anonymity and the setting, and we agreed that she was supposed to inform me beforehand in case she was not coming to a session. The patient did not pay for her therapy as it was funded by the Health Fund. The formula of the Health Fund-financed sessions at the clinic did not leave the option of 'make-up' meetings at another time. As a result, the patient's failure to turn up entailed missing the session and reducing the therapy time.

Three months before the end of the school year and while therapy was in progress, I suggested prolonging it. From April until May, the patient refused. She tried to break therapy and did not turn up for sessions. However, in June, she agreed to come back again in September and discuss possible ways of continuing therapy.

During the first session, a separate contract was established which stipulated that the patient should notify of an anticipated suicide attempt. Initially, the patient was surprised and insisted that such actions were unforeseeable, but having analysed her behaviour and way of thinking in such cases, we concluded that it was nevertheless possible.

Therapy in the context of transference phenomena

The patient was never late for sessions. However, she never took part in more than two or three sessions in a row. Following such a two- or three-session series, she did not turn up for the subsequent meeting. When I drew her attention to the fact, referring to it as 'getting closer and moving away', she laughed out loudly or, rather, 'laughed at me'.

I noticed that the patient's therapy was unfolding in a string of multiple short-term series which oscillated around particular themes. Interestingly, the patient usually failed to come to a session when we had just started working on a particular theme, which we only resumed when she came back again. I associated it with her need of taking a step back or distancing herself from a theme, as well as becoming accustomed to it, which was expressive of her fear of taking a definitive position and perceiving something more, in which she might need more time. Such situations took place when we started analysing her contact with the environment, when I asked who she felt closer to and more distant from and how this manifested in her life. On another occasion, she did not turn up when I had given her an assignment to write down two episodes which she observed made her sad or angry and two which made her happy or amused.

The patient took part in therapy for ten months. She came to 13 sessions out of the planned 24. She came to the meetings regularly, but following her own rhythm with one- or two-session intervals. A crisis in her therapy took place when the extension of therapy was proposed.

My meetings with the supervisor predominantly concerned countertransference. From the very first meeting onwards, it was obvious to me that the patient kept a considerable distance, deprecated the value of the meetings and likewise deprecated the therapist. I felt that the patient had adopted an attitude communicating 'Here I am, as you wanted me to, and so what?' The patient demonstrated external motivation to take part in the consultations by requesting written confirmation of her coming to the session as if, my hypothesis was, she needed an external justification for participating in it in case I did not turn up, gave up on conducting therapy or left.

In subsequent meetings, I often encountered her resistance and even anger. She categorically refused to do any assignments and was angry with me. For example, she spurted out negative opinions about herself (e.g. 'I am stupid'), and on such occasions, I had the impression that she was afraid to be evaluated and to reveal anything about herself, as this triggered fear of being criticised or assessed in any way. She voiced self-deprecating statements. Sometimes she was irritated and refused to answer questions. She expressed anger and helplessness at the same time. I think that as the patient felt helpless in therapy, she functioned similarly in relations with others.

I would notice that I also experienced helplessness, irritation and anger. I was helpless about the problem of the patient who saw no way out of the situation. Sometimes, I felt angry that Magda did not want to cooperate even though I was patient and continued proving to her that she was at a safe place. I was disappointed that she did not open up at all and that she had difficulty communicating efficiently (countertransference).

At a certain stage, when I noticed changes in the patient's behaviour, I felt curious and sympathetic. On various occasions, the patient showed more and more of her life to me. Sometimes, after she did not turn up for the session, she would call me up to say that she would be coming to the following one. I also saw positive changes in her functioning, which bolstered my motivation for further work. I could see that she no longer cut herself, and she talked about that too. Her mood was clearly elevated, and she responded positively to my interventions more and more often. A friend began to accompany her on her way to the clinic. The patient made an impression of becoming interested in therapy, especially in the unchangeably scheduled meetings offered to her. She saw that I was there, and I waited for her even when she did not turn up for the planned session. I always assured her that I was waiting or had been waiting for a meeting with her.

When towards the end of the school year, I proposed extending therapy, her reaction was fear. She did not come to the following meetings. Her housemother, who phoned the clinic then, confirmed that Magda was safe. She was overjoyed at the changes in Magda's behaviour at the CH. I found out that, among other things, Magda's depressive symptoms had subsided after a few months after the inception of therapy and that she had not undertaken any self-harm or suicide attempts ever since. Besides this, the girl had started to engage in relations with other residents and had even become a 'popular' person obtaining invitations to weddings and other important events. Furthermore, a dog had arrived at the CH and had been taken care of by none other than Magda. She fed the dog and took it out for walks. All this represented considerable progress in the girl's behaviour as compared to what she had been like before starting therapy. Another new thing in the patient's conduct was anger that she displayed in some interpersonal situations.

The course versus the assumptions of therapy

One of the most important objectives in my work with the patient was to establish, build and constantly sustain an alliance with her to give her a sense of security in her relations with the therapist and to supply a corrective experience for her which could later help the patient engage in more satisfying relations with others as well.

Upon coming to the clinic, the patient harboured strong resistance, declared external motivation and displayed a negative attitude toward psychologists and psychotherapy. I was certain that building an alliance would be an arduous process, but I did not expect that it would take so long. The patient's defences were indeed very strong, and she was reluctant to suspend them.

I assumed that my therapeutic work with the patient should consist of:

1. Delineating boundaries that had so far been absent in the patient's life and attempting to externally structure her life (e.g. by explaining to her what her social relations relied on, what they involved, what boundaries there were among them, what feelings were associated with them, etc.). I concluded that, in this case, the structuring of therapy and the clear, abided-by setting would be important, both in terms of the form and in terms of the content of the contract;
2. Supporting the patient by offering her attention and making her accustomed to direct focus on her and her current problems by verbal and nonverbal means and through fixed scheduling of the meetings, showing the patient that I was waiting for her and underscoring frequently that I was 'her therapist' and that this time 'was for her'. Initially, she responded to such assurances with laughter,

which I felt was an expression of uncontrolled emotions triggered by the experience of being at the centre of somebody's attention;
3. Channelling the patient's attention to herself by asking her questions about her functioning. I noticed that when I asked the patient detailed questions, I mobilised her to reflect on a given issue in her life. I realised that such therapeutic interventions somewhat contributed to the building and strengthening of the patient's ego; and
4. Identifying her needs and expectations and rebuilding her self-structure by devoting attention and interest to various spheres of her life. Throughout therapy, I expressed interest in her functioning, experiences and ways of responding.

I often showed or directly told the patient that she was important to me, that I was waiting for her and that I wanted to hear how she was doing. I strengthened her sense of belonging and catered to her need of fitting in and being important and appreciated. As a result, her self-esteem increased and her mood improved. She learned ways of coping with difficulties. First and foremost, she saw and was assured that 'people did not disappear' from her life - that even if she did not turn up for a meeting, they waited for her and appreciated her being there. During therapy, Magda began to transfer her behaviours and moods onto the peer group and the animal, a dog that she started to show affection for and to take care of.

Although when answering my questions the patient often said that 'she didn't care', I understood it as a repressive defence, a way of managing her needs for which there had been no room in her previous life. This reminded me of 'emotional numbness', one of whose symptoms is keeping emotions and feelings at bay, as one expects that indulging in them will result in being hurt when they are lost, destroyed or changed. I showed the patient that things could be different both here and now in therapy and in her adult life - that she contributed to relations with others, and I helped her build them.

In her therapy, she characteristically oscillated between getting closer and moving away, which was vividly exemplified in her missing out on sessions when the relation between us had become more intimate.

Initially, I hoped and planned that changes in the patient's functioning would be faster and clearer. However, as therapy unfolded, I came to accept slow changes in the patient's functioning.

Basically, it was only in the latest contact with the patient and her milieu that I realised that special changes had taken place as compared to the prior plan. The patient herself did not 'notice', however, that something positive had occurred in her life.

As compared to our first meetings, Magda's functioning had changed in terms of communication with her and her social relations; specifically, the patient began to initiate contact. For example, she phoned me a few times to fix appointments or to call off a session.

Understanding and diagnosing the patient

Therapy was launched within the psychodynamic framework and contracted for a short term of ten months, with breaks for bank holidays and winter school holidays.

At present, no systematic research is being carried out to identify the best therapeutic method for this category of patients. Such disorders have so far been approached within the psychodynamic or the biological perspective, and only scarce data have been collected concerning the concept of family relations and couple or family therapy.

As far as the psychodynamic aspect is concerned, the patient's capacity to grasp how strongly she influenced 'her own pathology' was very limited, and her only motivation to keep on working was to stop suffering or, as she had expressed it herself, to put an end to criticism or other's unfavourable and overlooking attitude toward her.

Typically because of the patient's adolescence, she is searching for her own identity, wherein she maintains resistance, especially vis-à-vis authority figures and consequently also the therapist and several other people (i.e. the staff of the CH).

The process of separation from her parents was literal for this girl, as she was abruptly taken away from her family home, which induced a deep sense of loneliness, isolation and depressive symptoms. Understanding the patient in terms of adolescence (i.e. puberty and the identity search) entails interpreting her symptoms in relation to the norms/standards for her age group. Within this framework, her dysfunctional symptoms should be explored in terms of disorders in behaviour and emotions (i.e. mixed disorders, as she exhibited impaired mood, depressiveness, suicidal ruminations and suicidal acts) and met the criteria of responding to severe stress and adaptive disturbances following several traumatic events in her life. She has been medically diagnosed in this way throughout the period of treatment and therapy.

Analysing the patient's functioning in terms of ego development, it can be concluded that her symptoms are characteristic of borderline personality development. The patient is capable of perceiving sensory reality, and, in spite of all, exhibits a relatively stable ego, as compared with psychotics, and is able to recover after temporary episodes of exceptionally strong stress. Nevertheless, as compared to neurotic patients, she presents a strong identity dispersal and relies on primitive defence mechanisms. Additionally, she is intolerant of frustration, cannot cope with frustration and anxiety (e.g. self-aggression, suicide attempts) and exhibits a lack of object stability and of observing ego, especially in stressful situations.

Consistently with the functioning characteristic of borderline-personality ego development, the patient panics when she feels too close to others. She is afraid of being fully absorbed and controlled, but on the other hand, when she feels separated, she experiences a traumatic sense of rejection. The patient is torn in the dilemma of 'seeking help' versus 'rejecting help'.

As the patient is very young, it is impossible to diagnose personality disorders in any conclusive way. Nevertheless, she meets certain criteria characteristic of borderline personality disorders, such as:

- anxiety- and tension-fraught interpersonal relations;
- impulsiveness (periods of alcohol abuse, eating disorders, suicide attempts);
- self-aggression, self-harm;
- lack of emotional stability (previously depressiveness, currently anger outbursts);
- feelings of emptiness and boredom; and
- persistent striving to avoid real or imagined abandonment.

The patient can also be viewed through the lens of schizoid personality features, such as the sense of loneliness, withdrawal and non-integration with others, the sense of being 'odd' or different (displayed in her response to the suggestion of extending therapy and in her prior tendency to avoid contact with psychologists), sensitivity to intrusion, fear of being abandoned, fear of being dependent, lack of pleasure-oriented activities and the limited capacity of expressing friendly and warm feelings.

Magda went through traumas at a very early, oral stage of development and experienced herself as an unwanted, or even hated, child. Schizoid cases are linked to problems involving the sense of security in the social world. The patient displays an inability to form bonds with another person and fear in social situations. Besides this, her skills of self-care and self-soothing are very limited, and she is incapable of recognising her own feelings. This is accompanied by depressiveness/dysthymia, which is all probability caused by exhaustion, despair and longing and likely resulting from being abandoned, disjoined and not needed. Concomitantly, she is self-deprecating, has a reduced sense of self-worth and diminishes the significance of whatever pursuit she undertakes in life.

In devising further ways of working with the patient, these diagnostic considerations and hypotheses should be taken into account. Even though, given the patient's young age, these are cautiously posited, the insights concerning the development of borderline personality should serve as relevant predictors for the future course of therapy.

It will undoubtedly be vital to maintain the therapeutic alliance and undertake attempts to prevent the patient from missing visits, threatening to quit or completely withdrawing from therapy, which was an important takeaway from supervision sessions. The patient can seldom be expected to spontaneously talk about essential and unpleasant aspects of her life. She can also be expected to be sensitive to all signals and interventions from the therapists. I also understand that mood changes are likely to occur in the future. Even at this stage in therapy, it could be seen that depressiveness had largely receded and the patient had instead begun to express anger, which can also be comprehended within the diagnostic conclusions outlined above.

It will be fundamental for the therapist to connect throughout the therapy period to the countertransference of feelings, especially the negative ones, so as to remain alert to her own potentially nontherapeutic responses at further stages of working with the patient.

Epilogue

The description above is a fragment of therapy records of a person from the environment which is most vulnerable to social exclusion risk: a broken family affected by juvenilisation and violence. Pathological models of social functioning, inconsistent upbringing methods and a simultaneous lack of support and warmth, or even the loss of family home, add up to an environmental context in which many young people grow up facing exclusion risk. They grow up lonely, in their own inner world of unexpressed experiences which are pushed out of consciousness. As traumatic experiences mount, childhood depression is often replaced by aggression towards oneself or others.

It is not easy to help young people who are stuck in their unique 'insulation' as they disaffect others and oppose their own therapy. Any bond such a young person establishes with another individual seems a success, as others are so difficult to trust.

Working with children and adolescents at risk of social exclusion is a challenge. It demands authenticity, patience and sustained attention from a therapist, an educator or a guardian. If the insights gained are superficial, then the desired change may not come to pass. If insights are obtained too quickly, then this may trigger fear and attempts to discontinue therapy or contact. Therapy takes a lot of meetings that patients often cannot afford to pay for.

Part III

Multidisciplinary perspectives on exclusion

Chapter 8

Transgenerational trauma, trust and emotional exclusion

Human beings are predestined to derive joy from their lives and to live in harmony with themselves and their environment. This is the oldest truth about ourselves which has been obscured in the human mind over the thousands of years of human existence. Around 40,000 years ago, our ancestors lived in tribal groups in which they formed and felt to be an immanent part. They felt important, needed, and they had a sense of belonging within the group. Every community member mattered for the survival of all, because everybody contributed to the gaining of food, the sustaining of fire and/or the protection of others in danger. They did not shun art, entertainment and pleasures. The few preserved artworks of the period, such as cave paintings and figurines, testify to our forebears' creative drive and practices. An ample interest was devoted to astronomy and constellations and also to the sphere of sex and fertility. Both females and males could have several partners at the same time if they chose so. There were no reasons to engage in rivalries, to indulge in speculations or to plunge into tangled relationships. People's lives were based on trust in their families or tribal groups and on the belief that everybody supported everybody else and learned and worked to further their own good and the benefit of all. Collaboration was expedient for gaining and distributing goods. External perils, such as the unpredictability of nature, had to be handled, and co-existence with other tribes (e.g. the Neanderthals) had to be arranged (Hoffecker, 2009).

It can easily be noticed that mindfulness—which is treated as an antidote to stress and mental problems today—was taken for granted by our ancestors. Mindful contact with nature was exigent to life, since perceptive intercourse with nature, careful observations of weather symptoms and the meticulous scrutiny of wildlife, therein animals and plants, provided basic information for survival and effective coping. Much of it involved intuitive insights and reliance on one's own emotions and feelings. New and unpredictable things could happen every day. Fear and anxiety appeared in situations of real danger, such as the vicissitudes of weather, the proximity of wild animals and/or hunger. Anger and rage had their palpable dimension, as they accompanied moments of necessary fighting. A motivation for searching was natural, while communing with nature occasioned joy, play and relaxation.

What is in our genes and ancestral memory?

Our ancestors did not go down with degenerative diseases. They were not as commonly affected by mental disorders as people in our times are. They did not suffer from depression, dementia, Alzheimer's disease and other brain diseases; neither were they plagued by diabetes, atherosclerosis, cancer or allergies. They were not morbidly obese as eating only served survival needs, and considerable physical activity helped them maintain fitness and health, as well as relieving stress (Wilczyńska-Kwiatek, De Meester, Singh and Łapiński, 2010).

In our times, degenerative diseases account for at least 90% of deaths worldwide. Stress, lifestyle and diet are their major risk factors. Relationships among people no longer fulfil the functions they did before: they are far less frequent, and they do not satisfy the human need for closeness and belonging, as shown in the previous chapters.

Our ancestors found natural bodily intimacy soothing, for it kept them warm in cold nights and gave them physical security. Mutual support was a massive benefit, and it was utterly unthinkable to bar over half of the group members from activities performed by others or to exclude them in any other way. Language was used for communicating in daily life, and relations were neither dysregulated nor hurtful to people to such a degree as these are observed to be in our times.

In the course of civilisational progress, people abandoned the nomadic lifestyle, started to work fields, settled in various areas and focused on producing food, as a result of which the human species began to experience stresses, diseases, wars and conquests. Basically, humans themselves produced these stresses and wars. We are a generation that not only experiences the memory of past wounds, but also anticipates future threats (Ulriken de Vinar, 2012).

Genes and memes are transmitted through various information channels.

De Meester's concept, as described in the latter part of this book, allows an explanation of how environmental and body information is transmitted via cell membrane fatty acids and blood cells.

Gene expression takes place, and behaviour (i.e. the phenotype which is subject to natural and cultural selection) is shaped. As De Meester explains, 'individual phenotype (behaviour) reflects the expression of genes and memes, which themselves influence each other. Fatty acids in cell membranes are to memes what nucleic acids in cell nuclei are to genes (i.e. biological sets of information)' (De Meester, 2018, pp. 3, 14).

Learning to exclude others

Up to about three years of age, children are open-minded, curious about the world, assertive with their needs and courageous. They offer unpremeditated altruism to others, take care of others, readily share their toys and propose playing games that are pleasurable to others. Children are only taught 'reciprocated' altruism several years later by family, society and culture. Children quickly learn that, in order to 'survive' in the contemporary world, one must display reciprocity and that non-reciprocation and being ignored and/or overlooked are painful. Empathy, which all of us possess to lesser or greater degrees, is sometimes taken advantage of in order to deliberately hurt others.

The first unexpected experiences of being excluded increase alertness. Hurt people usually give up trying to be included, and they isolate themselves.

However, as already mentioned above, those who experienced pain in their childhood and stumble over obstacles when seeking to realise their need of belonging and being recognised tend to exclude others. At later stages in their lives or in other (e.g. school-based) systems, teenagers consciously and intentionally use manipulative measures to control the sense of belonging in the group (Benenson, Markovits, Thompson and Wrangham, 2011). This kind of control of the sense of belonging has become a new variety of 'natural selection'.

Modern e-communication media and channels of establishing relations, such as Facebook, Instagram and Twitter together with the entire virtual reality, breed cyberbullying. People versed in exclusionary mechanisms control the composition of subgroups in which they belong. The main players in the struggle for attention and position in the hierarchy are usually individuals whose sense of belonging is still unstable as a result of past experiences. As a rule, they do not know how to take care of themselves and how to accept care and compassion from others. Their politeness is superficial and rationed, rather than commonly offered. Their selective compassion and care bestowed exclusively on the chosen group members do not augment actual personal or group resources. Instead, this secures a top position in the 'pecking order'. In such a structure, a person whose position in the hierarchy is high is less likely to fall victim to aggression or exclusion (Strycker, 2016).

Observations of everyday life indicate that bullying—which is a form of social exclusion—has become rampant and endemic in recent years. In 2017, a survey carried out by the Workplace Bullying Institute (workplacebullying.org/wbiresearch/wbi-2017-survey/) found that:

- 19% of Americans are bullied, and another 19% witness it;
- 61% of Americans are aware of abusive conduct in the workplace;

- 60.4 million Americans are affected by it;
- 70% of perpetrators are men; 60% of targets are women;
- Hispanics are the most frequently bullied race;
- 61% of bullies are bosses, and the majority (63%) operate alone;
- 40% of bullied targets are believed to suffer adverse health effects;
- 29% of targets remain silent about their experiences;
- 71% of employer reactions are harmful to targets;
- 60% of coworker reactions are harmful to targets;
- 65% of targets lose their original jobs to stop it;
- 77% of Americans support enacting a new law; and
- 46% report worsening of work relationships, post-Trump election.

There is no consensus as to whether contemporary exclusion practices originate in culture or in nature. I am inclined to believe that mass excluding is underpinned by both natural and cultural factors. For one, it can be driven by our natural instincts powered by the fight for survival. However, because we realise that our survival anxieties are unreal and the reality in which we dread the loss of position, the forfeiture of material goods and the depletion of resources is our own product, we may assume that exclusion is created by modern society. In some communities, exclusion is treated as a form of regulation and restoration of the order within the group—for example, if the group's functioning has been disturbed by a member's behaviour.

'Inheriting' the experience of exclusion from our ancestors

If people inherit the memory of trauma and are additionally faced with present stresses in everyday lives, difficult and painful experiences mount up and become more and more unmanageable. Depression and other mental disorders with which our times are fraught are affecting more and more people and are spreading across generations. The growing awareness urges us to immediately stop the flywheel of sufferings that afflict people all over the world and even to reverse the direction of these exacerbating processes.

The notion of transgenerational trauma is becoming increasingly popular. In this framework, trauma is conceptualised as a process in which anxieties and pain are transmitted to descendants by the generations which were directly exposed to suffering during war or other traumatic events (Yehuda and Lehrner, 2018; Danieli, Norris and Engdahl, 2016). Polish scholars Professor Maja Lis-Turlejska and Professor Katarzyna Shier (https://www.polityka.pl/jamyoni/1770624,1,polacy--narod-z-ptsd.read) argue that almost the entire Polish nation are traumatised as a result of the experiences of World War 1 and World War 2 and that our local history can indeed explain why Poles are pessimistic, have a negative mindset and do not trust others. In Poland, trust towards people other than family and close friends stands at the lowest level in Europe.

The concept of transgenerational transmissions can be corroborated by findings concerning the transfer of information, therein environmental information. Scientists are willing to look for a gene-transfer centre, which is obviously a mistake. In cultural inheritance (i.e. social and psychological characteristics of humans), rules and norms are transmitted memetically (Gerson, 2019; Danieli, Norris and Engdahl, 2017). I am convinced that the concept discussed in this book enables us to understand the foundations of human functioning and to devise treatments for the human psyche—the mind. Future psychological/psychonomic research on the human mind will probably draw on it, with a view both to trying to overthrow it and to harnessing it in order to save humanity.

Inheriting trauma

Trauma is experienced at several levels. Transgenerational trauma is passed down from generation to generation. A parent who survived the war or a crime incident may have difficulty sharing his/her history with his/her children. This reaction is known as the survivor syndrome, which is expressed in distrust of the world, permanent sadness, chronic sense of threat, fear of separation, focus on educational achievement and not setting limits for oneself and others. A child who does not know what happened to his/her family feels anxious and worried about such a parent. Unarticulated words and accumulated emotions are vented by the caregiver in sudden outbursts of aggression or hysteria. His/her responses are dominated by a fear of separation, which entails death or suffering. Children do not understand the prevailing atmosphere, but they strive to give their parents relief and avoid occasioning further tensions. Trauma is not talked about in the family, but its painful wounds are 'cultivated' through the specific functioning of at least some of its members. The child who bears the stigma of trauma behaves in specific ways as if 'expecting an impending catastrophe'. Feelings and attitudes are absorbed by children from their parents. The child functions the way that his/her parent functions, irrespective of what the caregiver's verbal messages are (Yehuda and Lehrner, 2018; Rutkowski and Dembińska, 2015).

In regions fraught with wars and disasters, entire communities bear the burden of trauma. In Poland and many other European countries, whole populations can be viewed as survivors. Each of us has heard family stories of wounds and tragic deaths happening across a multigenerational history of wars and conquests (Baum, 2013). Many are affected by the direct tragic history of the closest generation—such as addictions, violence and loneliness—which persist through generations. Traumatic experiences are one of the causes of the sense of social exclusion.

Reaching beyond the 'imprinted' information

For any change-based development to be possible, certain necessary conditions should be met. These conditions crucially include a resolve to follow the path of development, to revise schemes and to replace old habits with new solutions. Of course, this is challenging, if not impossible, to some people and especially at the beginning of their journey, because this requires both identifying deficits, obstacles and wounds and acknowledging them together with the deeply buried need of belonging. As humans have a capacity to feel a range of emotions—therein, also difficult ones such as anger, anxiety and rage—they probably possess adequate resources to handle these emotions as well. Such primeval emotions are, in fact, a response to real or imagined threats. Their source lies in the schemes of thought and behaviour, and they are strongly imprinted in the biochemical structures. When the self-strengthening mechanism is activated, other emotions are not allowed. Instead, they are sifted and deleted. To use other emotions, people have to implement other, new solutions based on very advanced psychological mechanisms. Scientists suggest that, in the future, the adult mind will be able to be cured of previous traumas and harmful patterns by blood changes or blood transfusions.

Even sceptics who have entered the path of self-development through meditation admit that they have noticed changes as early as after a mere few weeks of mindfulness training sessions. People go through soothing psychological and spiritual experiences and perceive an increase in their emotional and cognitive capacities. Their bodies respond by healing and growing, with the brain functions expanding to cover new areas on which people can draw in order to calm down and regenerate. As a series of studies have shown, the brain is constructed as our thoughts produce it. Therefore, the brain grows through the generation of new connections, dendrites and whole neurons (Singer and Engert, 2019).

Diaphragmatic breathing provides a noninvasive stimulation of the vagal nerve, which involves raising heart rate variability and reducing stress symptoms (Gerritsen and Band, 2018). Diaphragmatic breathing also enhances the general cognitive capacity of the brain and, thus, helps in making better decisions (De Couck et al., 2019).

Code of upbringing

In my view, parents—future parents in particular—should participate in educational programmes or be obliged to abide by a defined way/code of child-raising. It is especially important when they do not feel prepared for parenthood or did not have an opportunity to witness good parenting models in their own families. Children are far too often exposed to emotional trauma caused by exclusion in their closest communities, which has serious consequences over the following years of their lives. Having worked with parents as a therapist for over 20 years, I have observed that neither their education nor their economic status is linked to their personal predispositions and educational skills. Children tend to be emotionally excluded as a result of incidents associated with emotional experiences that slip out of their caregivers' control. The trauma of exclusion is often caused by a less intense but prolonged emotional experience of hurtful situations or relations generated by their loved ones. Emotional exclusion is neither featured in the classification of disorders nor defined by law. This is probably one reason why parents and caregivers are not aware of how serious its implications may be. In fact, severe value judgements or verbal criticism of children may trigger the sense of exclusion through excessive evaluation, subjective comparisons, emotionally deprecating or irritated commentaries, failure to devote attention and neglect of the children's importance and presence. When children's love for their parents is rejected or ignored, the pain felt by the children is compared to a 'broken heart'. The acuteness of the pain of rejection is directly proportional to the individual need for love (Lowen, 1988).

Children may experience this kind of exclusion from parents, siblings or other people without all parties realising this, or at least with the children themselves realising the fact only when they have grown up. However, if a child who struggles with math assignments is systematically called 'dumb' or 'ninny', this name-calling will deeply affect his/her further development in a way that is opposite to supporting and congratulating him/her for perseverance despite failures.

A metaphorical light is shed on this issue by the Japanese researcher Maseru Emoto, whose research has shown how human emotions or human consciousness influence the formation of water crystals. In his experiments, water which was 'exposed' to love, gratitude and harmonious sounds or images took beautiful, regular shapes; while water 'exposed' to verbal 'aggression' became 'ugly', developing an irregular or amorphous structure (Emoto, 2005).

Negative emotions work similarly to the brains of people who grow up in traumatic circumstances. Neuroimaging results show remarkable differences between the activity of the developed brains of people who grew up amidst acceptance and love and the brain activity of people who experienced negative emotions when growing up. The earlier a trauma is experienced, the greater damage it does to the brain activity (De Bellis et al., 1999; Jorge et al., 2004). The experience of medium-intensive but repeated emotional trauma is the major factor that curtails the optimum development not only of emotions, but also of knowledge and creative capacities.

Emotional traumas resulting from neglect and deprivation account for the largest percentage or the largest number of all traumas which afflict people. Developing 'tacitly' at family homes, schools and shared living spaces, after some time, these cause symptoms similar to those triggered by physical traumas and sexual or medical violence (Vetulani, 2017). Regrettably, these will continue to take their toll until parents are supplied with credible and scientifically corroborated recommendations and constraints concerning the ways of communicating, building relations and child-raising.

Chapter 9

Attachment and exclusion

Can a wounded attachment be salvaged?

To comprehensively understand what attachments/bonds are, we should usefully consult the psychological Theory of Attachment developed by John Bowlby (1969) and, of course, clinical practice. Building bonds with a loved one is a natural biological need that closely ties in with the evolutionally conditioned motivational system of the preservation of the species. Establishing and sustaining closeness with a caregiver secures individual survival at the early stages of human life. From birth onwards, a child has a certain sense of security which is maintained through the bond with his/her caregiver. For this attachment to develop correctly, the caregiver should be tuned-in with the child and self-conscious of his/her own and generational negative experiencesto to avoid transfering them on the child.

While the bond/attachment does not exist independently of a caregiver, a child is not a passive 'recipient' of his/her parent's behaviour. The parent can consciously work on his/her relationship with the child, and yet unconsciously transfer on the child his/her own internalised, unrecognised and unworked-through anxieties. If justified/unfounded or real/unreal anxiety (e.g. about the child's health and life) arises in the adult, it is identified by the child. There are various kinds of situations in which a child identifies anxiety. In one of them, a real threat to the child occurs—for example, when the mother disappears for a longer period of time from the child's field of vision, or when the child is hungry and cold. In the other one, the mother feels anxiety related to her care for the child (e.g. she doubts whether she is a good mother; she worries not only whether she properly looks after the child, but also whether she handles her relations with other people well; she is concerned about everyday matters and problems, etc.). When the mother does not reveal her anxiety, for example, by smiling and talking in a soft voice, the child experiences a dissonance. The child may feel it both when experiencing real physical and physiological discomfort and when co-feeling his/her mother's anxiety in response to everyday situations. Although the mother teaches her child to cope 'bravely', the mother's feelings, which are sensed by the child, possess the real power of communication and teaching (Byrne and Russon, 1998).

A child is connected to his/her mother with strong family bonds and a loving relationship. Every change in the mother's emotional system will bring about a change in the child's system. There is a very pictorial Polish proverb that captures the essence of this process. Conveying the sense of 'what youth is used to, age remembers', it literally goes 'what the shell soaked in when young it smells of when old' and insists that people's features, especially the negative ones, are acquired in childhood and adolescence. Until a child matures and becomes an aware adult, s/he 'collects' what others communicate and uses external response schemes.

Similarly, averse experiences in attachment relationships which a child faces over the first three years of his/her life are often traumatic experiences. Interestingly, traumatic events take place in families that transfer this trauma, for example, through alcohol addiction, experiences of violence, exclusion and the like. It seems obvious that in dysfunctional families, traumatic events (e.g. accidences) will more occur frequently. Apart from traumas correlated with the family line, a child may be confronted with entirely random traumatic situations that affect all people, such as natural disasters, wars and crime. They impact systems of emotional and behavioural regulation, 'furrowing' particular channels of connection among them. If a person experiences more soothing and security than threats in childhood, his/her systems of emotional and behavioural regulation are smoothly harmonised, and these furnish the person with multiple resources—providing a sense of security in regular everyday life and initiating alert responses when faced with danger. In response to a threat, a high-functioning person—who abundantly uses the system of security and soothing—as a rule, effectively mobilises this system and either fights or flees. When desiring food or pleasure, such a person activates the mechanisms and resources of the drive and achievement system in order to achieve satiation and pleasure.

Children in families with a long or complicated trauma history more frequently rely on the mechanisms and resources of the threat and protection system, which not only helps them 'cope with' the problem at a given moment, but also 'anaesthetises' and enables them to survive in no-pain. A recognised threat automatically activates the defence mechanism which protects against the experience of pain. Usually, the response is, in fact, no reaction at all—such as in, for example, the freeze response or tonic/collapsed immobility (Kozlowska, McLean, Walker and Carrive, 2015).

Painful childhood experiences: attachment and trauma

Painful childhood experiences can be fully or partly forgotten as a result of defences used by the mind. Information inscribed in our bodies will 'memorise' such events better than our conscious minds (De Meester, 2019).

Long-term effects of such acute early experiences can surface in later childhood or in adolescence as emotional disorders or disturbing behaviours. Such instabilities tend to result in criminal deeds and/or mental disorders in later life (Garbarino, 1990).

Alan Schore states that disorganised attachments experienced in childhood are a predictor of post-traumatic disorders in adolescence and adulthood (Schore, 2002). In this kind of bond, the caregiver's endeavours to provide a safe and favourable setting for the child's development are interrupted by periods of uncontrolled emotions, such as anger, despair or fear. The caregiver's unworked-through problems are transferred onto the child not only through emotions received by the child, but also through stressful and traumatic experiences that the child is exposed to. The adult's unpredictable behaviours are dangerous for the child, because the child's emotional system is not mature enough to interpret and understand or to oppose these.

The Polyvagal Theory (Porges, 2003) stresses that the vagus nerve is responsible for people's responses to stressful and traumatic situations. It is a cranial nerve that is built of afferent motor and parasympathetic fibres. It innervates most of the parasympathetic system, e.g. such as the thoracic and abdominal organs. It consists of two parts: a dorsal part which is unmyelinated and the ventral part which has myelin sheaths. The two parts serve different functions (Kozlowska, McLean, Walker and Carrive, 2015). The unmyelinated part operates the most primal behavioural responses—such as the freeze response or the inaction in the face of threat—and the evolutionally more advanced system of fight-or-flight responses, which depends on the parasympathetic system. The myelinated fibres of the vagus nerve operate the third system, which is the system of social cooperation. In a stressful situation, the first response is to seek contact with another person, which entails activating the system of social engagement and seeking security. If for one reason or another, the person does not obtain the soothing effect by means of the social engagement system, then the brain activates the earlier systems: fight-or-flight or, ultimately, dissociation and withdrawal.

Dissociation as an effect of a childhood trauma

Dissociation is the loss of conscious control over some thoughts, feelings or behaviours. In a child, dissociations are part of the natural developmental process at a certain stage of growing up, with phenomena such as fantasising and incarnating various characters (e.g. fairytale protagonists, animals, toys, etc.) being the developmental norm. A range of derealisations—suspending or changing time and space, memory or perception disorders and an overall difficulty in integrating various functions of the body—all mark a natural developmental stage. Such symptoms disappear in the course of time. Yet in children who experience psychological trauma, dissociative symptoms persist, change and intensify as they grow older, which leads to serious disorders in the psychical sphere (Schore, 2009).

Adaptive dissociation is understood as a defence mechanism that is necessary for survival. Pathological dissociation shows in an entrenched, inadequate and harmful pattern of bodily responses to subjectively perceived threats. As a consequence of traumatic experiences, relatively permanent deficits and disorders appear in the integration of somatic, motor, perception, emotion, memory, consciousness and identity functions in children. Some authors (Courtois and Ford, 2009; Drozdowski and Weigl, 2011) claim that the body which is exposed to repeated threats, negligence and abuse from a parent or a significant caregiver produces an incorrect model of equilibrium. Disordered self-regulation manifests in excessive excitement and in dissociation states which alternate in a child.

Attachment and the experience of exclusion: what is attachment?

Traumatic events are recorded and pushed into oblivion. In a review of studies on biological disorders that take place in response to traumatic stress, Van der Kolk (2018) enumerates changes involved in disturbed brain functions. Neurohormonal effects include changes in the level of noradrenergic and serotonergic neurotransmitters and endogenic opioids. They include an elevated release of catecholamines, impeded MAO action, dysregulation of adrenergic receptors, a drop in serotonin secretion and an increased secretion of opioids when faced with stimuli associated with trauma. Changes in memory include amnesia and hypermnesia. Neuroanatomical effects are, for example, the reduced effectiveness of the hippocampus, which later decreases in volume, the activation of the right side of the amygdala when recollecting, the activation of the sensory areas of the right hemisphere and the reduced activation of the Broca area during hypermnesia or flashbacks (Van der Kolk et al., 1996).

In fact, these effects are brought about by very strongly imprinted information which was 'recorded' due to intense emotions that accompanied it. Any association with them triggers these symptoms. The fact that experiences are recorded in the body is also confirmed by the renowned French microkinesitherapist Dr Daniel Grosjean (Grosjean, 2020; Baum, 2013).

In his Neuroaffective Relational Model (NARM), Laurence Heller (Heller and LaPierre, 2012) emphasises that good social relations are predicated on achieving a balance between the scrutiny of one's own feelings and the scrutiny of other people's feelings. To sustain relationships, one must monitor one's own inner impulses and, at the same time, develop receptivity to other people's states. Building such reciprocal relations requires constant effort and mindfulness of oneself and others one is close with. A deficit of closeness is perceived as an early childhood relational trauma. Children who do not experience the close contact they need go through the same process of trauma as that involved in traumatic experiences of violence. Such experiences cause body tension, activate the nervous system and unsettle the body's biochemical balance and bioelectric potential. Thereby, the child is unable to assess the situation of attachment deficit or disturbance as resulting from the environment's inadequate response to his/her needs. Being abandoned or ignored is, thus, experienced by the child as resulting from his/her own defectiveness. This is a personal failure which the child transforms into later feelings of worthlessness, helplessness and shame. Feelings and emotions which appear in this process are usually contradictory; for example, the desire to be close and taken care of goes hand in hand with helplessness or anger with the parent. When basic needs are permanently unfulfilled, systems become dysregulated; the distorted self-image is perpetuated and improper contact with the self becomes entrenched. A young person becomes increasingly convinced that s/he is not valuable enough for his/her needs to be met. As a result, s/he stops communicating needs and expectations, his/her motivation slumps, and the system which seeks change and effective coping is thoroughly wrecked. The child—and later, the adolescent—does not reveal his/her feelings in fear of being hurt again and losing the relation with his/her significant caregiver. By not revealing him/herself, s/he surrenders his/her own self, and, consequently, his/her life turns into a mere physical/biological existence with a superficial ego. S/he loses, conceals or disguises his/her authenticity, gives up on sincerity and abandons the belief that s/he has the right to have and communicate his/her own needs. Practically, s/he does not experience peace, relief, security and felicity at all. If these symptoms continue in adulthood, then they block the inner development of a person and his/her access to self-consciousness (Moretti and Peled, 2004).

In such circumstances, the person is not in touch with his/her emotions, body and other people. Those who have learned to function in deficit develop defences that make them believe that they are 'different than the rest' and do not need other people to live and work. Sometimes they even negate the point of there being a community as such. Nevertheless, such people often focus on satisfying others' needs and live through these needs. They are dependent on others or of schizoid character. They either do not know their boundaries or allow others to cross them as in the case of a symbiotic character. They do not know how to take care of themselves, their feelings and their wishes. They repress the 'inner child' and become demanding 'adults'. Their prevailing feelings are sadness and regret; they may even feel that they are hated by others, while they usually hate themselves. In such circumstances, it is very difficult to engage in any kind of relationship with others, as the longing to be with others atrophies, or contact with others breed anxiety. These processes also affect sexual identification, with sex sometimes not being manifested and sexual needs being repressed or misunderstood/exaggerated as in the case of an oedipal character. The person does not derive pleasure from being in a sexual relationship, or this relationship exclusively serves to 'maintain' physical closeness with another person (Johnson, 1994).

Heller discusses 'intelligent survival styles' (Heller and LaPierre, 2012) which are initiated in environments that are insufficiently tuned in with the child. The 'intelligent child' splits off from his/her own needs, for not having needs forestalls the experience of having their realisation denied.

Children's 'intelligent' and ostensibly independent attitudes take shape in response to the avoidant attachment to their mother. Bowlby's attachments styles were broadly discussed following a so-called 'strange experiment' in which mothers and their children had been observed in new situations with strangers, with the mother's and the child's heart functions monitored when the child was being left alone with a stranger and then during the mother's return (Ainsworth, Blehar, Waters and Wall, 1978; Levine and Heller, 2012).

Although the avoidant style is depicted as not providing a secure basis of development, in Polish culture, a 'self-reliant' child is, in fact, a desirable role model of upbringing. Children are trained to cope on their own in difficult situations, to not 'cry for no reason' and to not be a 'crybaby'. Children are praised for solving problems by themselves, which regrettably also concerns those that are too difficult for their level of maturity.

Avoidant attachment and the sense of exclusion

Children's forced 'self-reliance' is also formed when their mothers fail to spend quality time with them, which is a precondition of building a security-underpinned bond. Sometimes, mothers work long hours, leave children in daycare institutions for hours on end or leave the family for several months, for example, going away for work. When entrusted in the care of people who are not engaged in building close relations with them, children feel abandoned, desperate and lonely. For a while, they try to fight for access to their mothers and signal their needs. Yet when they are neither satisfied nor noticed, children give up and stop demanding attention from and intimacy with mothers, and instead begin to cope by curbing their need of security and restraining their feelings and expression.

Mothers' avoidant behaviour also contributes to the development of children's acquired avoidant behaviour while in contact with them. This takes place when a mother does not know how to maintain and communicate closeness to family members, because she has experienced a lack of care, when she does not believe that she performs her mother-role well, when she has no trust in herself and when she does not recognise her own emotions and cannot express them.

As a result of avoidant attachment, children avoid closeness and do not express their emotions, suppressing even the positive ones while accumulating the negative ones. Children may not reveal their stress on the outside, but it is physiologically detectable anyway. When children can no longer bear the accumulated tension, they explode, whereby they deregulate themselves and hurt others.

People who experienced avoidant attachment in childhood do not necessarily feel excluded. Usually, they do not realise that they had their inability to build relationships with others imprinted in the upbringing process. In fact, they grow up lonely and remain outside of most relationships that are available to their peers. They do not experience close bonds with other people, and if they engage in any relations at all, then their relations tend to be superficial contact, short-lasting or based on ingrained polite conventions and, as such, are barely sustainable. Such people usually become workaholics and sometimes develop other addictions as well. They may come across as professionals and experts in their fields, but they are afraid of criticism. They make an impression of mysteriousness and attractiveness, but they cannot build lasting, intimate relationships. They suppress their need for closeness. They cope with stress on their own. They dislike bodily contact, such as touching and being touched, given which their sexual practices aim to release tension rather than experiencing pleasure. They do not recognise their needs and do not know how they can be communicated. As a rule, they cannot set boundaries for others and are eager to satisfy other people's needs instead of their own ones (projection). Although they do not join groups, they are pained when they are excluded from them—for example, when they are not invited to co-workers' informal get-togethers. On one hand, they feel relieved because they do not know how to function in such relationships, but on the other hand, they are aware that others also withdraw from contact with them, perceiving them as unapproachable and lacking directness. Basically, they function all the time at elevated levels of physiological tension and permanently sustain alertness in social situations, although they do not display their emotion. Avoidant attachment predicts prospective changes in depressive symptoms and in anxiety symptoms (Lee and Hankin, 2009). In physiological tests, they have high outcomes in systolic blood pressure and diastolic blood pressure, while low outcomes in the heart rate (Wilczyńska, De Meester, Singh and Bargiel-Matusiewicz, 2010). This is what differentiates their apparent quiet from genuine quiet and independence. In fact, they do not trust others and monitor themselves both in public situations and in intimate relationships.

People with the avoidant model of attachment tend to locate the causes of their situation outside rather than within themselves, while they actually do not invest in relationships and are afraid to love, reveal affection and cultivate it. They fear rejection, but, at the same time, they expect or even provoke it. Their inaccessibility and 'boycott' of bonds and close relations cause their relationships to fall apart. They may also inadvertently contribute to breakdowns of relationships of other people around them. They often assess potentially close relations between people as impossible, fake or threatening (Wilczyńska, 2019).

Anxious attachment and an ongoing threat of losing relationships

Anxious attachment is characterised by entirely different responses, as it entails efforts to strongly bond with another person—first and foremost with the mother. When a child is being raised by a mother who herself experiences strong emotions, in particular anxiety, the child picks up the anxious attitude from her and displays it even in common situations in life. An anxious mother is overprotective and often oversensitive to the child's signals, because she is too self-absorbed. She is afraid to leave the child alone or to let him/her explore the environment, because she believes it is dangerous for the child. As a result, the mother's strong and ungrounded fears for the child contribute to the child clinging to her.

When the mother is engrossed by her own anxiety, she fails to notice the child's real needs. When the mother's motivations in moments of anxiety are unclear to the child, s/he may develop a perception of reality as unknown, threatening and harbouring some ghastly mysteries, which are better left unknown and from which the 'knowing' mother seeks to shield the child.

When children's anxious behaviour begins to be a problem for themselves (e.g. when they refuse to join a social group, do not want to stay at the kindergarten or at school, etc.), family members realise that there is a problem and try to 'familiarise' the children with situations from which they have been sheltered so far. Sometimes, such mothers endeavour to teach their children 'brave' behaviours by encouraging them to play with unknown children or to stay alone with a stranger, such as a babysitter. As a rule, this produces rather reverse effects, as the children burst out crying and clutch the loved one in panic. Sometimes, such behaviours—learned and excessive as they may be—are used to pressure people to maintain the status quo.

On one hand, the anxious functioning model develops as a result of the inconsistency of the mother, who accompanies her child with a strong bond even when the child does not need it. On the other hand, this also occurs when, on the contrary, the mother is in the habit of leaving the child without necessary support in situations when the child really needs her assistance. Children who are raised in this way tend to enforce the satisfaction of their needs by crying and throwing tantrums, often in an exaggerated manner or in advance, as they are uncertain whether their mothers will indeed be around when they want it. In new situations, in peer relations and/or at school, they withdraw, with their conduct often diagnosed as an instance of 'school phobia', or become victims of other children (Guttmann-Steinmetz and Crowell, 2006).

As adults, such people are prone to react very emotionally and can be described as 'softies'. They tend to regard other people as insensitive and to demand more attention and tenderness for themselves. They need bodily contact and touch most of the time. In adult life, they engage in toxic relationships with partners in order to avoid being alone. They are very sensitive to all symptoms of rejection in relationships with their partners. They perceive a threat of exclusion whenever other people are present, because they could potentially be their competitors for a close relationship. They are jealous of other people around—of friends, siblings and acquaintances. They need to be assured and reassured of another person's love, acceptance and exclusiveness. They control and test the availability of the person with whom they are in a relationship through means of phoning, texting, checking availability on social media, etc. They focus on the deficit or insufficiency of care and love rather than on the positives of their relations.

Disorganised attachment: 'I don't know who I am and I don't know who I am not'

Disorganised attachment forms when a relationship simultaneously involves hostility and helplessness. People's experiences include traumatic events, therein both physical and emotional violence (Main and Salomon, 1986). Children are the target of violence/abuse, witness sexual abuse or violence against their loved ones, and/or interact with addicts. They feel threatened by a parent, even though they crave to satisfy their need for security in the relationship with the parent. Such children may become insensitive, especially when their experiences repeatedly breach their fragile structure. Feelings which are aroused when a child sees his/her drunken father kick his/her beloved dog or hurt another family member deeply wound the child's mind, the memory of which may be repressed, though it will linger within the child's system, inscribed in the unaware mind and the body.

People who have experienced disorganised attachments have problems with focusing, paying attention, memorising and recalling things. They are alert, but they do not know how to behave in unknown situations. They are confused when facing things they have not anticipated. They develop strong control over their environment as a way of coping with what they are experiencing, whereby they adopt the role of caregivers, family saviours, heroes, etc.

Children and adults who have grown up in a disorganised relationship do not trust either themselves or others. They have lowered self-esteem and have a self-image as an evil person, one who is blameworthy, dangerous, wicked and incompetent. They often display self-destructive behaviours and perform destructive acts against other people and the external world, such as animals, nature and objects. The point is they have learned to build relations that are hurtful to themselves. Their frequent responses include submission or, the other way round, aggression. As a rule, they cannot recognise most of their emotions; they do not understand themselves and their behaviour, and they have no awareness of their bodies and bodily sensations. Without being aware of it, they misrepresent reality. They can be both the victims and the perpetrators of violence. If they feel acute emotional pain, then they can plunge into states of disinvolvement from the situation, such as fainting and obliviousness, as discussed above. They develop addictions and alleviate their pain with chemical substances. Rejection is part of their lives, because they have experienced it multiple times—being excluded, ignored and then excluded again. Exclusion and self-exclusion in their nonadaptive experiencing of life have become a regular element.

Chapter 10

Non-attachment factors in the forming of relationships

The new generation and the old influences

Bowlby's Theory of Attachment is a framework that describes relational traumas or 'potentially traumatic events' within a child's close environment (Bonanno, 2004; Bonanno and Mancini, 2008).

A kind of faulty mother-child attachment partly determines the child's future emotional disorders and is regarded as a predictor of disturbed functioning in the future. In fact, people's functioning in adulthood is determined not just by their type of attachment to the mother but by a constellation of several conditions. Genetic and epigenetic conditions are of utmost relevance in this respect, including the receptiveness of the nervous system, emotional regulation mode, transgenerational transmission, the experience of traumas unrelated to attachment, chronobiological and chronopsychological determinants, etc.

Even a secure attachment can mutate into an avoidant or anxious one if a person experiences severe stress, traumas, pain and loss, such as strong social or school stress, rejection, death, serious or sudden illness, rape, harm, loss of consciousness and/or the accumulation of stressful situations linked to a threat to one's own or loved ones' life and/or health. Such experiences make for 'emotional gates' (Boolean gates) through which certain thoughts, particular behaviours and unaware conduct patterns are formed or selected. Certain patterns of thinking and action are imprinted in ways which the organism and the person recognise as stable and 'logical', because they are accompanied by intense emotions associated with particular events in the past. They are most resistant to coping strategies if they concern early childhood experiences, because people's yet-undeveloped brains were then not mature enough to understand the event or help the organism handle strong sensations, such as terror, hunger, emotional or physical pain. If the experiences of repressed childhood trauma are not worked through in therapy or self-therapy, they will always linger in the individuals' and their families' experience.

The current rate of heart diseases and mental disorders in societies has capped all-time records. The co-occurrence of cardiac and mental morbidities is by no means coincidental. Depression, anxiety disorders and brain diseases prevail among the latter. Their causes are attributable to the stressful pace of life, wrong nutritional habits and harmful environment with its electro-smog pollution and disturbed electromagnetic field (De Meester, 2020). Social psychologists associate the increasing depression rate among young adults with the widespread use of smartphones and information technology instead of cultivating direct contact with people.

In her research, Joan Twenge (2017) has found that experiences of contemporary societies, in particular, of the youngest generation known as iGen, radically differ from those of their predecessors. The former do not feel pleasure, soothing and calm when in a group or in the company of other people. Young people isolate themselves, spend less time together partying or meeting up and even less frequently get drunk and have sex.

Today, people fear being inadequate and excluded, that is, being unapproved of and unaccepted the way they are or the way they want to be. They crave feeling important and valued (i.e. belonging), but, at the same time, they are afraid of rejection. Young people would like others and society to notice their uniqueness and sensitivity. Inferably, they do not understand that society is unable to provide them with what they need, because society itself is plagued by the same disease. Consequently, young people are distressed, oversensitive and immature, postponing as long as possible the moment of leaving the family home and starting to live on their own. They try to meet social standards and are more conformist, because they want to be fair and to avoid exposure to risk. They are also tolerant and inclusive in the sense of formally accepting otherness, equality and freedom of speech. They also mention their own otherness and their own way of life, because this is what furnishes them with a sense of identity, especially in virtual reality. They have their own attitude towards sex and partner relationships, living their lives in compliance with their individual values. Supposedly, they need these values, ideas and characteristics in order to construct their self-images in social media, irrespective of how much or how little these images correspond to what they really are. At the same time, they are isolated and not eager at all to put themselves on the line for the sake of ideas, whether their own ideas or those of other people. As their own security is their central concern, they are less engaged as citizens. They are afraid of cyberbullying but endeavour to keep up with the input on social media. Between 2013 and 2015, American teenagers spent as much as six hours daily using social media (texting, video-chatting, surfing on the Internet and playing video games). In 2015, the feeling of exclusion rose by 48% in girls and by 27% in boys, as compared with 2010. Between 2009 and 2016, the depression level in boys increased by 21% and in girls by 50% (Twenge, 2017). Additionally, the number of teenagers who report that they do not enjoy their lives is increasing as well.

The portrait of young adults which emerges from recent studies shows them as loners who cannot support each other or experience strength that comes from belonging. They do not feel that they belong either to families or to social groups. They fear rejection and feel excluded, in a way. They aim to survive in a world that offers them everything and nothing at the same time. To survive in good health will probably be possible to those of them who will find their strength in belonging or self-belonging through self-development and to those who will be strongly supported in this venture by others, parents, teachers and therapists. The problem is, however, that parents and teachers are also confused about the new realities and in their own sense of belonging.

Intergenerational transmission of trauma

Trauma can be experienced even before one is born. At around the seventh month of prenatal development, the human nervous system controls activities, thinking, feeling and body movements, as well as develops the capacity for music and speech reception. In other words, the nervous system is already developed enough to receive stimuli from the environment. This is the time in which the foetus is already prepared for surviving outside the mother's body if need be. From this last prenatal period up to within two years after birth, witnessing violence has a meaningful and long-lasting impact on an individual's cognitive development. This has been shown, for example, by Michelle Bosquet Enlow of Boston's Children Hospital, who carried out a longitudinal research study on these issues (Bosquet Enlow et al., 2012).

According to the latest discoveries in science, trauma can be transmitted as an experience of preceding generations. This happens through handing down models of emotion, behaviour and, in particular, relation-building, and through transmission at the cellular level (De Meester, 2020).

Transgenerational transmission does not affect a person directly (indirect transmission), as it is usually passed down in unrecognised ways through the family system. War survivors transfer onto their children certain emotional response schemes and types of behaviour in both everyday and extraordinary situations. What has come to be known as the 'survivor syndrome', which is triggered by war or another severe trauma, has a few important characteristics which, when exhibited by parents, affect their children. These features include, for example: distrust of the world, an abiding sense of threat, the fear of separation, a lack of clear boundaries, etc. Families in which trauma has been experienced do not talk about trauma, even though they 'cultivate' the painful wounds of this trauma. As their major characteristic, families who have gone through serious traumatic experiences practise what is referred to as the conspiracy of silence, indirect communication or being silent over some themes when older family members do not want to talk about them, and younger ones either do not ask or do not want to listen about them. In such families, unarticulated emotions are released from time to time in the form of aggression, hysteria or other uncontrolled behaviours of family members. Separation, which may mean death or threat, is felt. Children do not understand the prevailing atmosphere of 'expecting an unknown impending disaster' and often try to relieve their parents by avoiding causing any additional sorrow or tension. This reverses the expression of care in the family, with children taking care of parents and trying to alleviate their suffering in difficult moments. As a result of parentification and 'mothering' the parents, the natural process of separation and individuation does not take place. The children usually undertake intense lifelong education.

However, children in survivor families do not learn how to effectively function as separate human beings, and family relation patterns can be transferred onto the following generation. This is reflected in the difficulties that descendants encounter in engaging in and establishing relations in the future.

In 'survivor' families, traumatic memories are not completely removed from the mind and continue to resurface in dreams, anxieties, obsessive thoughts, parapraxes, ruminations and emotional reactions. People who consciously do not remember traumatic past events are nevertheless affected by them, which is revealed in various behavioural, cognitive and emotional disorders. Such responses are observed in the following generations as well.

Research shows that forgetting is rarely complete, and a lot of trauma victims who suffer from, for example, PTSD experience remittent memories of these events. In clinical practice, complex determinants of trauma which involve psychological and memetic aspects are recognised. The inheriting of memories and experiences is a relatively new discovery, as is the finding that body memory, which records and retains these experiences, makes diagnosis and treatment possible. Anne Ancelin Schutzenberger (2014), a psychologist, teacher and researcher at the University of Nice, France, has studied psychogenesis as a therapeutic method for multigenerational trauma for many years now. She has discovered phenomena which, until today, were difficult to explain in scientific ways; specifically, she has found that the older generation ingrain in the younger generation certain 'programmes' which exert significant influence on her patients. She has established that the patients' repeated patterns of functioning are underlain by the circumstances, traumas and dates of events experienced by other family members. The transmission of such programmes is always associated with the experience of emotional problems. According to Schutzenberger, the trauma of the following generation involves emotional stress of a parent, a grandmother, a grandfather or their other children who experienced conflict or a problem which they failed to handle in their lives. Distress may arise in the offspring of the following generations: it is passed down automatically and manifests itself in problems or even somatic illnesses of another family member. Healing, that is, liberation from nonadaptive patterns, is possible if one becomes aware of the family's emotional history.

The baggage of the collective unconscious

In literature, art and even in psychotherapeutic practice, we encounter trends that suggest intuitive treatment of a person as part of the collective unconscious.

Alejandro Jodorowsky, a France-based Chilean of Russian descent, is a well-known composer, dramatist and filmmaker. He has directed several films, including *The Rainbow Thief* and the cult classics *El Topo and The Holy Mountain.* In 2019, the *Watkins Mind Body Spirit* magazine recognised Jodorowsky as one of the '100 Most Spiritually Influential Living People in the World'. Jodorowsky proposed a therapeutic system that uses the power of representations/imaginations and symbols to liberate individuals from difficulties on their way to self-perfection. Jodorowsky claims that we are all heirs to and victims of our genealogies. He believes that human individuality is produced by rehearsals of the past and is then shaped by family, society and culture. This culture and its legacy are indispensable at the early stages of human development, but later they become a barrier that separates the individual from the collective consciousness. The collective unconscious, which combines the past and the future, is an expression of humanity's improvement process. In this paradigm, a child is not 'the parent's property' and a carrier of certain genes, but rather an independent being that seeks to achieve awareness and participate in the evolution of humankind in his/her own way. The therapeutic techniques proposed by Jodorowsky combine meditation, art, dream analysis, magic, alchemy, special language, the sense of humour and even tarot cards (Jodorowsky, 2014).

It seems that characteristics are transmitted through nongenetic avenues not only from parents to children, but also from generation to generation (Hirst, Yamashiro and Coman, 2018). Parents unconsciously reproduce the same patterns and hand down the same beliefs which many generations of their family have cherished. Until these patterns are recognised and worked-through emotionally, some past traumas remain active in the family unconsciousness of consecutive descendants. Strong traumas experienced by previously living people produce effects in the lives of rather different people many years later. This shows that some unrecognised aspects can be transmitted and quite palpably affect the physiology of a biological living organism (Baum, 2013).

Therapists cite cases in which children represent ancestors who were unable to solve a past trauma (e.g. abandonment, ostracism), and this unrecognised mental aspect recurs in the descendants' life, so to speak, 'demanding' recognition and active closure. People transfer not only their individual histories but also ancestral experiences and/or limitations imposed by relatives, such as eating habits, suspiciousness to some diseases, energy resources, etc. (Cohen, 2006).

How to recognise the mind in the body

Microkinesitherapy: maps of experiences in the body

New techniques of microkinesitherapy show that it is possible to work upon patients' psychological problems in other ways than dialogue and recovery of awareness in therapy. As the treatment of several mental disorders is based on psychotropic drugs, and consciousness is also essentially affected by various psychostimulants, psychedelic substances and narcotics, it is obviously acknowledged that chemical particles can work, at least temporarily, as therapeutic means and alter behaviour. Nevertheless, the scientific world has found it difficult to accept an approach in which micromassage is used to free the body from trauma or from memories of painful experiences. The well-known French microkinesitherapist Daniel Grosjean (2020) explains that microkinesitherapy aims to reactivate, in as far as it is possible, the repair mechanisms present in all living beings and commonly recognised by biologists. In this approach, embryology opens up new perspectives and perceptions for us.

This concept is based on embryological and neurochemical knowledge, which tells us that the nervous system is made of the tissue which forms around the second week of embryonic development. This is the ectoblastic tissue which, as the very name suggests (ecto = outer), covers the embryo producing epidermal cells. Over the following weeks, these cells are condensed into what is referred to as the neural plate in the thoracic area at the dorsal surface of the embryo. Subsequently, the neural plate transforms into a neural groove which will develop into a neural tube, i.e. a precursor of the spinal cord. It is the part that enables the embryo to interact with the external world through sensitive sensory neurons and motor neurons.

Microphysiotherapists posit that there may still be communication among the epidermis, the neural plate and the circuits of the spinal cord's sensory and motor neurons. The therapy they apply consists in reintroducing a neural impulse to the disturbed circuits in order to release the area where change has been identified (skin resistance) and removing the obstacle. The triggered impulse must circulate in proper neurons and lead to proper synapsis; in this respect, the method is consistent with techniques used in reflexotherapy.

The laws of biology state that in order to produce an antibody (i.e. a repair mechanism), the corresponding anti-gene, the cause, must first be identified. Psychotherapy is informed by the same premise, as verbalisation, that is, conversation with the patient, restores memories of certain emotional experiences in order to find and identify the cause of the patient's nonadaptive functioning and thereby to either eliminate or to integrate it. This work is performed at the mental level, that is, at the level of emotions associated with thought, which are indeed produced by the mind. Similarly, manual therapists can intervene by attempting to detect traces of events that caused a mental disorder. In this way, Grosjean's approach combines the psychological aspect with the neurological aspect, which can be an identifiable physical factor localised in the body.

Direct re-information, (according to Grosjean, it is synaptic re-information), helps safely identify the disturbed area where dysfunction arises in the same ectoblastic tissue, and this re-information activates the desired repair mechanism. Patients recognise that, because, in the following days, they will feel fatigue corresponding to this very particular period of convalescence in which one's energies are used not for functioning but rather for self-repair.

Chapter 11

Biopsychosocial factors

Biochemical processes, mind and body

The body, along with the entire human psychophysical functioning, is an essential sphere of life that changes as the sense of belonging develops. In all probability, most readers of this book take good care of their physical health and bodies. They cultivate healthy dietary habits, exercise, take regular rest, relax or use effective stress-relieving techniques. They consciously approach their sexuality and derive satisfaction from this sphere of life as well.

Over centuries, concepts of the human being have located the mind in the body, which, as a physically palpable structure, was viewed as primary and preexistent. Most of us subscribe to the notion of *mens sana in corpore sano* and, consequently, look after our bodies so that they support our psychological functions.

Below, I take the mind to denote an entire spectrum of psychological processes and phenomena, including the experience and sensation of the self and the world, complete with all aspects of the emotional sphere, cognitive processes and behaviours.

On this take, self-belonging is an expression of mental health and optimal mind balance. It is a way of life developed self-consciously by each individual, also referred to as internal recognition of his/her existence as a full meaning in integration with the mental/spiritual or physical environment in which a person feels belonging.

My argument below aims to elucidate the relations between our mental functioning and physical functioning, proneness to illness and healing, and susceptibility to changes as dependent on the type and way of mind 'programming' at the early stages of people's development or in the past in general. Individual phenotypes denote the expression of memes, manifesting in people's behaviour. Like the genotype, phenotypes are subject to natural selection, which is, in this case, spatiotemporal and sociocultural. As the term indicates, memes are transferred environmentally, through education/instruction and personal development.

The phenotype is under the influence of the environment (external contribution) and the development (internal contribution) of the individual. Genes are imprinted from the time of conception, whereas memes start to imprint themselves from the time of inception, eventually reaching balance with genes at adulthood. Some refer to this stage of development as 'wisdom'. From there, self-conscious beings are capable of 'creating' new information/memes which ultimately will be transferred to the next generation of humans as a group, i.e. Humanity (De Meester, 2018, 2019, 2020).

The circadian rhythms of interaction between memes and genes are reflected in a number of physiological parametres of the heart and the central body/mind probe of an individual (circadian rhythms of heart rate and blood pressure with characteristic parametres of sinusoidal response, amplitude, phase, frequency, to competing influences). Medical symptoms are expressed in bioelectric activity or the body's electromagnetic field (EMF): electrocardiograms (ECG/heart), electroencephalograms (EEG/cerebral cortex) and electromyograms (EMG/peri-skeletal muscles).

In this study, we go beyond the prior models of the body and the mind as equidependent, or of the mind as dependent on the body. In our framework, the reasoning is underpinned by a solidly grounded concept developed by Fabien De Meester, in which the mind is located in and transmitted thanks to cell membrane fatty acids.

De Meester argues that consciousness and the mind can be studied at the level of cell membranes. In this new framework, the Mind is precedent and shifted to the forefront, with the Body as secondary in terms of both historical chronology and rank. De Meester (2018, 2019) spells out the fundamental principles of biological information technology (bIT) in his articles.

In solid sciences, the body is approached as a holographic projection of the mind, a vision corroborated by interdisciplinary experimental teams that have carried out research at the borderline of psychology, physics and energetic medicine. In this perspective, the mind and the body are absolutely inseparable, and, without doubt, the mind is formulating the body.[1]

To understand the processes which human beings undergo consciously, unconsciously or self-consciously (i.e. intentionally and actively), we must study the human being in a broader observation field. If, as psychophysical concepts hold, we resonate with the universe (the world, nature, the cosmos, etc.), the mind has primacy and the body follows it. The manner in which we experience, feel and think resonates in the cells of our bodies. In all living beings, the mind's functions are linked to unsaturated fatty acids through allylic double bonds and vibrational electron resonance. The mind naturally works in ways resembling the ECR (electron spin resonance) spectrophotometer; that is, it resonates at a precisely defined frequency of electromagnetic waves (e.g. sunlight) in a particular electromagnetic field (e.g. geomagnetic field).

According to De Meester (2018), cell membrane fatty acids, or rather their allylic double bonds, are capable of fractally absorbing and emitting tytes of information (-1,0,+1). Singlet oxygen is a high-energy electronic state form of oxygen that has the ability to capture electrons from allylic double bonds typical of fatty acids (DHA in particular), thereby producing a spin that can travel all along the fatty acid carbon chain and eventually passing/jumping from one side to the other of the cell membrane thanks to a physical phenomenon called 'tunnelling' of the electron spin, being—or, more precisely, behaving as—a wave-particle.[2]

In this way, the coding of information in double fatty acid bonds and then their transmission between individual organs of the body, especially between the heart and the brain and back again, are explained.

Memetic information about the mind is stored in every cell and affects the mental functioning of people and their bodies.[3]

Plasmatic membranes of animal species include four fatty acids with allylic double bonds. Specifically, they are linolenic acid (LA; C18:2ω6), arachidonic acid (AA; C20:4ω6), eicosapentaenoic acid (EPA; 20:5ω3) and docosahexaenoic acid (DHA; C22:6ω3).

When studying Bio-Info Technology, De Meester noticed that syllables and letters of the alphabet correspond to the information registering/coding capacities of AA and EPA and to the information processing capacities of DHA, while LA is used to generate logic gates. AA has 40 possible spin configurations, which is exactly as many as there are single phonemes in natural languages. EPA has 121 possible spin configurations, which is equal to the number of characters in alphabets of natural languages. DHA has 365 possible spin configurations, which, to a large extent, corresponds to the possible number of biphonemic clusters or syllables. At the level of the mind, human Cartesian communication essentially uses sounds (speaking) and characters (writing) (De Meester, 2018).

These observations concerning human functioning can be analysed in biochemical research, while the mind's processes can be observed, registered and have their bioelectrical activity/electromagnetic field (EMF) examined by means

Table 1 Fatty Acids and Corresponding Brain Waves

	MUFA	*EFA*		*HUFA*		
#db	1	2	3	4	5	6
FA[4]	OA C18:1ω9	LA C18:2ω6	ALA C18:3ω3	AA C20:4ω6	EPA C20:5ω3	DHA C22:6ω3
ν(Hz) Calc.	1.8	3.2	5.8	10.5	19.0	34.0
ν(Hz) Obs.	0.2–3	3–8	8–12	8–12	12–27	>27
Name	Delta	theta(*)		alpha	beta	gamma

Courtesy F De Meester (2019).

of electrocardiograms (ECG/heart), electroencephalograms (EEG/cortex) and electromyograms (EMG/skeletal-pericerebral muscles). Electroencephalogram-biofeedback (EEG) is commonly used to record and to stimulate brain activity in psychological patients. Basically, it registers brain waves, which, at the membrane level, correspond to the vibrations/shifts of fatty acids, which themselves depend on the number of allylic double bonds of fatty acids (see Table 1; De Meester, 2019).

Components of the mind

The first component of the mind is the so-called emotional memory of RAM (random access memory) type, which is located within the heart, imprinted in special stiffened lipid networks or rafts and serves as the mind's 'black box'. Information that comes through them is picked and selected by what are known as Boolean gates (i.e. simple principles of the yes/no type). They govern the mind throughout one's lifetime unless attempts are made to restructure and reorganise them. Such information becomes deeply imprinted at an early stage of human development as a result of strong emotional experiences. As such, it provides unique 'instructions' for further functioning in later periods of people's lives. This is where attitudes, defences and nonadaptive schemes come into being. They form an unrecognised filter through which subsequent experiences and information are sifted.

Strong emotions and an insufficiently developed brain are the key two components that, among other things, cause the recording of fairly persistent information in logic gates.

The primary information is saved in lipid rafts located in the heart. It is coded into the 'simplest' way in phospholipids there; therefore, they only allow for a simple and unambiguous assignment of information: Yes/No, Pleasant/Unpleasant, Safe/Threatening notation.

The second component of the mind is cognitive. It is shaped in the brain mainly through astrocytes, which work as microchip units or CPUs (central processing units) and ROM (random operating memory) and are channeled by the circulating/communicating red blood cells. ROM is subsequently processed in the brain and, at the same time, methodically filtered through the logic gates in the heart. Given this, human behaviours at any given moment will result from a unique personal balance accomplished by the individual and involving information from the critically thinking brain (cognitive) and from the heart (emotional) (De Meeester, 2019). Therefore, in adult life, they can be partially changed through consciously undertaken individual effort invested in the restructuring and reorganisation of structures and schemes.

Erythrocytes are responsible for gas exchange (oxygen and carbon dioxide) and for the transfer and exchange of the smallest units of information (tytes of informions). Information received from the environment is connected with the brain through an external surface of brain cells or astrocytes.

Cognitive/brain informions undergo selection at the level of heart logic gates, after which they are distributed to all peripheral tissues. Then, after the information is delivered to the peripheral target tissues, the erythrocytes follow the reverse route, transferring the information from the tissues back to the heart and the brain.

We should realise that most of the programmes and schemata discussed above usually become imprinted during human development and growth before 21 years of age. Even very young children perform coding unintentionally, i.e. without consciously controlling information processing. They take over their parents' and other authorities' beliefs and behaviours, making them their own. Brain waves that are synchronised with particular fatty acids capture information at certain stages of human development. These processes are involuntary or unintentional, because the brain of a young child mainly functions at the lowest frequencies of EEG waves (0.5–4 Hz), i.e. so-called delta waves. Between two and six years of age, the child also functions at higher frequencies of theta waves (4–8 Hz), alternating with the normal activity states of alfa waves (8–12 Hz). At the age of 12 to 14 years old, the brain enters the phase of beta waves (12–35 Hz), which are characterised by active and focused attention, up to gamma waves (above 35 Hz; Lipton, 2010). Delta and theta waves foster considerable suggestibility, and, consequently, children code a lot of information simply automatically, just by copying the information into their own systems. The stronger people's emotional engagement is, the more permanent structures of beliefs and functioning they form in their systems of world reception and understanding. Thus-built logic gates (Boolean gates) select and form subsequent information which appears at later developmental stages: an 'emotion' or, in software terms, a Boolean gate is associated with something which is already known/imprinted.

The brain functions here only as a processor and a cognitive tool necessary for the dynamic processing of information (a 'kinetic partner'), while the body is the vehicle of processed or unprocessed information, set as the mind/body programme (a 'thermodynamic partner'). The brain processes the information in conformity with what the individual has learned throughout his/her life about what information should be processed and how it should be processed (De Meester, 2020). Often the information comes from collective information (e.g. brainwash).

The human body may cumulate unconscious, conflicted or repressed information (Grosjean, 2011).

Understanding the significance of fatty acids in our lives

Fatty acids are also instrumental in protecting people against degenerative diseases. Fatty acids play a significant role in human beings' cognitive, social and emotional functioning. They are the main building blocks of the brain and the nervous system, as well as all of the body cells (as components of cell membranes, which has been underlined above). The central and peripheral nervous systems contain high concentrations of fatty acids. Their general content is estimated to stand at over 60%. All axons of nervous cells are surrounded by a myelin sheath, which is mainly composed of fat, whose quality affects neural transmission and the speed of the transmission of impulses. If the myelin sheath is too thin or damaged, communication among neurons is slowed down up to 50-fold or disabled.

Polyunsaturated fatty acids account for as much as 20% of the dry mass of the brain and for over 30% of all the fatty acids in the nervous system. Omega-3 fatty acids, especially DHA, play an important role in the synthesis and degeneration of neurotransmitters (Wilczyńska, 2019).

The decrease of the DHA content in the brain (in the test of the proportion of fatty acids in the blood) is implicated in the reduction of people's capacity to learn, remember and receive auditory and olfactory stimuli. Changes in the proportion of Omega-3 fatty acids in people's diet and, consequently, in their tissues are associated with the increase of depressive and aggressive behaviour, as well as the lowering of cognitive functions. Bernard Gesch of Oxford University has researched the relations between nutrition and aggression for years in an attempt to reduce criminal inclinations in prisoners by dietary means. The study carried out by Gesch and his team involved 231 young inmates at the HM Prison Aylesbury, a penal institution for violence-prone young offenders. The diet of half of the sample was radically changed. They ate varied meals which were supplemented with vitamins, mineral salts and indispensable unsaturated fatty acids (80 mg of the EPA and 44 mg of the DHA, daily). The diet of the other participants was not modified, and they were given a placebo. Empirical evidence was obtained that the level of aggression in the test subsample of the young inmates who took supplements was considerably reduced. The number of brutal incidents in this group dropped on average by 37%, while in the control subsample of offenders, the level of aggression did not change. Interestingly, after the completion of the experiment, the aggression level rose again. Besides, it has been estimated that proper proportions of fatty acids contribute to decreasing the incidence of some degenerative diseases, such as dementia and Alzheimer's disease. Supplementing the diet of pharmacologically treated depression patients with Omega-3 acids has also been found to improve their outcomes (Gesch et al., 2002).

As a matter of fact, the effect of fatty acids on human health and longevity has been known for many years now. Unsaturated Omega-3 acids have antiallergic, anticarcinogenic and antiatherogenic effects and support treatments of several conditions which plague modern societies.

According to new research, humanity is at risk because of common degenerative diseases that mainly afflict leaders. They are both mind- and body-sick and, as a consequence, not sane. A decision-maker should, by definition, display an ARA:EPA ratio of 1:1. This should be a civil obligation (ibid.).

Restoring the proportion of fatty acids in diet/blood that is natural to humans and was typical of our ancestors can be a preventive means against most degenerative diseases. While in the bodies of our ancestors, the ratio of Omega-6 and Omega-3 (Status Omega 6) was 1:1, now it reaches even 20:1 in Western societies (Wilczyńska, 2019).

The phospholipids concept and the role of the red blood cells

Some of these unexplained phenomena can be explained by referring to the biochemical and psychophysically conductive mixture of phospholipids, xanthophylls and microelements contained in the red blood cells (RBC) which circulate in the human body. The red blood cells transport and disseminate oxygen along with spatiotemporal and socioenvironmental information across the body, thereby determining the mode of behaviour, the phenotype. This is nothing else than the mind which science has been looking for and which, while not found in the protein particles of genes, is being discovered today in the lipids of red cell membranes. It is indeed high time to take De Meester's (2020) insistence seriously that scientists should focus on the evolutionally selected substrate of the mind, i.e. on the lipids of red blood cell membranes and their components, paying particular attention to the evolutionally selected allylic double bond.

Usually, no circumstances in life which affect human functioning happen randomly. These are additionally well programmed by our unconscious and inscribed in the body. The restoration of health and liberation from traumatic history is possible through coming to understand the sources of our subconscious programmes and through using proper tools to modify them, for example, in the processes of biological purging of memetic carriers: 'Knowing that RBCs carry the mind (memes) to virtually each and every part of the body, past historical observations/legends may soon turn into real Science all the way from nutrigenetics/genomics (diet/regimen) to psychomics (psychology/psychiatry) derived phenotypes' (De Meester, 2020).

As information is acquired in the way described above, socialisation and acculturation processes can take place. According to Geert Hofstede, culture entails mental wiring of the mind, i.e. a quick and interactive adaptation of a child to the changing environment (Hofstede, 1997). Fundamental behaviours, beliefs and attitudes which are perceived in the parents are 'inscribed' in the child's mind and are unconsciously reproduced until they come to be consciously noticed and replaced with other ones. Regrettably, the already existing paths probably cannot be changed, but they can be phased out, while newly built paths can be reinforced, and new connections with the old ones can be created to foster changes in the perception and experience of the world.

Therapeutic work aimed at comprehending and shaking off past burdens can avail itself of techniques used in ISTDP (intensive short-term dynamic psychotherapy, practised and studied for example by Josette ten Have-de Labije and Robert Neborsky, 2017). One of these techniques is the separation of patients' pathological superegos (introjects, mainly internal critics or aggressors coming from their parents) from their healthy egos (so-called observing egos). Therapists can work effectively if they utilise information about the parents, as in going back to the second generation.

Professor Richard Nisbett of the University of Michigan insists that we should apply ourselves to the practice of fractal, spiral or cyclical event analysis. Inattention to the cyclical nature of the unconscious results from our narrow and linear perception of time and analytical cause-and-effect thinking, which prevails in Western culture. The human being is approached in quite different terms in Eastern cultures, where time is perceived as cyclical as a result of holistic thinking and contextual information processing, which can be used in therapy (Nisbett, 2003).

De Meester's (2018, 2019, 2020) groundbreaking study shows how 'the mind is transferred' by the blood. This has been experienced firsthand by transplant recipients who received new interests and habits 'transferred' along with the donors' organs. Memetic information, which appears before genetic information, programmes the human body.

We absorb information directly from the environment through receptors to blood vessels.

The red blood cells do not carry genetic information as they have no nuclei, but they certainly transport oxygen and memetic information. Allylic double bonds of unsaturated fatty acids in lipid membranes of the red blood cells are unique information-carrying transistors. They have all the characteristics necessary for translating spatiotemporal and socio-environmental information into biological information.

What resources for coping with everyday situations the mind has at its disposal depends on the information recorded in the heart and the possibilities of the brain. As already mentioned, the information in the heart forms critical gates (Boolean gates) which select data on the basis of strong emotional responses recorded in it. If people have been abandoned or ignored, if they have experienced scorn or violence from adults or witnessed violent acts, it is difficult for them to obtain information and emotions which are incompatible with the rigidly fixed gates. They usually have the emotions, feelings and related behaviours which have been imprinted to help them survive. Frequently, these emotions and responses are from the fight-and-protect system and the sadness-and-loneliness system.

Notes

1 Obviously, the point lies in influencing the behaviour, psychophysics/phenotype or biochemistry/genotype of the same being. Contemporary physics has shown that these two states resonate at a speed (1E44s-1) exceeding the speed of light itself. Accurate clinical measurements (e.g. by SQUID) are capable of capturing dimensions of the magnetic information field that surrounds each and every one of us (extending at the radius of at least several metres) (Dr Meester, 2019).

2 Such type of biological microprocessor, if highly efficient, would require a high amount of single oxygen to maintain a high steady-state concentration of active spins (recording/reading/processing speed) and, in turn, a high circulating concentration of spin traps to avoid fatty acids peroxidation and destruction (aging).

3 Fractals are basic mathematical formulas for growth and organisation that occur in nature. Their characteristic feature is self-similarity, which means that the whole is encoded (interference and phasing patterns) in every part (cell membranes), and all parts together make up one, interconnected whole (the mind). Like the body (cell nucleic acids), the entire mind (cell-membrane fatty acids) is located in every cell. Starting from this assumption, De Meester (ibid.) concludes that, by using an appropriate magnetic field, allylic double bonds of fatty acids (the mind) can be encoded as well as routinely produced in silico (computer chips) or on right carriers (e.g. CDs) by means of perpendicular cohesive electric field (e.g. laser light). Imprinting/loading of the mind boils down to the conscious and/or unconscious encoding/transfer of tytes of cell membrane fatty acids.

4 Cell membrane fatty acids of lipid bilayer structure and their expected/estimated shifts/vibrations in resonance, based on their proper number of allylic double bonds. MUFA: monounsaturated fatty acids, EFA: essential fatty acids, HUFA: highly unsaturated fatty acids, #db: number of allylic double bonds, FA: fatty acids, OA: oleic acid, LA: linolic acid, ALA: alpha-linolenic acid, AA: arachidonic acid, EPA: eicosapentaenoic acid, DHA: docosahexaenoic acid. (*) ALA is not usually found in animal cell membranes; LA and CHL (cholesterol) appear as an evolutionary substitute of characteristic #db=3 of the logic gate in biological information technology (bIT), focused at ±8 Hz in the standard EEG and corresponding to the first harmonic frequency of Schumann resonances (7.83 Hz) (ibid.).

Chapter 12

The mind in the body or the body in the mind

Where is the mind located?

This chapter develops on the concept of the mind. It presents scientific data which help explain where the mind is located, how people obtain information from the world around, how this information is processed throughout their lives, how it is recorded and transferred onto others, and how it shows in people's behaviour. While people are self-aware of some of this information, part of it is inaccessible to people's consciousness. The information may affect people's functioning in their systems and their mental and physical health to varying degrees. Becoming aware of the data inscribed in the mind represents the first step towards changing them and thus towards modifying individuals' functioning in ways that make it possible for them to live a more satisfying life. Importantly, some of this information is so durable that—without knowing how to retrieve it—it is difficult to imagine reorganising it and, thus, changing and developing.

Locating the mind and identifying the ways in which the human psyche is formed provide the key starting point for new research on improving the condition of people in contemporary societies.

Over recent decades, researchers have been preoccupied with studying the possibilities of the human brain in hopes of answering these yet unexplained but important questions about the mind/psyche. Neuroscientists and philosophers have often inquired where consciousness and unconsciousness are located, how they are constructed and how and when they are formed.

So far, the notion of the mind has been described by researchers as the totality of the 'primarily conscious' activities of the human brain, such as perception, thinking, memorising, feeling emotions, learning and regulating attention. The brain has been defined as the basic tool for making sense, interpreting, explaining and decision-making (Gazzaniga, 2013, pp. 78, 110). Although scientists have distinguished the brain as the physical organ/body part from the mind as its content (in the sense of feelings, thoughts, needs and motivations) for some time now, they have no clarity either about to what extent the brain is an explaining tool and to what it is an object of cognition or about which is contained within which (in essence, can the cognising subject be the object of cognition itself?) (Frith, 2011).

There are some good popular-science biopsychosocial explanations of health and illness, one of the interesting discussions being Paul Martin's 1997 *The Sickening Mind: Brain, Behaviour, Immunity and Disease*. In this book, the author demonstrates experimental and scientific work that proves that the mind has a tremendous impact on the immune system, and health and illnesses (Martin, 1997).

Notably, the brain is becoming accessible to examination in our times of the advancement of neuroscience. It is something material: it can be measured and weighed, and the activity of its regions can be observed. Moreover, the neuroscientists introducing the latest 'brain neuroimaging' technology on the market shows how the machine/computer learns about *Homo sapiens* and not the other way around (De Meester, 2020).

For its part, the mind has seemed something immaterial and yet undefined by psychology or any other science. Researchers of the previous decade wondered what had been first, whether matter (e.g. neurons) shaped the mind or whether, perhaps, the mind shaped the brain in order to act with its help.

Most hypotheses are based on as-yet obvious explanations that development follows a plan inscribed in the DNA code, and while genetic information (genotype) contains an overall scheme of the construction and functioning of the organism/brain, it does not explain the particulars of what will happen further when environmental/cultural factors come into play.

Answers to the questions above are as paramount and fundamental as the sense of belonging is to individuals, their survival and development. In the past, people who were excluded died because they were unable to fend off for themselves without their tribe and without the possibility to reproduce their species. In our realities, socially excluded people are doomed to social death. They have no family and no loved ones who will spend time with them and support them when looking for a job. They are labelled oddballs, recluses and loners who isolate themselves and do not want to establish bonds with others.

The tendency of being interdependent makes it unusually easy for people to include and exclude one another (Markus and Conner, 2014).

Although the system is cultural and social, its regularities are still being explained based on evolutionary theses and natural selection.

Some developments mounting up in contemporary societies, such as mental and brain diseases which have been a serious social problem over the last several decades, are not explainable by the evolutionary theory. If Darwin's theory were to explain the phenomenon of depression, scientists would likely suggest its decreasing tendency, as adverse features contributing to diseases and death should be disappearing rather than afflicting ever bigger human populations across the world. Therefore, inferably, another kind of memetic information transmission contributes to the spread of depression.

According to the neuroscientist Michael S Gazzaniga, we came to the world furnished with abstract moral principles and a readiness to acquire other rules (Gazzaniga, 2013, p. 147). The commonly adopted position was also that the brain created the mind rather than the other way around. Gazzaniga suggests that it is the brain that, in a way still unknown to us makes the formation and operations of the mind possible (ibid., p. 112). A specific 'interpreter' is this part in the brain that produces the sense of the unity of experience. Chris Frith shares these views and personifies the human brain, stating that the brain can solve, act and guess, and explains how the brain shapes our mental world (Frith, 2011, p. 174).

In order to explore and describe the mind, researchers have so far focused on the structure and functions of the brain as responsible for human functioning in the scope of motivations, emotions and personalities. If we endorse the hypothesis that every traumatic experience 'leaves a trace in the brain' and that trauma is intergenerationally transmitted, we should conclude that emotions, feelings and even memories are 'inherited' in a way (Dias and Ressler, 2013) and should theoretically leave a concrete 'trace in the brain'.

Researchers have suggested that gametes contribute to the transmission of the memory of behaviour and emotions. It has been shown in observational research on people and in the already mentioned experiments on rodents. Psychiatrists expose that acquired risk factors (as in depression and mental diseases) are intergenerationally transmitted. They can be transmitted through non-genomic and epigenetic mechanisms to subsequent generations, potentially contributing to a cycle of disease and disease risk (Klengel, Dias and Ressler, 2016). Thus, there are clues that once again emphasise the rank of the mind occurring as prior to the brain.

The Japanese physicist Seiji Ogawa has discovered the possibility of brain magnetic resonance imaging, whose effects depend on the oxygenation of blood (Ogawa, Lee, Kay and Tank, 1990). Blood maps have been generated and, owing to them, maps of the functional activity of the brain. The maps show which neurons of the brain respond to mental processes by electrochemical signals. In this way, functional MRI is used to map olfactory, visual, auditory and tactile sensations, cognitive functions and emotional responses. Imaging is made possible by the magnetic properties of haemoglobin. FMRI is used, for example, in psychology, in neurology and in neurobiology to diagnose mental diseases and organic brain dysfunctions in clinical medicine.

Separate brains and the shared mind

Let us recapitulate the most important findings and proceed to further conclusions. Firstly, intergenerational transmission concerns the information which was/is linked to strong emotions or to recurrent difficulties associated with certain emotions. These pieces of information are carried by the mind. Secondly, this information is usually unrecognised but resurfaces across individuals' lives as a difficulty or an obstacle in life. It can be consciously analysed and processed by the brain, if individuals have a possibility of such an insight. Thirdly, the information of the mind is transmitted in a non-genetic way. Fourthly, the process of psychotherapy helps people return to the memory records from early developmental stages, including those which were not fully recognised, which makes it possible to rediscover them and acknowledge or heal and reorganise this information in ways that are more beneficial to people than before. This information is easier reached if one knows the information recorded in particular individuals; more is discussed below. Only integrated, recognised and reincorporated experiences enable individuals to establish their boundaries anew and self-develop. Fifthly, child-raising processes introduce information that is encoded as new records in the mind in its durable memory part. This process may occur through kinds of relations, through the use of particular words/language and through nonverbal communication, voice vibrations, gaze and touch. Sixthly, modern Bio-Information Technologies will be capable of programming both the computer and human minds. The production of bionic organs and artificial neurons that behave like the real ones has already commenced (Abu-Hassan et al., 2019).

Psychotherapy may not be enough if trauma is implicated in the memory of shared past experiences, as in the case of generational trauma. Imaginably, people's histories involve feelings and emotions layered over generations, anger, shame, guilt, pain and loneliness, which result from exclusion or the lack of the sense of belonging. It may be exigent to 'return' to this shared 'memory' of the mind in the process of healing.

It will be impossible to understand certain processes and proceed to a higher level of development without bringing together cultures and civilisations in this process. What we all share are the most fundamental feelings of love and compassion or the common roots of humankind, which can be found, for example, in music, especially music at certain frequencies (e.g. 432 Hz) (Dubey et al., 2019; Calamassi and Pomponi, 2019).

It can thus be concluded that even though we each have a separate brain and a separate body, we all share some experiences, for example connected to the traumatic events of our common ancestors, which manifest in people's minds.

Although the cells of living organisms contain basically the same gene information (genotype), the cells of various tissues differ from each other, manifesting their diverse phenotypes. Genetic information can be used in various ways due to epigenetic mechanisms. As people who have been nearly identical genotypically for generations, we differ phenotypically, for example in the colour of the skin or of the eyes. The phenotype is also comprised of temperament and susceptibility to particular diseases. As already discussed, we can inherit not only the genetic material, but also some trauma and programmes of functioning. Epigenetics was ascribed the major role in these processes, even though it was not yet determined back then how this happens memetically (Carey, 2012; Sillivan, Vaissière and Miller, 2015). Today, we have a considerable certainty that not only genes but also memes, i.e. culturally acquired information, are inheritable.

Darwin or Lamarck?

In today's approaches to human development, Charles Darwin's science of genetic transmission and Jean Baptiste de Lamarck's science of memetic transmission are set apart. However, natural selection and cultural selection do not have to be contradictory, as a matter of fact (Gould, 1991). Daniel Dennet relies on Dawkins's concept of the meme to argue that this contradiction does not exist if we adopt the notion of the meme as a unit of cultural heredity, and the gene remains a unit of natural heredity (Dennet, 2016).

Psychology falls back on evolution to explain rivalry, conformity and altruism. The evolution-based approach is tantamount to a selfish approach, in which humans rely on intergenerationally transmitted schemes and unconsciously use information about the 'proper ways of responding' for the sake of survival. In this way, emotional logic gates come into being and subsequently constrain people. In Darwin's model, natural selection does not promote compassion and help for other people, even though Darwin himself believed that such care should be cultivated despite entailing the loss of the 'advantage' of natural selection.

Manifestations of evil proliferating throughout the history of humanity have been explained by referring to the self-centred 'human nature'. Experiments conducted by Philip G Zimbardo and Stanley Millgram have shown that social surrender to this evolutionally conditioned nature (e.g. submission to the commands of authority) can breed viciousness and aggression to the point of taking another person's life.

Today, the application of solely the tenets of Darwin's theory in teaching and education is becoming a serious limitation to human development. People who are deprived of genuine attachments and rely on rivalry and achievement, rather than on trust and cooperation, lose their potential. A considerable portion of the interdependent part of society mainly consume and admit that they 'steep themselves' in their prosperity. When I look at a picture that presents the evolutionary development of human beings from prehistoric figures to today's *Homo sapiens*, I increasingly frequently see the last link of this evolutionary chain represented as a human being holding an alcoholic drink, slumped in depression or staring at a computer screen. The sad conclusion is that it is not our future; it is the present which we inhabit.

The good news is that Lamarck's theory of memetic heredity is taking on new hues, as a matter of fact. Notably, it is owing to Lamarck that the epigenetic concept of inheritance of acquired characteristics was endorsed. According to it, people have a chance for development by producing so-called good memes which contribute to human development. Consequently, people can proceed to higher levels of development, create, inspire others and finally win by combining compassion or humility and strength, whereby they can reduce the incidence of mental diseases and other woes of contemporary generations.

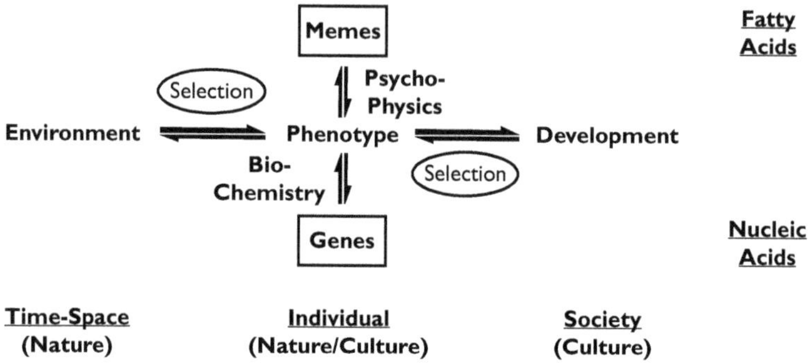

Figure 12.1 Natural Selection and Cultural Selection (De Meester, 2020). Courtesy F De Meester (2019).
The individual phenotype (behaviour, temperament) reflects the expression of genes and memes, which influence it and each other. Thus, the phenotype is subject on one hand to natural (temporal-spatial) selection and on the other to cultural (societal) selection.

For the purposes of this study, I use the notion of memes interchangeably with a more precise term denoting the type of social/cultural information transmitted through the mind, namely, informions, a coinage borrowed from the framework developed by De Meester (De Meester, 2020). De Meester believes that natural/cultural selection of species according to Darwin only makes sense it if refers to the same selection which concerns informions according to Lamarck (see Figure 12.1).

Understanding how memes correspond to genes in determining the phenotype and how they consequently shape behaviour and responses at the cellular level may probably help us identify, understand and alleviate psychological problems.

The genius of phospholipids and the location of the mind

Returning to the aforementioned magnetic capacities of the red blood cells (cell membranes), today, we know much more. The key information for exploring their special properties lies in the fact that the mammalian red blood cells are the only cells that have no nuclei and as such do not carry genetic information contained in proteins (the cell nuclei of an organism). However, they can transport oxygen and memetic information, owing to their electromagnetic potential. Knowing that blood vessels are the first to appear in the process of embryogenesis, we can also conclude that the mind preceded the body.

Information can be transferred by the mother to the child via erythrocytes. Fatty acids of red blood cell membranes become a similar 'information conveyer' for memes as nucleic acids in cell nuclei are for genes, i.e. sets of biological information (De Meester, 2018, 2020). Fatty acids of cell membranes can carry psychological, social, cultural and environmental information owing to electromagnetic processes.

Similarly to genes, which are composed of four nucleic acids, memes are built of four fatty acids. This means that information is to be found both at the level of the cell nucleus (genetic information) and at the level of plasmatic membranes (memetic information). The four types of chemical information imprinted in animal species (A, C, G and T[1]) have their equivalents in the four sources of physical environmental information (LA, AA, EPA and DHA).[2] How exactly the mechanism of mind → body communication works (i.e. in what way the mind transmits instructions to the body) has not been discovered and described in detail yet. However, it is basically impossible to miss the parallelism between the possible configurations of electron spins in the allylic double bond of membrane fatty acids (-1, 0-+1) and the electron coupling of nucleic acids in DNA (A-T & G-C). In both cases, the presence of electrons in the environment makes it possible to process and reproduce/reedit data for the sake of the interaction of the environment/mind and genes/body. The Bio-Info Technology encompasses the processing (registering, storing, searching, aggregating) of data at the mental (memes/psychophysics) and the bodily (genes/biochemistry) levels of the phenotype (ibid.).

Visual, auditory, tactile and other (for example, geomagnetic) information is received, processed and then registered owing to the specific structure of the lipid layers of membranes and the properties of respective fatty acids. The processing of information is a cognitive process that demands an input of energy. First, information is translated in cells, that is, sequenced at the molecular level into handy units of information, informions, which are subsequently transported to the brain and then to the heart and back to the peripheral tissues. The allylic double bond of membrane fatty acids is a perfect vehicle for informions, since it makes it possible to transitionally store discrete units of electron information in cell membranes and to find and to process them (De Meester, 2013).

Extensive research in biochemistry and molecular biology has provided us with considerable knowledge about fatty acids and their critical functions for the human organism. For over ten years, I have accompanied the biochemist and molecular biologist Dr Fabien De Meester in his discoveries concerning the mind, and Fabien has accompanied me in discovering the functions of fatty acids. We inspire each other with our respective disciplinary knowledge.

Drawing on several years of research, observations and analyses, De Meester has developed a comprehensive theory of identifying and locating the mind and of the transfer of information by means of fatty acids contained in the membranes of all cells, a theory evoked throughout this book (De Meester, 2018, 2019, 2020).

What are those mysterious phospholipids?

Plasmatic membranes of animal species mainly contain four fatty acids with allylic double bonds: linolenic acid (LA; C18:2w6), arachidonic acid (AA; C20:4w6), eicosapentaenoic acid (EPA; 20:5w3) and docosahexaenoic acid (DHA; C22:6w3).

Polyunsaturated fatty acids are built from hydrocarbon chains of different lengths with several double bonds. The bonds are separated by single methylene groups. The designation of a particular family (Omega-3 or Omega-6) of fatty acids depends on the position of the first double bond starting from the methylene group. The position of the first double bond (omega) distinguishes the Omega-3 family, which includes alpha-linolenic acid (ALA), eicosapentaenoic acid (EPA) and docosahexaenoic acid (DHA), from the Omega-6 family, including linolenic acid (LA) and arachidonic acid (AA). It is estimated that these double bonds influence the flexibility and plasticity of fatty acids (Wilczyńska, De Meester, Singh and Bargiel-Matusiewicz, 2010; Wilczyńska, 2019).

Fatty acids (phospholipids) which are included in cellular membranes can temporarily serve as a substrate of the mind. Allylic double bonds of unsaturated fatty acids are a unique electronic system that acts like a transistor. According to De Meester (2020), it possesses all the properties which enable the transcription of environmental and social information, as well as all of the temporal and spatial information, into biological instructions. It is this information that determines human behaviour. Biological instruction regulates the process of a genetically controlled combination of elements.

Cell membranes are composed of two kinds of fatty acids: unsaturated acids with their characteristic allylic double bonds sequenced in the 'cis' formation and saturated acids, which basically act as an insulator.[3]

Within the Bio-Information Technology, linolenic acid (LA), concentrated in the heart, is used to produce logic gates. It has only two double bonds, through which information is selected at a very basic, emotional level.

AA and EPA acids have more double bonds, and their role is most pronounced in interpersonal communication as their properties make it possible to encode information at the level of language and speech.

DHA is the most sophisticated fatty acid since it possesses the largest number of double bonds. For this reason, it supports processes of conceptualisation and the generation of innovative solutions. In the course of evolution, the carbon chain of unsaturated fatty acids was lengthening. As a result, the number of allylic double bonds was growing and, consequently, the functions of the brain were becoming ever more complex (De Meester, 2013, 2020).

The latest observation-based findings indicate that the mind differentiates human beings (therein, the evolutionary ancestor, *Homo sapiens*) from other animals at the level of time/space and environment/society. It is one reason why we must devote attention to the evolutionally selected substrate of the mind, specifically to the allylic double bond of fatty acids selected in the process of evolution.

Our mind is being recorded in biological matrices

Cell membranes spontaneously form biological matrices. These, in turn, are mathematical matrices for isothermal data (informions or tytes), which can only be transferred and recorded at a particular body temperature. The totality of processes that occur in cellular membranes, which easily transition into fluid motion, makes it possible to obtain preserved, statistically significant and complex information by means of the biological Information Technology (bIT) (Amos, McCaskill and Rasmussen, 2011). Thinking ahead, we can imagine that the brain will not need the body/mind.

Rigid lipid rafts referred to as logic gates manage the mind throughout one's lifetime, contributing to the individual's characteristic ('intuitive', automatic) responses based on the yes-versus-no choices. They are encoded strong primal emotions, such as anxiety, fear, anger versus soothing or joy versus sadness. Notably, soothing and joy mirror the sense of belonging, while fear, anger and sadness have developed in response to rejection, threat and/or exclusion (Wilson-Mendenhall, Barrett and Barsalou, 2013; Wang and Pereira, 2016). In fact, emotions and experiences associated with them can be described in two lucid, independent dimensions as pleasant/unpleasant and generating calm/tension. As we shall see further in this argument, this binary system of opposite emotions is compatible with the function of chemical substances that maintain it.

Imprinting in logic gates takes place at the early stages of individual development, in childhood and early adolescence, while experiencing situations in conjunction with strong emotions or repeated emotional experiences. At this time, the brain is not yet fully formed and is incapable of coping with these on its own. They later work as a kind of filter which admits mainly the information that can get through these logic gates. Affective reactions become programmed and involuntary, but they are also shaped by experiences in life (Ekman and Cordaro, 2011). They are assigned to some situations, people or events.

In this way, ways of responding to difficult situations associated with traumatic experiences are recorded. Previously imprinted rigid reactions, which are often intuitive or unreflected, tend to be repeated, while all other ones are prevented.

For example, a person who experienced exclusion and emotions involved in exclusion in the past will identify social situations and respond to them in a very simple, black-and-white manner. Besides this, s/he will spin his/her own scenarios and conjectures around potential situations, as well as spending time on futile ruminations on possible solutions (negative) or on re-experiencing the past or anticipated sensations. Expectedly, systematic entrenchment in these schemas is accompanied by mental problems, including depression (DeJong and Fox 2019). Stereotypes and prejudices are underpinned by a similar mechanism. If, in childhood, interactions with certain people involved one's parents' strong emotions (e.g. anxiety or aversion of strangers), such information is imprinted in the system of logic gates.

Societies and the principles they use contribute to the formation of Boolean logic gates. Other factors include educational methods, consciously or unconsciously transmitted social knowledge and norms and rules of conduct founded on previously experienced models.

From Columbus to Copernicus

De Meester shows how the mind's ROM is processed in the brain and, at the same time, methodically filtered through the heart and logic gates. As an effect, the resultant, which is balanced information coming both from the brain (cognition) and from the heart (emotion), determines responses/behaviour rendered in the expression of the circulating units of ROM/red blood cells (see Figure 12.2).

Therefore, whether and to what degree a given individual will be capable of controlling his/her behaviour is predicated on the capacity of his/her brain or the cognitive apparatus to control his/her heart or emotions. Very often this process requires the 'unlearning' of the mind, particularly on its most stable level, the lipid rafts in the non-cognitive mind.

Therapeutic work, therein self-therapy, consisting in the elimination of one's 'attachment' to emotions can be expected to be an effective path to liberating the mind of the 'brainwash' type of information from the past. This may be supported by parallel work with the body through breathing and selected techniques of removal of tensions/bad memory.

It is also worthwhile to realise what current memetic impacts affect our minds through electromagnetic vibrations, if we are not sufficiently anchored in our own potential. Some of them are generated by pernicious electro-smog (e.g. mobiles, laptops, wireless routers, fridges, etc.).

In 2018, the United States National Institute of Health published data which indicate that electrosmog (EMF) is harmful to mice, which come down with cancers more often. We can easily imagine its influence on the human mind, especially since its operations are based on electromagnetic communication. The latest research results suggest that the incidence of carcinogenic and neurodegenerative diseases and depressions is increasing in connection with growing emissions of various artificial electromagnetic fields (Becker, Selden and Guarnaschelli, 1998). Some people may be especially sensitive to

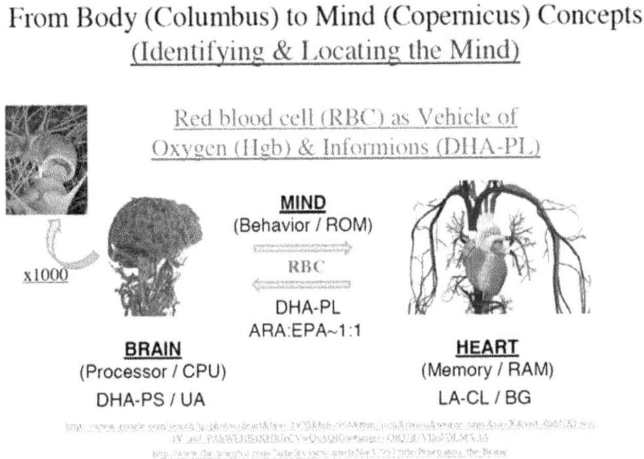

Figure 12.2 From Body to Mind Concepts. Courtesy F De Meester (2019)
Red blood cells (Hgb) as oxygen and informions transporters (DHA-PL); BRAIN (Processor/CPU), DHA-PS/UA; MIND (Behaviour/ROM), Red blood cells, DHA-PL, ARA: EPA ~ 1: 1; HEART (Memory/RAM), LA-CL/BG (Boolean gates).

electromagnetic smog (Electromagnetic Hypersensitivity Syndrome, EHS), as reported by Swiss Harmony, which cites the opinion of the World Health Organisation (WHO) and the International Agency for Research on Cancer (IARC) in 2011 (https://swissharmony.com/what-is-electrosmog/.)

In fact, every human being emits a magnetic field. Its parameters vary, depending on a person's health status, emotions and attitudes. When we stay with our loved ones, we co-feel emotions, which is referred to as empathy, the activity of mirror neurons or emotional contagion. The emotional contagion effect increases in affiliative dyads, such as relations of mother and infant, a couple, or an individual and his/her dog (Katayama et al., 2019).

The transmission of information with certain psychophysical parameters takes place in close relationships between partners. In everyday interactions, information is transmitted, captured and systematically imprinted if it is coherent with a person's own system of schemas. Every human being's reception of sensory (auditory, olfactory, visual, etc.) impressions in the same environment differs, depending on the imprinted RAM-type Boolean gates and on the kind of linear transformation proceeding form the mind to the cognitive brain. In the state of infatuation, this proneness to absorb mutual information increases due to reduced criticism and enhanced receptivity. Similarly, memetic information that partners obtain from each other in a romantic relationship (husband, wife) is then transferred onto their child. People who live in intimacy share not only the space of their home but also the same memetic information.

In the human organism, the process of transmitting and capturing information can be described with more accuracy. Cell membranes in all tissues divide what is inside the cell from its external environment, and they envelop oganelle. For example, the endoplasmic reticulum is a sizeable scaffolding made of a two-layered membrane. The membrane encloses the cell nucleus like a unique antenna, owing to which physical information (mind/electron spins) can closely and directly interact with chemical information (body/genes), and this, in turn, influences the gene transcription/translation and ultimately affects human functioning—behaviour. Three possible configurations of electron spins in the allylic double bond of membrane fatty acids (-1, 0-+1) are typical of the human being. In comparison, robots are incapable of generating/self-reproducing information, and they obtain binary instructions (0, 1), so they are entirely dependent on their programming and their functioning is predictable and independent of the environment.

Fatty acids versus speech and thinking

Due to Noam Chomsky's work, language has come to be viewed as a biological object in philosophical inquiries. Chomsky believed that because we did not have well-defined and coherent notions of what 'body', 'matter', 'the physical' and 'the mental' were, their theoretical utility was negligible. Furthermore, we were not in the very least equipped to study relations among them (Chomsky, 2000, p. 106). Although Chomsky believed that both the mind and the language were biological, he could not explain their interconnectedness (Chomsky, 2002, p. 62).

According to De Meester, depending on allylic double bonds, each fatty acid is responsible for processing and storing information at a different level. He has calculated that AA has 40 possible spin configurations, that is, exactly as many as there are single phonemes of sound in natural languages. EPA has 121 possible spin configurations, which is equal to the number of characters in the alphabets of natural languages. DHA has 365 possible spin configurations, which largely corresponds to the possible number of two-phonemic units (syllables). De Meester's findings help us verify the following hypothesis: Languages have evolved naturally and then culturally to become an optimal tool for verbal communication (De Meester, 2019, 2020).

Thus, each syllable has particular vibrations and makes parts of words of various meanings. Words are building blocks of notions and sentences, yet before they appear, they pass through the selective sieve of logic gates contained in the heart in the form of the already mentioned lipid rafts. The brain communicates with the hearth via erythrocytes which circulate in the bloodstream.

Thus, thinking of oneself is also a vibration of electrons, like emotions and language. People have learned that it is beneficial to relish good experiences, and it is such experiences that they would like to multiply. They negatively respond to events in life which they have not expected; they complain, hunt out difficulties or glorify them. The sense of belonging and the sense of exclusion are self-beliefs and self-representations which have become stuck in logic gats and select all the incoming information through this specific screen. They select information, whereby they automatically bestow emotional colouring on it and prepare a response to it.

Notes

1 ACGT is an acronym for the four types of bases found in a DNA molecule: adenine (A), cytosine (C), guanine (G) and thymine (T). A DNA molecule consists of two strands wound around each other, with each strand held together by bonds between the bases. Adenine pairs with thymine, and cytosine pairs with guanine. The sequence of bases in a portion of a DNA molecule, called a gene, carries the instructions needed to assemble a protein. *National Human Genome Research Institute*: https://www.genome.gov/genetics-glossary/acgt.

2 Linolenic acid (LA; C18:2w6), arachidonic acid (AA; C20:4w6), eicosapentaenoic acid (EPA; 20:5w3) and docosahexaenoic acid (DHA; C22:6w3) (Wilczynska, De Meester, Singh and Bargiel-Matusiewicz, 2010; De Meester, 2018).

3 Unsaturated fatty acids can be linearly encoded, and as such, they can form a linear mathematical equation. Formed in the network of the cellular membrane, they make up physico-chemical matrices where *infromions* (i.e. information from the environment) are recorded in bonds as *tytes* of information. Thus, they follow a given person's individual logic of matrix algebra and themselves provide logical *or* illogical information, if needed (ibid.).

Part IV

Building belonging

Chapter 13

Building self-belonging in schools

Work with teachers

The appreciation of and compassion for the child, combined with fostering the child's conviction that s/he is a relevant part of the family or another system in which s/he lives, are key factors in building the child's sense of belonging. These are also preconditions of people's comprehensive development, therein of their preparation for self-reliant life. I understand self-reliant life as a meaningful life that is respectful of the self and of others and involves self-appreciation, regard for other people and the recognition of every person as a complementary part of a given system. In this sense, the system denotes the microsystem of the family or of the closest group, the macrosystem of the world or the universe, as well as one's real place on earth or in the spiritual realm.

The more taxing the experiences a child or an adolescent has faced in life, the more urgent and exigent it is to establish a positive, or at least a non-conflictual, relationship for/with him/her, one in which s/he can come to feel that s/he belongs and, consequently, acquire the sense of relevance and develop an inner consent for self-expression. The sense of belonging gives people the freedom to express their feelings and needs, and it breeds the sense of security, for example, by fixing boundaries (Wilczyńska, Januszek and Bargiel-Matusiewicz, 2015). All the experiences of humiliation, scorn, pain, anger, hatred and despair which ensue from damaging attitudes displayed by others, usually the closest family, in the past and which, when unrecognised, accumulate in people tend to transform into resentment for or contempt of the self and the external world. This is vividly exemplified in the case of the Orphan, who, in fact, has never been an orphan, but has lived in enforced isolation from the system in which she grew up, experiencing anxiety, despair, aversion and contempt toward herself and others.

Differing from J. Bowlby's Theory of Attachment, the concept of the sense of belonging practically shows that the individuals' need of belonging can be fulfilled, and their relevance and being a meaningful part of the system can be asserted, at any stage of their lives. In addition, some relationships can be replaced by others (cf. Baumeister and Leary, 1995). The possibility to build one's sense of belonging at any moment in life, which hinges on one's readiness to do so and/or on favourable social circumstances, encourages an optimistic belief that motivating and engaging other people and institutions other than family as such in the process can not only be effective, but also recommendable and desirable.

Until recently, the prevailing idea was that some personality traits are tolerably stable descriptors of individuals and reliable predictors of their future functioning outcomes. This notion still underlies the (sometimes not really ethical) recruitment procedures which companies marshal to select employees based on predefined personality 'profiles'.

School as a friendly place to build the sense of belonging

In the initial phases of children's lives, family members make the children experience, or prevent them from experiencing, themselves in their belonging. In mature families such, as those with self-aware parents who have mature childrearing attitudes, children develop a belief that they have an emotional and cognitive coping potential and that they are capable of using this potential in their daily lives. Children become convinced that they belong and that they are part of their family systems. This is a very important experience because it subsequently serves as a foundation upon which to build the sense of belonging among peers and at school.

With such potential and personal resources, they start their educational path. Importantly, this condition of a complete sense of belonging is the feeling that one belongs with oneself and is, thus, self-accepting, self-trusting and self-reliant. If one bestows care and love upon oneself, one will offer care and love to others as well. Self-recognition as a complete being capable of self-soothing and of achieving goals and plans in life is the next stage of experiencing. Such individuals feel that they are themselves and gratefully and self-consciously register the fact that they decide for themselves, choose what to create in their lives and how, know what they want to participate in and how and realise with whom and on what terms they wish to be and to live. This represents a state of peacefulness and the ability to use the present moment to build one's future without fears and to harmonise one's body after experiences of stress.

Almost 25 years ago, I set out on a research journey to explore how the sense of belonging is built. Every year, several thousand patients have used state-funded counselling and therapy services at a psychotherapy facility which I opened for children, adolescents and their families. The histories of families, child-raising problems, school difficulties and mental disorders which I have amassed serve as precious materials for my argument in this book. Together with a team of dozens of specialists, I have carried out survey research and longitudinal studies, examining our patients at various stages of their development. Our collaboration with schools and teachers, whom we support in coping with difficult school-based situations and in helping students who need to have their sense of belonging strengthened, has been an opportunity to glean a range of valuable observations and insights.

Children who have experienced a painful rejection have far more difficulty realising that they need help. As the examples cited in this book have shown, young people who feel rejected by their peers do not discern either any solution to their problem or possibilities of obtaining help. If adults or peers perceive this problem, the positive experience of a significant relationship they provide can help such people rebuild their sense of belonging. As described above, the healing process can be commenced when the crisis is recognised or when an essential problem is solved. Because children are not able to do it, this is the responsibility of adults, parents, teachers, psychologists, etc. Consequently, the young will be able to go through the process of building their belonging in this system or in any other system in the future.

However, we have observed that teachers do not know much either about supporting others' sense of belonging or about the construct of belonging, as a matter of fact. As a result, they seldom consciously engage in supporting belonging in students, children or teenagers.

Teachers cite a range of excuses, such as the lack of time caused by packed curricula, work overload and a reluctance to assume excessive responsibility. As a rule, however, they do not realise that the process of building belonging neither is as difficult, time-consuming and as complicated as they believe it to be nor places any extra obligations on them.

One of the experiments which I will describe later has discovered that everybody can support children in building their sense of identity and that it is not only possible but also recommendable at school, as it optimises children's functioning, activates their potential and strengthens their self-esteem, good mood and motivation to study. Everyday support can be provided by any significant person from the individual's closest environment (e.g. acquaintances, neighbours, colleagues, classmates and members of informal groups), family members, educators, teachers, etc. Professional support is provided by psychologists, therapists and physicians.

We have discerned that the greater the difficulty young people in need of support faced and the longer they were entrapped in their suffering alone, the more helpless they and their professional helpers felt.

Even if there are educators, teachers or psychologists eager to support, the process requires enhanced patience and special determination.

The Italian psychiatrist and psychotherapist Antonio D'Andrea (2010) reports that owing to affiliation processes in a system, in the family, children can feel that they are descendant members in groups to which they belong. The feeling of being relevant to the system and of personally fitting in is channelled through relationships with significant family members. If there is no such person in the family, other people from the children's environment can assume this responsibility (Eck, Schoel and Greifeneder, 2018).

When I conduct workshops and talks for teachers, I usually explain what the sense of belonging involves and in what ways teachers and educators can bolster or build the sense of belonging amongst their charges and students. Recently, I have noticed that teachers themselves need lessons or therapy in how to feel relevant, how to develop self-confidence and how to be self-reliant. Teachers more and more frequently enquire about self-development possibilities because they perceive that the knowledge and competence they acquired in university teacher training programmes and in non-formal education are not enough for them to cope with several difficult life- and/or work-related situations. Most of them realise that even the best professional training for educators did not make them feel important and valued. Even when they are perfect teachers, they sooner or later notice personal obstacles and very challenging situations with which they are unable to cope by relying exclusively on the knowledge they have acquired. If teachers themselves do not really feel that they belong, to their system, to the school as their workplace, to their families or to themselves, sooner or later, a moment comes in their careers when they are faced with an insurmountable problem. They begin to doubt in their potency or even in the purpose of their work and/or life. Increasing numbers of teachers grapple with professional burnout, depression and anxieties, rather than experiencing satisfaction. Some of them enter the path of self-development and self-search when meeting therapists, and it is only then that they perceive the meaningfulness of what they do and come to a self-understanding.

The study described in this part and some assumptions of self-help may be useful in everyday practice.

Teachers play a fundamental role in child development. Social relations which are established by people with high levels of belonging are consciously built, and their dynamic course is regulated as they unfold. Individuals are mindful of themselves and of partners, students, friends, family members and life partners, in relationships, are aware of and honour their own and other people's boundaries, take care of and respect themselves and others and obtain respect and care from others.

Chapter 14

Prevention and self-soothing

Self-compassion and mindfulness for psychological well-being

Human survival needs to be particularly based on new resources of coping. Options heralded by futurists in their visions of our not-so-distant future are fascinating and apparently unavoidable but sometimes scary. Namely, futurists point to biotechnology as a chance for the survival of the human species. For example, nanocomputers in the human body are supposed to diagnose problems and prevent diseases even before they develop. People's intellectual, mental and physical capacities will be perfected and enhanced. Relationships and communication will be possible in all fields and across several planes (Kurzweil, 2006).

Before the biotechnology revolution comes into effect, ways of coping must be activated here, now and with recourse to currently available means. Some therapies and relaxation techniques are known to beneficially influence the development of the brain and emotional regulation. Various forms of meditation, in fact, such as techniques and exercises originating in mindfulness and mindful compassion training, serve as ways of achieving harmony and 'returning' to the state which was once our ancestor's natural and obvious condition. These techniques now have remedial, therapeutic and preventive functions ascribed to them.

We actually resort to traditional Eastern medicine, which cultivates such interventions.

In broad lines, meditation techniques serve to slow down the pace of life and to give people room to experience the present moment without judging, rushing themselves and others, developing a sense of guilt or feeling regret. The effectiveness of mindfulness-based cognitive therapy has been proven in several studies (Kabat-Zinn, 2003; Gilbert, 2010; Braden, 2017). Briefly speaking, people learn how to train their minds in order to avoid reproducing nonadaptive or harmful patterns and to find peace and harmony. Besides this, these techniques are used to support therapies for depression and anxiety.

Similarly, resuming healthy, research-confirmed eating habits or adopting supplemented diets aids the treatment of mental disorders, therein of depression. Polyunsaturated fatty acids accompany certain minerals and vitamins as indispensable components of health-promoting diets.

The building and supporting of the human soothing system is a fully aware, approving and loving attitude to oneself and to other people around. If one approaches oneself in a self-loving manner, the old response pathways blur out and others are created and strengthened by soothing and healing. Adverse emotional activity is phased out.

When we study the early development of human beings in our times, we notice that the first postnatal period is one of the most harmonious periods in people's lives. We are born receptive and ready for cooperation. We are moral and eager to do favours for others.

A compassion-focused approach

A new approach to the human being as compassionate, tender and sensitive offers a path to maintaining soothing and security for oneself and for others as well. Over the last two decades, there has been an increasing interest in the concepts of the compassionate mind and mindfulness. This is correlated with current brain research, which has shown that mindfulness and compassion training produces palpable effects, such as changes in brain structures and functions, which support human development and soothing emotions (Singer and Engert, 2019).

Pro-health attitudes to the self have been conceptualised by Dr Kristin Neff of the University of Texas. Her construct of self-compassion is affiliated with and complementary to the concept of mindfulness (Neff, 2003a). Although self-compassion is a relatively new approach to the self in Western psychology, it is not, objectively speaking, an entirely novel notion as it has been borrowed from Buddhist philosophy, where it has been cultivated for over 2,500 years now (Makransky, 2012).

Self-compassion has been observed to help people distance themselves from self-destructive ruminations, while discovering and expanding soothing and a benevolent and forgiving self-attitude. As a result, people can develop new ways of approaching themselves mindfully, kindly and lovingly and of treating themselves as integral members of the human community. There is ample evidence corroborating the insight that compassion is an emotion that is rooted in the story of the human species. Compassion has evolved in humans as a kind of a caring response to another helpless human being (Goetz, Keltner and Simon-Thomas, 2010).

Until recently, compassion was not perceived in terms of its positive impact on the individual who expressed it and was not considered a priority value (Makransky, 2012). Rather, it tended to be identified with mere pity for the weaker or the suffering, with asymmetrical power relations inscribed in it.

However, compassion is actually an expression of sensitivity to one's own and other people's suffering, which entails an obligation to act or at least to attempt to alleviate or prevent suffering (Gilbert, 2014 qtd. in Dalai

Lama, 1995). It is a multidimensional process comprised of four key elements: awareness of suffering (cognitive component), compassionate care, emotional arousal (affective component), a desire to see relief (intention) and a concrete response or readiness to help and assuage suffering (motivation, action) (Jazaieri et al., 2013, 2018). While Western philosophical thought distinguishes compassion for others from compassion for oneself, the Tibetan word *tsewa*, an equivalent of compassion, does not differentiate between compassion shown to the self and to others (Hańczak, 2017).

Healing and prevention techniques based on mindfulness and compassion have been adopted as therapeutic tools in Western countries as well (Kabat-Zinn, 2013; Germer, 2009). The practice of compassion beneficially influences emotions and improves people's mental well-being. Paul Gilbert, one of the major researchers of compassion and the founder of the Compassion-Focused Therapy (FCT), emphasises that compassion should be understood as an intersection of three flows: of practising the skills of offering compassion to oneself, of being compassionate to others and of accepting others' compassion. The latter kind of compassion seems to be the most difficult kind, because several people associate it with the image of themselves as weak and with the reception of pity from others. It is also connected with the fear of dependence on others, with the inability to ask for support and attention and with the incapability of using support and attention granted by other people (Gilbert, McEwan, Matos and Rivis, 2011).

People who have experienced social exclusion find it nearly impossible to develop self-compassion. They have developed or imprinted schemas of thought and action which are limited to self-defence against being potentially hurt again.

Belonging as a resource and as a process

Supposing that people who have experienced social exclusion, and who often exclude others when feeling threatened, could change this self-perceived situation and/or heal themselves through their compassionate minds, we would have to adopt some essential premises. We should assume that individuals were aware and that the resumption of a fully normal life was possible through expressing their pain and then through the meaningful wish to alleviate it and to fundamentally change their attitudes towards it. This would entail their preparedness to discover and to accept their pain/the wound and to show compassion and care to themselves without evaluating, comparing and promising.

Having read this book this far, the readers certainly realise that if such a change were considered by a suffering person, the excluded person would not feel excluded, the depressed person would not have to be on medication; the lonely person would not feel lonely, and an anxious person would not have any fears.

However, a person who is being excluded has no inner strength, a resource that would help him/her confront himself/herself and feel part of his/her important system. The system/group senses this 'deficiency' in the individual, and 'the vicious cycle is complete' in this way. The data cited in the foregoing parts suggest that people are excluded for reasons which are not fully evident either to the excluded or to the excluding parties, yet social and individual schemas which perpetuate this process are nonetheless reproduced (Benenson, Markovits, Thompson and Wrangham, 2011). Exclusion takes place when the group does not feel that the individual 'fits in', and the individual who feels that s/he 'doesn't fit in' is excluded. The lack of the 'sense of belonging' resource is, paradoxically, a metaphorical key opening the metaphorical door to the system/group. It looks as if, at his/her unrecognised level, the individual 'decides' that s/he is not part of the system and does not belong, while at the level of awareness, s/he experiences the pain of exclusion.

Belonging and exclusion are human resources, and besides this, they are also processes that produce and lead to these resources. At the first stage of working with excluded people, the major task is, thus, to change their inner sense of belonging, which cannot possibly happen without an actual experience of inclusion in the group. Therefore, the parallel investment in changing both the resource and the process is requisite.

If the individual is not aware of these processes or is too young, s/he often does not comprehend what process is actually taking place. Support should come from the outside before emotional insulation or post-traumatic stress sets in. In this way, the system works for the benefit of the individual while simultaneously repairing itself (Figure 14.1).

The sense of belonging based on self-compassion can be fostered in a few ways. Firstly, self-compassion can be activated through reproducing one's early experiences with the parent/family or through re-examining family roots or the record of emotional stories. Another possible way involves achieving self-compassion through treating oneself, one's needs and feelings with care which is usually showered on a young child. Finally, compassion can be experienced, trained and memorised through an actual experience of being included in real relationships. The implementation of these strategies should be aided by the person who the individual perceives as a representative of his/her relevant group or system. This function can also be fulfilled by a school staff member, a psychologist, a therapist or an educator.

Inclusion can be initiated by the group or can be independently attempted by the individual. In the latter case, the individual needs to understand his/her situation, have insight and be resolved in action. It is also possible to change one's target group, for example, by joining a religious or a

Figure 14.1 Sense of Belonging (Be) in Three Systems of Emotion Regulation (Adapted from Gilbert, 2005).

parareligious organisation. Importantly, whatever pursuits are launched, it must be made sure that these are undertaken in compliance with and in recognition of one's own needs rather than as replacement behaviours.

People being excluded mainly experience pain, perceive themselves as defective, fail and worry. Given this, support for them should be based on patient assistance, authentic understanding, acceptance of imperfections and unconditional love. Experiencing oneself as part of a community and the realisation that all people go through the same feelings and emotions also give relief and breed a sense of security.

The practice of self-compassion precludes self-criticism, severe evaluations, egoism, narcissism and egocentricity. Individuals who are compassionate towards themselves and others do not reject doubts, confusion or negative feelings which surface in the process, and they do not identify with these either. Rather, they try to be aware of and prepared for a variety of possible feelings (Neff, 2003a; Leary et al., 2007).

Kindness to oneself as a member of a collective

The concept of the compassionate mind is based on three major components of self-attitude which is first practised by the therapist for the individual so that s/he learns self-compassion. The first component is self-kindness and self-leniency as opposed to self-criticism and self-judgement. The second component is the awareness of common humanity as opposed to isolation. The third component is mindfulness as opposed to over-identification (Neff, 2003a).

In Western culture, we are accustomed to focusing on kind and understanding attitudes to others rather than to ourselves. This is an effect of contemporary cultural patterns, which highly value self-reliance, self-efficacy and support for those in need. Interestingly, support is primarily offered to individuals who openly manifest their difficulties and needs and can talk about them. Examinations of Facebook portals suggest that such people receive a lot of support from others, and some of them even 'exploit' this in order to obtain as many 'likes' as possible for their posts or websites.

Excluded people do not reveal their weakness in order to prevent this from becoming a reason for further exclusion. Exclusion is hidden and shameful. We do not teach children how to talk about it; nor do we educate them on how the need of belonging manifests itself, even though such knowledge could prevent several problems. Educational trends are rather opposite, as a result of which individuals are demanding and critical about themselves, as well as prone to harshly judging themselves for mistakes. As a consequence, the spiral of self-criticism and inadequate self-requirements escalates and is particularly observable in people with anxiety disorders and depression (Johnson, 1994; Hańczak, 2017).

Self-kindness is founded on leniency for and the recognition of one's own weakness or imperfections. It involves an awareness that we are not always capable of executing certain plans and meeting some expectations, especially those that are imposed from the outside. Self-kindness helps us protect ourselves against self-criticism, keeps overwhelming emotions at bay, supports our self-understanding and helps us regain balance. If we accept our mistakes and inadequacy and cast off regrets, disappointments and representations, we will find it easier to develop self-leniency. If we endorse ourselves and our lives the way they are at a given moment (i.e. while implementing the decision to change and 'rebuild' them without judgement and evaluation), our stress and frustration will be considerably lessened (Neff and Germer, 2017).

The awareness of common humanity as opposed to isolation is an extremely important concept that helps people experience themselves as an integral part of a community. Hence, the process of including an individual must indispensably involve the promotion of experiences of real inclusion and the consistent maintenance of this contact. People who are being excluded do not want to be at the centre of others' interest, because even minimum information about being recognised in the group is sufficient for them.

Mindfulness as opposed to overidentification helps distinguish conscious focus from an excessive identification with emotional states and experiences. In mindfulness, the present moment is experienced in a simple and balanced way (Brown and Ryan, 2003). This kind of attentiveness is characterised by awareness, a non-judgemental attitude and concentration on the present moment in close contact with the self rather than with the external circumstances (Kabat-Zinn, 2013). The Covid-19 pandemic has literally shown that all people in the world share the same experiences: the sense of human survival, land, weaknesses and resources of individuals and societies, fears, social inclinations, etc. As the virus Covid-19 has spread worldwide, healthcare workers are vulnerable to psychological distress. Mindfulness is the foundation of self-compassion insofar as persons can only respond self-compassionately when they know that people are struggling. Compassionate people deal with unfriendly events in a more emotionally regulated way. Their reactions are less extreme, and they have greater self-acceptance and internal control (Leary et al., 2007; Hedderman, O'Doherty and O'Connor, 2020).

The accompanying emotions are recognised as existent, but they are not value-ranked, suppressed or exaggerated. Mindful self-compassion entails a calm examination of one's own thoughts, sensations and emotions. Mindfulness promotes detachment from outside factors in order to scrutinise one's own suffering and then to offer compassion to oneself. Such a mindful approach to one's experiences is contrasted with overidentification with one's sensations, especially with negative emotions, persistent thoughts on a given situation or state and ruminations. People who excessive identify with what they are experiencing have a tendency to believe that success proves their strength and failure, their weakness (Neff and Gremer, 2017).

These three components are intimately interconnected, interact with each other and exert reciprocal influences, adding up to the compassionate state of mind (Neff and Germer, 2017; Neff, 2003a).

A person who develops self-compassion abandons self-criticism and self-judgement, and this contributes to lowering the level of negative emotional states (Dzwonkowska, 2013). Increased mindfulness reduces egocentricity which causes individuals to feel isolated from the rest of humanity and breeds a sense of hurt. Similarly, a strongly critical attitude to the self exacerbates one's sense of inferiority, which, in turn, strengthens the feeling of isolation. Self-kindness offsets some of this hostile self-awareness, which then helps one get closer to other people and feel connected with them (Neff, 2003b). Gradually, one begins to accept the thought that one is a part of the world and becomes accustomed to kindness and mindfulness.

Recognising one's own system of emotions and behavioural responses

The initiation of various behavioural responses associated with physiological and emotional reactions has been described in the context of compassion training by Professor Paul Gilbert (2005). Gilbert developed an evolutionary model to demonstrate the utilisation of the three systems of emotional and behavioural regulation in coping with different life situations.

The threat and protection system

According to Gilbert and Choden, people have motives and goals as they go through life. Different emotions are like the 'weather' during this journey. Individuals need to cope with these if these lead to unwanted behaviour. In this evolutionary understanding, the brain is the main generator of emotions. This system of emotional regulation is linked not only to a particular area of the brain, but also to the body's chemistry (i.e. as in the production of hormones, such as adrenalin and cortisol) and to and with the corresponding behaviour. 'This is not our fault but our responsibility' say the authors (Gilbert and Choden, 2014). This is a bit of a different explanation than initially introduced in this book; however, the three circles of emotions may be a good reference to show how people react in their social systems, family, small groups and society.

Anxiety, fear, anger and aggression are natural emotions that served to protect us against attackers and enemies, the wild beasts of the past. When this 'threat and protection' system is overused because of permanent stress, its operations lead to reverse effects. In contemporary people, anxiety and fear do not fulfil their protective function but, instead, work in destructive ways. Anticipated dangers are often confined merely to our imaginations, and the preventive response of defensive stiffening precludes the application of other solutions. All of the energy is directed to stir alertness or to freeze motionless to avoid feeling pain (i.e. freeze response or opioid analgesia). Alternatively to the freeze response, flight or fight reactions can be activated as well.

Possible reactions in situations associated with very strong stress include fainting, numbness and or tonic/collapsed immobility. Kasia Kozłowska and colleagues (2015) have studied the defence cascade and found that these coping responses are an outcome of activating or deactivating certain neural connections and that these are most probably related to a prior strong stress stimulus. The preprogrammed reaction paths imprinted in the permanent memory of the mind will automatically release fear and anger in respective situations. The activated/erected stiff logic gates (Boolean gates) let only certain emotions, and consequently defined behaviours, through. People who experienced traumas and painful events early in their lives have elaborate threat-protection systems.

Importantly, if the experience of pain is chronic, as in cancer or, for emotional pain, in a permanently damaging life situation, it can contribute to personality change. This can also happen in the aftermath of traumatic events, deep stress and in mental disease. In such circumstances, researchers have observed that hostile or distrustful attitudes toward others and the world, withdrawal from social life, a permanent feeling of emptiness or hopelessness, tension and irritation make inroads into people's 'natural' functioning. Triggered by the sense of threat, these symptoms can later contribute to psychosomatic diseases which were first described by Franz Alexander as the Chicago Seven. Originally, these included, for example, essential hypertension, hyperthyroidism, gastric ulcers and bronchial asthma. Today, the list has considerably grown to include several other conditions (Stora, 2015).

People who have painfully experienced exclusion are eager to use the threat and protection system. On one hand, this system 'shelters' them against involvement in new situations and new reactions. On the other hand, it helps them to attack and defend themselves. However, the permanent reliance on this system precludes going 'beyond the imprinted information'. Consequently, the need to constantly identify possible threats and to respond to them is sustained. The world is repeatedly discovered as threatening, and the utilised defence system is self-reinforced. Dominant emotions include sadness, distrust, anxiety, anger, loneliness and refusal to experience pleasure with other people.

Angry behaviour and aggression are not necessarily instrumental, as shown in the chapters reporting my research. Aggressive behaviour may serve to gain attention and be noticed and considered important in the group.

Adaptive uses of the threat and protection system involve an accurate recognition of risks and effective coping through the expression of emotions and engagement in action. The realisation that a developed and sensitive threat and protection system activates the best known and ingrained response pathways in various situations is the first information that serves to change this scenario. Angry and irritable responses can be relinquished for the sake of summoning other emotions. Change is importantly aided by resorting to a supportive collective or to a real or imagined place of security.

The drive and achievement system

The motivation and reward system is another system used by people. When people perceive that some of their behaviours entail rewards, they can attempt to expand the repertoire of such behaviours to sustain positive reinforcements and, for example, obtain others' continued attention. Called the drive and achievement system (Gilbert, 2005), this system is comprised of ways of regulating emotions, thoughts and behaviours for the sake of achievement, such as the realisation of desires and needs.

Most people have needs that they want to realise, they wish to develop, to climb the ladder of scholarly or professional advancement, to live in prosperity or to relax in luxury. People desire to win contests, earn money, drive good cars and have attractive partners. The culture we inhabit rewards certain 'booties' and accomplishments with attention and special interest. Achievement entails experiencing positive emotions of joy shared with others or involves 'basking in the glory' of victory.

Dopamine, which is called a reward hormone, is the major factor in this system. Embracing the drive and achievement system is also one of the indirect ways of coping with the risk of social exclusion. If an individual is regarded as a socially attractive person, if s/he is a renowned doctor, actor, contest winner, discoverer or a talented athlete, s/he will obtain correspondingly ample social attention, which will induce in him/her the feeling of being important and valued (Figure 14.2).

Many people who were rejected at the beginning of their life's journey have, nonetheless, achieved their coveted goals and have had success appreciated by others. They did so owing to their determined drive and achievement system approach. Achievement can result from conscious and deliberate action, but it can also be a 'side effect' of a life passion.

Fame and recognition become tickets to the world full of people. They help one feel noticed and, at least for some time, deliver one from oblivion and suffering in loneliness. A similar function is fulfilled by exertion to 'perfectly' meet social expectations and standards in pursuit of the socially defined success in family and work life. Dreams about starting a family and making a brilliant career become a promise of a sense security and a happy life, as well as a guarantee of appreciation, respect and love. Accomplishments bring satisfaction and ensure a relatively stable position in the social group, but usually, these do not entail an inner sense of coherence or one's own inner self-soothing.

The soothing and commitment system

Using the third system, called the soothing and commitment system, people arrive at the state of soothing, peace, harmony and kindness to themselves

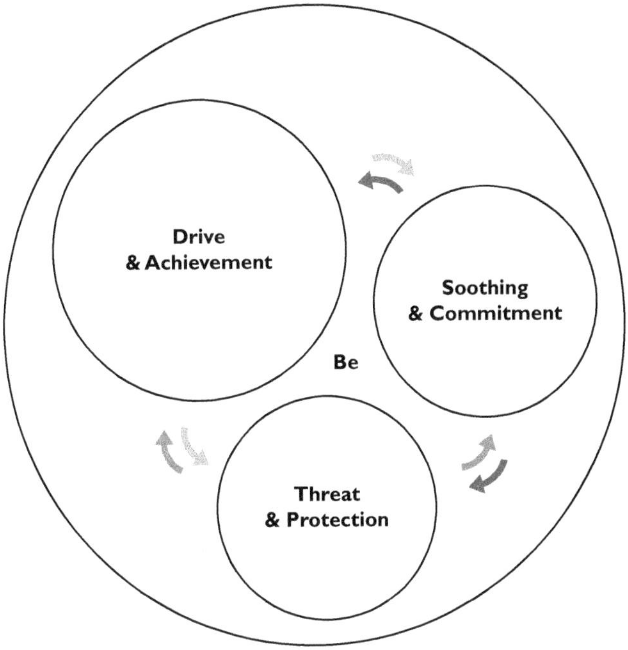

Figure 14.2 Sense of Belonging and Motivation to Achieve, to Reduce Strain.

and others. This is a state of unforced joy that accompanies a receptive experience of the world. The states typical of the soothing system are best exemplified by a natural condition in which a mother loves and takes care of her child, and the child mutually experiences loving and tender care, which brings happiness to the mother. Oxytocin and some endogenous opioids are hormones that uphold relaxation when released.

Similar states can be achieved in meditation through exercises that help people appreciate themselves as important in and to their own lives. Expressions of gratitude, appreciation, care and compassion enhance the sense of soothing. As a result, this makes us feel a sense of safety, belonging and attachment to other people and animals. This also motivates us to be helpful and obliging to others, which is a natural effect of being liked, looked after and secure.

This state should not be confused with slackness or the loss of alertness. This is a state where the senses are naturally sharp, reactions are attentive, and the person feels energy for action and, thus, commitment. The sense of security and soothing prompts a natural motivation to be helpful and obliging to others. Because people do not perceive any threat, they neither seek security nor feel compelled to achieve, to blaze trails or to fight for survival

(Depue and Morrone-Strupinsky, 2005; Eck, Schoel and Greifeneder, 2018). People who function within this system do not feel the deprivation of the need of belonging, since they have everything they need within themselves.

People can reach states of soothing and security either on their own or with support from others. Yet the complete process of self-building first demands the recognition, reconfiguration and reorganisation of structures in which emotions are implicated.

If we are aware of the dynamic coexistence of and the balance among these three systems of emotional and behavioural regulation, we can use and thereby strengthen the one we choose. Any self-conscious regulation of emotion and behaviour is predicated on the recognition of the situation and of one's own response schemas, real needs, imagined final state (e.g. solution, closure, continuation, etc.) and 'means' (e.g. emotions, thoughts, behaviour) by which this state is to be achieved. It is also crucial to identify possible obstacles or difficulties related to the imprinted information or action schemas associated with emotions and cognitive processes. The will of recognising and casting off behaviour patterns which further neither development nor soothing is central in this respect. Putting an end to problems involves an understanding of suffering, forgiveness and gratitude on the path towards acceptance and kindness.

Devoting attention to oneself and recognising oneself as an important member of a community entails deep self-awareness and self-experience as a living organism and a human being. For this reason, change processes should be based on the training of conscious breathing, nutrition and body care, all of which stimulate mental development both in the individual and in the relational dimensions.

Investment in the soothing and commitment system helps experience new adaptive emotions, feelings and reactions which produce the sense of security. As a result, these expand the range of future responses in various situations, fostering different reactions than before on the way of building new relationships.

Chapter 15

Working therapeutically with socially excluded adolescents

A case study

An experimental longitudinal study was carried out in clinical conditions on a sample of adolescents at risk of social exclusion.The study aimed to find how young people's functioning changes when under the influence of belonging-enhancing therapeutic techniques, as compared with other interventions used in traditional clinical psychology and psychotherapy.

Sixty F91- and F92-diagnosed teenagers enroled at the facility were recruited to the research sample. According to the ICD-10 classification of mental disorders, both diagnoses concern behavioural disorders and emotional-behavioural disorders. Their major symptoms include, for example, initiation of physical fights, eruptions of anger and serious violations of social norms. The adolescents primarily came from disadvantaged backgrounds, from broken homes and from families with an alcohol problem. Some of them were inmates of educational and correctional facilities to which they had been committed for to their prior criminal offences. All of the respondents were aged 14–16 years old. They had reported at the therapeutic facility in order to start therapy, and they were on the 'waiting' list, with an estimated waiting period of six to seven months. Teenagers and their guardians were invited to participate in the research project while waiting for admission to individual therapy.

All of the participants and their guardians consented to take part in therapeutic and instructional meetings and to undergo testing.

The sample was randomly divided into six groups of ten adolescents each—three main 'thematic' groups of 3×20 participants—which were supposed to participate in weekly sessions run by two therapists/psychologists over six weeks. All the respondents completed psychological tests before participating in their sessions, directly after the termination of the sessions and then three months and six months later. Besides this, a short test was administered to assess each participant's mood by means of the UMACL (UWIST Mood Adjective Checklist), a tool for measuring emotions, before and after each session.

Additionally, the Ambulatory Blood Pressure Monitor (ABMP) was used in the study to examine the parametres of heart functions.

During the study, the respondents who participated in the sessions did not use any other forms of therapy.

Following the initial/preliminary tests, the participants were divided into three groups:

- the eudaimonic E group (two subgroups of ten participants);
- the hedonic H group (two subgroups of ten participants); and
- the control C group (two subgroups of ten participants).

All groups started their sessions at the same time. The sessions were held in the afternoon when classes at school ended, and these lasted for 1.5 hours each.

The therapeutic facility-based study

Each of the experimental groups had different therapeutic interventions administered to them which actively involved the participants. In the control group, the subjects' participation was passive as they were offered lectures on psychology-related themes. Each group was divided into two ten-person subgroups that were led by two therapists.

The eudaimonic interventions consisted in discovering and supporting the adolescents' skills and potentials related to their talents, development possibilities, abilities or interests. The sessions aimed to establish the sense of meaningfulness, to let the participants perceive previous and possible future achievements and to help them learn how to balance experiences, make future plans and set long-term goals. The programme was geared towards supporting young people's inner motivation, appreciating their strengths and identifying their skills. This tied in with the development of the drive and achievement system.

The hedonistic interventions consisted in working on the improvement of moods, the general balance of emotional sensations, an increase in satisfaction and learning through pleasant feelings. The sessions aimed to activate the sense of security and to practice flexible, kind and nonjudgemental attitudes toward the self and others. The participants focused on themselves and on others, exercising politeness towards the other participants. In this way, emotions and experiences characteristic of the soothing and commitment system were supported.

In the experimental groups, precedence was given to building direct, supportive relations with each participant and to supporting kind relationships among the participants.

A series of general development lectures (e.g. on interpersonal communication, psychology in films and proverbs, etc.) were offered to the members of the control group. Their participation was passive; meaning, direct individual contact with the attendees of the sessions was not established.

The sessions were conducted while the patients were waiting for inclusion in a therapeutic group or for a place in individual therapy conducted by the facility.

The study involved structured interviews with the participants, followed by the measurement of all the variables monitored in the experiment, i.e. mood, anger, emotional intelligence, sense of belonging, stress coping strategies and perceived time perspective. The subjects' heart rate variability and various heart parametres (i.e. systolic/asystolic pressure, pulse/HR) were also examined.

The participants' mood was measured before and after each meeting, and the heart parametres were tested during the sessions.

All the variables were measured again upon the completion of the programme. The measurements were carried out in the experimental groups and in the control group one week after the end of the sessions. Delayed and long-term effects were tested by measuring all the variables after three months and six months following the end of the interventions.

Upon the conclusion of the research project, all of the participants were given an opportunity to find out about their test results and to consult a psychologist individually. The participants were offered to take part in therapeutic sessions and meetings organised by the facility.

The studied variables

Mood and its dynamics were assessed by the UWIST Mood Adjective Checklist (UMACL) developed by Matthews, Jones and Chamberlain and adapted to Polish conditions (Goryńska, 2005). The scale measures tense arousal, energetic arousal and hedonistic tone. The expression and increase of anger were assessed by means of the self-descriptive *Skala Ekspresji Gniewu* (SEG, Anger Expression Scale/AES) by Nina Ogińskia-Bulik and Zygfryd Juczyński (2001), which was developed to test children and adolescents above 11 years of age.

Heart rate variability was assessed by Ambulatory Blood Pressure Monitoring (ABPM), a noninvasive device recommended by the circadian rhythm researcher Professor Franz Halberg of the University of Minnesota.[1] A relatively new, compact and light (215 g) TM-2430 model was used. Abilities, competencies and skills fostering effective coping with the demands of the environment were studied by means of INTE (Schutte et al., 1998), an emotional intelligence questionnaire adapted to Polish conditions (Jaworowska et al., 2005) and dedicated, among others, to adolescents older than 14 years of age.

In order to establish adolescents' strategies of coping with stress, the *Jak sobie radzisz?*[2] Scale (Juczyński and Ogińska-Bulik, 2009) was used, in which the definition of coping draws on the transactional model of stress, as proposed by Robert Lazarus and Susan Folkman (1984). The sense of belonging and the need of belonging were measured by the Sense of Belonging Instrument (SOBI), an original tool constructed by Bonnie M Hagerty and Kathleen L Patusky (1995), which was translated and adapted for the study on Polish adolescents with the author's consent (Wilczyńska, 2013).

The perceived time perspective was assessed using an abbreviated version of the Short Zimbardo Time Perspective Inventory (SZTPI-PL). This questionnaire explores the positive future perspective, the negative future perspective, the present hedonistic perspective, the present fatalistic perspective and the future goal-oriented perspective (Zimbardo and Boyd, 2009).

The unexpected results of the experiment

The results of our study helped describe the immediate, delayed and long-term effects of the implemented interventions in all of the research groups. These effects could be assessed on the basis of comparing the differences between the research groups at given stages.

The findings for the last stages (that is, as in delayed effects after three months and long-term effects after six months from the conclusion of the programme) proved statistically significant and surprising. Generally, no results improved on the completion of the sessions, even though the participants had experienced pleasure and satisfaction in sessions, as reported in their feedback.

The comparison of results after six months from the conclusion of the programme with those from before its commencement shows that energetic arousal (EA), hedonistic tone (HT), emotional intelligence (INTE), self-esteem (SES), the need of belonging (SOBI) and the sense of belonging (SOBI) in the eudaimonic group (E) dropped as compared with the control group results.

While the results in group H implied that the participants functioned better than the E group members, the scores of the H subjects were also observed to worsen upon the completion of the programme. The results for energetic arousal (EA) and hedonistic tone (HT) decreased. At the same time, the values for two variables—external anger (SEG) and systolic blood pressure—increased in comparison with the control group. The effect size was slightly lower than in group E (0.28 to 0.34).

The functioning of participants in different groups could be compared across time by comparing effects at consecutive stages. Three months after the conclusion of the programme, group E exhibited a significantly higher result for systolic blood pressure and a significantly lower result for 'Time Perception—Past Negative', as compared with the preceding stage. Similarly, in the hedonistic group, a higher result for systolic blood pressure was noted; at the same time, the results for the fatalistic-present time-perception and external anger (SAG) increased in this group.[3] Something special happened to the experimental group members and which made the effects of the sessions deteriorate rather than improve after the conclusion of the programme.

The dynamics of changes in symptoms that had appeared in the adolescents in response to involvement in the series of sessions surprised the research team. The experimental study not only confirmed the prior hypothesis about differences in the functioning of people from different groups, but also showed something more; specifically, after the completion of the programme, some variables describing the functioning of the subjects in the experimental groups not only failed to go back to the initial level, but also paradoxically reinforced the participants' initial self-beliefs.

One explanation of this finding is that the participants experienced the sense of exclusion after the end of the group sessions, because the relationship was not continued. At the same time, they did not join in the activities of any other group in their environment or, alternatively, this inclusion was not satisfying. Supposedly, the findings were associated with the interruption of the established relationships and the feelings of regret and sadness that this triggered. James Garbarino (1999) has reported that anger is often a masked form of sadness in young people who experience traumas and difficult situations in their lives; this kind of response is the 'most adaptive' for them, because it helps them protect themselves and their feelings. Our participants exhibited their protest against the termination of the relationship and responded to the adverse environment to which they were compelled to return.

However, it cannot be ruled out that the conviction about being excluded, which is manifested in the low sense of belonging, the low need of belonging, low mood and self-esteem and/or elevated anger levels, is so strong and internalised that participation in the programme not only failed to change this belief, but also made the subjects react by bolstering these features.

It looks like the achieved effects were the total opposite of what had been expected. After six months since the conclusion of the programme, the greatest differences in functioning were noted between the eudaimonic group participants and the control group participants. The eudaimonic group subjects reported definitely lower energetic arousal and hedonistic tone, as well as a decrease in emotional intelligence, the sense of belonging and the need of belonging in comparison with the scores of the control group respondents. The E group participants felt the termination of the group most acutely even though all of the subjects had known from the start that the programme was going to end. In fact, what they experienced after the conclusion of the session series was separation from important relations—that is, the sense of 'exclusion'. No changes were revealed in the control group.

Interestingly, the participants behaved differently after the termination of the group, depending on their specific group. The subjects in the eudaimonic group responded with sadness, lower mood, decreased vigour, diminished self-belief, reduced reported need of belonging and a drop in the sense of belonging. The respondents in the hedonistic group primarily exhibited elevated external anger, besides decreased mood and vigour. This suggests that, while the participants responded to the termination of valuable relations by personal sensations, they, in fact, reacted in ways that they had learned in the programme. The eudaimonic group subjects emphasised the difficulty related to the inability to achieve their aims by a decrease in self-belief and vigour. The hedonistic group members, who had learned how to express emotions during the programme, responded with increased anger.

For the interpretation of the findings to be accurate, we must remember that the project participants were patients with F91 and F92 diagnoses in a psychological facility; all of them had experienced strong exclusion from their environments, first at their homes and families and then in school and community systems. Many of them did not live at home with their loved ones but were residents of correctional facilities for young people. They were not only excluded people, but also the excluding ones, which was expressed in their aggression and delinquent behaviour, such as armed robberies, thefts, brawls, assaults, etc.

These research findings imply that socially excluded adolescents find it challenging to learn co-feeling and care for the self and others. Nevertheless, such training and learning are possible, which is indicated by the overall participation of adolescents in the project. Close and tolerably positive relations with significant others taught them to name their emotions, to recognise these and to share these with others (see the description of the eudaimonic and hedonistic sessions in the following chapter), which afforded them spontaneous, readily available joy during the sessions. However, since this was all new to them, the information and feelings related to the ways in which they could support themselves and build relations with others did not fall on fertile soil in their psyches/minds. The novel and good emotional experiences did not register for long in the memories of the participants. On the contrary, the experimental group subjects responded in the opposite way, as if mobilising forces to remove the new experiences the way viruses are removed from the infected body by proliferating 'immunological bodies' to trigger the body's enhanced defence reaction. Thereby, they buttressed their prior beliefs about themselves. The information and experiences concerning them being valuable, important and appreciated people with whom others were eager to spend their time and to whom others offered their attention were not only ignored but actually driven away with a tremendous force.

Our research results corroborate the notion that people who are socially excluded or are at the risk of exclusion have a fixed internal self-image and likewise a response schema in social situations. It can easily be noticed that, before the commencement and after the completion of the programme, the participants predominantly relied on the threat and support system for their emotions and behaviour. This is implied by their hostile attitudes, anger, lowered mood, reduced self-esteem, low need of belonging and low sense of belonging.

Nevertheless, they willingly took part in the sessions and reported that they liked being there. They also reported a need to continue or to take part in such meetings in the future.[4] This indicates that, for the sense of belonging to be sustained, people must feel that the relationship is maintained and can be continued in the future. This relation must be founded on direct, non-conflictual interactions in which warm eye contact is established with the person and a friendly timbre of the voice is maintained. Observations and research results imply that voice can serve the same function as touch (Lowen, 1988).

The sessions were regularly distributed over a six-week period at one-week intervals. Each session lasted 1.5 hours and followed a similar pattern. The same procedure was applied to all groups. During a session, all of the participants and the two moderators sat in chairs arranged in a circle. Each session began with each person discussing his/her mood and locating the self-perceived level of this mood on a 1-to-10 scale, where 1 meant a hopeless mood and 10 was the best imaginable mood. If the participants found it important, they could state the reasons for their mood. The participants also recounted what had happened to them recently, including on that day, and what events, thoughts and social situations (e.g. meetings) could have affected their current mood. In sessions with groups E and H, direct relationships were constructed and the sense of belonging was supported.

Thus, the empirical data from the study did not substantiate the motivational theory of the need of belonging (Baumeister and Leary, 1995) and some tenets of the relational model of coping with stress (Lazarus and Folkman, 1984) in adolescents at risk of social exclusion (Baumeister, Brewer, Tice and Twenge, 2007, Twenge, Catanese and Baumeister, 2003; Twenge et al., 2007).

It was demonstrated in the situations above that resilience could play a rather deceitful role. When new soothing patterns of thinking, feeling or behaving were emerging, they were cancelled by the youth, and the primary attitude was strengthened.

The ideas behind the hedonistic interventions

Sessions with the hedonistic group focused on recognising one's own emotions and needs and on satisfying these. In each session, the subjects were supposed to recall and realise the pleasant thing/s that had happened to them over the preceding week. This made them analyse each day of the week in terms of positive events, gratifying feelings, relaxing time, meeting nice people and experiencing pleasure. Initially, this exercise was not a simple task, as the participants did not notice anything positive in their lives or had difficulty not only recalling, but also communicating such information. Still, such pleasant moments were becoming increasingly accessible and more easily retrievable from memory as one meeting progressed to the next. The practice of sharing good and nice moments with others contributed to an increase in the subjectively felt positive affect during the formation of closer bonds among the participants (Wilczyńska and Piękoś, 2014).

Positive experience training was also a constant fixture of the sessions. In order to trigger positive emotions and pleasant moods in the participants, the study applied Positive Experience Training (PET), a therapeutic method developed in Germany by Dr Rainer Lutz of the University of Marburg and employed, for example, in depression therapy programmes. The method consists of eliciting positive experiences and memories by pleasant stimulations of the various senses: smell, taste, sight, hearing and touch. Such exercises make subjects focus on the present moment and relax. PET has been shown to help reduce depressive symptoms and increase coping capacities in hospitalised patients (Dudek, Grabski and Siwek, 2003). The main aim of such training is to put participants in a good mood by affording them opportunities for savouring pleasant bodily stimuli, recalling positive emotions and moments in their lives and sharing those with others. In brief, it involves stimulating the hedonistically conceived feeling of happiness and subjective well-being.

Sharing nice memories and experiences with others in a group increases the sense of community and belonging, inspires trust in others and encourages other participants to recall similar positive memories. A mindful approach to one's own feelings and a caring and kind attitude to the self are supported in this exercise.

The adolescent sample in the study eagerly took part in positive experience training. Each session focused on sensations provided by another sense. The first of these was with concerned smell—a sense which is strongly connected with emotions and helps one code emotions of varied quality together with the events associated with them. During training, the adolescents could relish various smells of fruit, vegetables, oils, incense sticks, coffees, natural teas, etc. The participants were experiencing sensations induced by nice-smelling props when closing their eyes and recalling pleasant memories. Subsequently, the subjects shared the memories linked to the smells and talked about which smell was most pleasant to them. All this took place in an atmosphere of unhurried peacefulness. The following PET sessions focused on taste, hearing and sight. In each of them, the therapists presented various props that were then sensorily explored by the subjects. The hearing-focused session was very special, as the adolescents brought along their favourite pieces of music—those they had liked in

childhood and also those they liked at the current time. Each participant presented a part of 'his/her' piece and talked about the impressions it inspired in him/her while looking for other associations with other positive experiences
together with the group.

The involvement in sessions with hedonistic interventions was very attractive to the participants. Boys and girls had an opportunity to relive pleasant memories from the past and current experiences, as well as sharing these with others. They also appreciated the inclusion of their 'own' music as part of the session. They indirectly expressed their outlooks on life and their sensitivity through music. It seems to have been an important moment, because individual music preferences varied widely. The participants were also curious to see how very different music genres triggered strong emotions in others. The session offered a site for the coexistence of different music styles and the expression of mutual respect.

There were also exercises in which the participants received positive feedback about themselves. In this way, they had an opportunity to experience the sense of power coming from the community and from belonging. The participants anonymously (as they were embarrassed to use their own names) wrote what they liked about the others on sheets of paper, and the group were supposed to figure out whom the particular positive features addressed. The reading and hearing of positive information about themselves bolstered the participants' self-esteem and their sense of being accepted by others.

The draughting of individual lists of pleasures was another important point on the hedonistic agenda. Such lists catalogued things, people and activities that made the participants relaxed, cheerful or excited. In the session, each person produced his/her own list of 'mood-enhancers'. The participants were supposed to organise them, for example, in categories of a 'calming/exciting activity', 'minor/major pleasure' or 'time-consuming/time-economical'. Having draughted his/her own list, each participant received an agenda for the following week and had to plan at least one item of pleasure from the list for each day. The planned pleasant activities were supposed to be executed over the following days. Monitoring their mood after performing the specific pleasant activity was an additional assignment for the participants.

Exercises which served as interludes engaging the entire group were also used. These tasks raised the level of energy in the team and fuelled the participants' motivation for further work. These included riddles, designing a video clip together, producing a board game with the team, etc. Such pursuits built the sense of belonging and community and created space for sharing positive feedback and releasing creative potentials.

When the programme had run its course, all of the participants expressed their regret and sadness with the sessions finishing so quickly and declared their desire to take part in further rounds of the project if possible. In their written feedback, the adolescents emphasised that they had felt they could influence the sessions or that they had a say on their content and course, enjoyed themselves and obtained an opportunity to see themselves in a good light and meet other people (Wilczynska and Piekos, 2014).

The aims of the eudaimonic interventions

The eudaimonic exercises were designed on the basis of the Self-Determination Theory (Ryan and Deci, 2000). Consequently, these mainly focused on the achievement of mental well-being through evoking the needs for competence, belonging and autonomy.

The sessions were devised so as to provide the participants with the maximum amount of opportunities for making their own decisions and choices, both in terms of the sessions at hand and in terms of analysing their choices in real life. This is one way of boosting teenagers' internal motivation to participate and engage in meetings. The programme also aimed to raise the adolescents' self-awareness through the discovery of needs, values and short- and long-term goals that the group members wanted to accomplish. Thematically, the interventions concerned certain values, such as helping, health, love, friendship and development, which can be relevant to fostering mental well-being in young people. Some sessions involved meditation and visualisation which helped the participants develop a sense of strength and competence (Wilczyńska and Piękoś, 2014).

In the beginning, each participant presented him/herself in the manner of his/her choice. The idea was to highlight the features and skills which were common for the entire group and the ones which were distinct for particular individuals. This exercise was meant to draw the participants' attention to individual differences and unique traits of every person, thereby contributing to increased autonomy (individual strengths), as well as foregrounding the mutual intragroup adjustment and bolstering the sense of belonging through showing the commonly shared characteristics and skills.

Each session had its own leading theme. These included: My strengths, My friendships and loves, My passions, My goals, My helping and gratitude.

The subjects also had plentiful opportunities to reflect on their positive features on the basis of what others said about them, of what they themselves knew about themselves and of which activities gave them satisfaction. In this way, they brought their traits to light (e.g. a good organiser or a capable, patient negotiator) and also relied on their brief acquaintance and mutual observations to write about the positive features of their group mates. They wondered and planned how they could use those 'strengths' of theirs (e.g. effective organisation of parties, solving conflicts among their acquaintance) and draw on them in relations with other people (e.g.

organisation of conferences, at court, in childcare, when deciding about their career paths and work lives).

The participants tried to 'predict' their future on the basis of the features they presented. Besides this, girls and boys had an opportunity to play at being 'analysts' of their own and other participants' possibilities in the future. When 'brainstorming', they came up with plans for utilising their character traits in the future. This also served as feedback for the participants and as a reinforcement of their positive strong sides. Everybody has their own potential in themselves which must simply be 'discovered' and developed. Listening to themselves and observing others helped the subjects achieve inner harmony, satisfaction and self-fulfilment. The participants were supposed to reflect on how they could use their (subjectively) most important strong features in the following week and were asked to plan relevant events. These assignments were discussed in the following session, focusing on how the subjects had executed the task, which of their strengths they had used and how they had felt in those situations.

Some exercises were devoted to reinforcing the sense of self-competence through visualisations and meditations associated with the sense of inner strength, for example, by using metaphors. Stories also had a relaxing influence.

Our aim in implementing the eudaimonic interventions was to promote the sense of autonomy in the participants. Given this, it was crucial to boost the adolescents' self-trust and accountability for their and to provide them with opportunities for deciding for themselves. We encouraged them to freely express their thoughts and articulate their opinions in the group without self-criticism. These rules applied to all sessions.

The interventions focused on reinforcing the participants' autonomy also consisted of planning their own goals and recognising and realising their passions. They discussed goals that other people set for them and the reasons why people set any goals in the first place. It seemed important to distinguish internal goals, i.e. ones we define ourselves as driven by our internal motivations and subjectively important values, from external goals, i.e. ones which are dictated by the environment, other people and institutions. The participants noticed that imposed goals sometimes overlapped with internal goals. We also analysed motivations behind different goals: the desire for wealth, professional growth, health, friendship, family, success or knowledge. This called for deeper reflection on the part of the subjects. What came in handy in this regard was an exercise in which the participants were asked to imagine themselves winning one million dollars. The exercise aimed to raise their self-awareness in relation to values and motivations behind goal-planning. Their answers were neither assessed nor criticised, because the point was that they should understand what implications particular choices had. For example, when a participant envisioned buying a new luxury car or going abroad to study, we inquired,

'Why does it matter so much to you?' in order to elicit the values endorsed by the participants and direct their attention to possibilities of self-determination on the basis of what motivates us.

The subjects also thought about how goals could be pursued after they had been chosen. They envisaged themselves ten years later and, importantly, in the best of the possible options. This meant that each participant activated imaginations concerning their future situation in which all his/her plans and dreams would come true and all goals would be achieved. We talked about those visions while asking each individual the following: 'Who are you?"', 'Where are you?', 'Who are you with?', 'What are you doing?', 'What people are around you?' and 'What are you busy with?' Spinning such visions of themselves in the best possible scenario encouraged the participants to think of long-term goals and to speak about them in front of the group.

An internal belief that engaging in various activities makes sense is an important part of the sense of autonomy and self-determination. Given this, we looked for internal motivations, and the participants tried to replace expressions such as 'I have to' (external motivation) with 'I want/choose' (internal motivation). We all know that teenagers often say 'I have to', for example: 'I have to go to school', 'I have to study', or 'I have to tidy up my room'. However, they could reformulate some of these challenges into 'I want' if they analysed the matter at hand in terms of 'what would happen if this did not take place—if you did not go to school, if you had no job and/or if you did not earn money?'.

Every participant described his/her passions and hobbies. We noted these passions down on slips of paper side by side with their strengths in order to combine resources and to think about how these passions could be used in the future. We also explored whether the participants included these passions in their ideal visions of themselves ten years hence.

Fostering the sense of belonging as an indispensable part of individual mental well-being was an important aspect of the eudaimonic interventions. The sense of belonging is connected with the feeling of community with the group, in terms of adjustment and appreciation. It is also shaped by the individual's trust in the group, when one can freely present oneself in the group without any increased fear of rejection. This goal was pursued chiefly by exercises involving the entire group or subgroup, where individual and shared features and skills were identified. Besides this, the participants looked for potentials in themselves and others and had an opportunity to appreciate them. The sessions included assignments that were to be solved together, with the participants supporting and helping one another. Additionally, ideas that engaged the entire group were implemented.

The participants were also expected to prepare anonymous feedback for others, which was read in the group and all the participants were supposed to figure out whom it addressed. This kind of exercise essentially affects the sense of self-worth in adolescents and is a way of fostering non-competitive and cooperative attitudes in young people.

'My helping', a game that had already been used in other positive-psychology interventions (Lyubomirsky, King and Diener, 2005; Layous et al., 2011), was the participants' favourite exercise. They drew lots with names, and the person they had drawn would become their 'charge' for the rest of the session while they turned into discreet 'helpers'. Their tasks were, all undercover, to support their charge, to pay attention to his/her behaviour and emotions and to help him/her, but in ways which did not enable the charge to immediately realise who his/her helper was. This exercise aimed to stimulate the sense of belonging, to train empathetic perception, to sensitise the participants to the needs of others and, in particular, to engender self-competence in the participants as people who are capable of helping and contributing.

The eudaimonic interventions were concluded with a meeting in which each participant said what they had liked the most and the least. What mattered to them was that they felt they had had an influence on the course of sessions, that the sessions had been ordered and harmonious, and that it had been possible to freely yet deeply think on the possibilities of shaping the future and on one's own choices.

Conclusions and recommendations from our research on the development of the sense of belonging in adolescents

The effectiveness of therapeutic techniques depends equally on the choice of interventions and on the severity of disorders or of the reported problems. The programme described above was designed for a group of several dozen teenagers who had been admitted to a mental health facility due to emotional and behavioural disorders, including serious run-ins with the law. The boys and girls came from incomplete families or from families with alcohol and/or substance abuse. A few of the participants had been committed to young offenders' institutions as a result of their aggressive or criminal deeds.

Carrying out an experiment involving the teenagers was a considerable organisational challenge to the researchers. It was not certain whether the teenagers would attend the planned sessions. It was also a new experience for the members of the experimental groups, as they had never taken part in any similar programme before. We were pleasantly surprised to see that the subjects regularly attended the sessions, except two people who missed two of them. At the same time, the research results after the conclusion of the group sessions were unexpected. In the experimental study, the effect of the reinforced sense of belonging not only disappeared or failed to occur after the completion of the project, but also even dropped below the initial level.[5]

It was concluded, however, that the programme had fulfilled its educational function. The participants verbally confirmed that they had learned to recognise their emotions, strengths and skills. This is an important change because research on social exclusion shows that emotional numbness and insulation (i.e. the inability to relate to one's own emotions) are among the major symptoms of exclusion. It was emphatically shown in the description of the first group study reported in this book. The members of the group (cluster: school problems and substance abuse) that experienced exclusion most acutely were unable to identify their qualities and emotions, and they 'coped' with the sense of exclusion by joining underprivileged groups of the same profile and by resorting to alcohol and other substances.

The results described in the three studies[6] teache us—teachers, psychologists, educators and therapists—some important lessons which can be translated into a series of fundamental implications:

1. Socially excluded people have negative and rather enduring or imprinted beliefs about themselves which are difficult to change within a traditional, time-limited therapeutic programme.
2. In order to develop a sense of belonging, people need others who, though not family members, provide them with a sense of importance or show interest while recognising them as members of a given community.
3. The sense of belonging is formed and sustained in and through direct, positive relations with others. These relations should be characterised by care for another person, which is expressed, for example, by direct and kind eye contact and timbre of the voice.
4. If relations are experienced and then lost without being replaced with other ones, the sense of belonging decreases, self-esteem drops, mood worsens and anger grows.
5. The sense of belonging can be fostered and sustained in an authentic relationship that does not have to be intense, but should be tolerably positive and constant within a given life cycle. This means that this relationship is available in the time and space in which the person finds him/herself, for example, throughout the period of study at a given level of education.
6. Adolescents who feel excluded feel that they have no ways of coping on their own in the situation of being rejected or excluded by others.
7. School and educational programmes should include instructions on how to devise training for students to help them recognise the need of belonging in themselves and in others and how to satisfy this need.
8. Programmes for teachers and parents should include knowledge and guidelines concerning the ways of fostering the sense of belonging in children and adolescents and the ways of building the sense of community among people, within and outside family, in real life.

In conclusion, it is important to educate people about the need of belonging and its manifestations. Sensitivity to all symptoms of the suffering of others resulting from loneliness or exclusion should be instilled and kindled in people. The signals of suffering caused by exclusion are very subtle and barely noticeable to others. Excluded people do not talk about their sense of exclusion, and those who brace up and articulate their sense of exclusion are likely well on their way to leaving exclusion behind. Frequent responses to the sense of being excluded include aggression, as in young people, or isolation. Excluded people cannot cope with the sense of exclusion on their own. The processes of exclusion can be effectively reversed and the sense of belonging can be supported through resorting to the ideas of self-loving and compassion-based therapies: the recognition of exclusion-related suffering of other people (children, adolescents), offering care (to oneself and others) and then the implementation of relief-bringing activities. The sense of belonging cannot be developed without fostering a real community of people in a given environment, system and situation in which preferential treatment is precluded and nobody is passed over.

Notes

1. Professor Franz Halberg was one of the pioneers of modern chronobiology. The author and co-author of over 3,500 publications, he was nominated several times for the Nobel Prize. An active researcher at the University of Minnesota until the end of his life, he died in 2013 at the age of 94. Professor Haberg was the author's teacher of chronobiology and chronopsychology with the focus on heart rate variability.
2. The name of the scale includes a play on words and can mean both 'How are you coping?' and 'How are you doing?'.
3. For intragroup comparisons, the effect size ranged from 0.41 to 0.88. The highest values of Cohen's *r* (above 0.7) were found for the systolic and asystolic blood pressure (stage VI, group H) and for the fatalistic-present time-perception (stage V, group E).
4. The following subchapter describes the exercises used in the experiment, the selected techniques of eudaimonic and hedonistic interventions, and the references to the participants' feedback.
5. After the project, all the participants were included in therapeutic programmes and meetings run by the facility.
6. 1) Study among adolescents in schools; 2) Case study; 3) Study among the youth in social exclusion risk.

Chapter 16

Positive individual human development

Adults, experience, role and responsibilities

Building belonging is possible at various stages of human development.

One of the ways to do this is to undertake an effort of understanding and starting a solitary and independent journey to reclaiming oneself in this world, that is, to regain the sense of belonging, which is a fact after all, for we are all part of an interdependent an interconnected whole. All we need is to recognise this, to emotionally endorse this fact and to let ourselves perceive ourselves in other people.

The other and basically parallel way is to show and teach people how they can bring up their children while supporting their sense of belonging or how they can correct and repair past mistakes. Therefore, it is the responsibility, first, of parents and of schools and, then, of employers to foster the conditions and rules of coexistence in which young people will not feel alone but will believe that they form a system in which everybody depends on everybody else in a way, and all people function together while acknowledging one another's existence.

Spiral human development

Key stages in the development of human belonging can be described in terms of four major areas bound up with particular time-space frames of an individual's development. They are identifiable in human development from childhood to adulthood. These are certain levels/spaces of life which provide the most important points of reference for human development at a given age. Even when one of these stages is currently being experienced and explored as the fundamental space and time of development, the remaining ones also matter. The latter may be linked to family or environmental information that reaches individuals in the process of growing up or developing.

Individuals' development follows a spiral trajectory where people find themselves at a certain level, but all of their belonging-related experiences associated with other levels/spaces affect them as well. This is visualised in Figure 16.1.

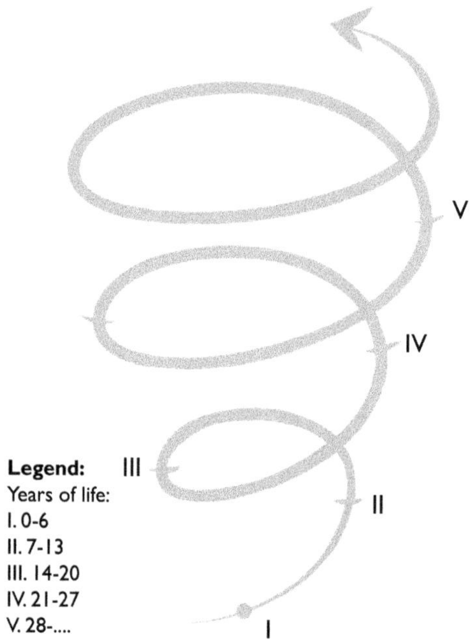

Figure 16.1 The Spiral of Personal Development.

In this way, starting from the first stage, an individual progresses to the following phase of his/her life and, with his/her prior experiences as the fulcrum, explores another broader space that is already a certain perspective of his/her own attitudes, beliefs, dominant emotions, feelings, etc. If at any of the stages the need to belong is withdrawn, the development of the sense of belonging and human functioning may be affected throughout the later stages. At the same time, it is possible to return to previous experiences in any phase in order to integrate them, undertake therapy and embark on the path of self-development and flourishing. This happens through the self-conscious processes of reconstruction and reorganisation of the structures of the mind.

Healing old wounds

The identification and reconstruction of lingering past memories/experiences or painful wounds that became fixed in a child's structure of the mind consist in locating them in a mature structure that is capable of opening up to them again in order to cure and heal them. The following stage of integration and reorganisation helps include the prior experiences in the structure of the mind in a new way, owing to the reorganised system of values, goals and needs. This is a kind of investment in the new reconfigured system. For example, the sense of rejection experienced in childhood is reproduced by an adult, but, since it occurs in the individual's mature structure of the mind, it does not cause the same harm to the person. The wound of exclusion can be reexamined and nursed or therapised through transposing past experiences or recent traumas onto a new structure (i.e. identification and restructuring), usually in collaboration with a psychologist (Lowen, 1988). The rebuilt sense of belonging and care helps integrate experiences, that is, include/incorporate the healed wounds as one's own part, while feeling secure and taken care of. This is made possible by the reorganised structure in which space has opened up for self-experience as a sufficient and belonging individual who is important to him/herself and to others and who feels part of the system/group/community (the reorganisation of structure and the integration of experiences). At the stage which caps the previous two, what has been achieved in the process up to this point is cultivated. Individuals experience themselves in various roles in life, making sure that they are compassionate and mindful of their own and others' needs (self-development and self-flourishing). People are then creative and aware of their contribution to the joint work of creating the world or correcting their own worlds and of taking care of themselves and others. If an adolescent develops properly or feels that s/he belongs, the last phase of flourishing appears by itself and usually coincides with the entry into adulthood. This is the stage of permanent self-caring, self-compassion and self-belonging in harmony with others.

A person's social and individual development is grounded in the four following stages:

- early childhood (1 to 7 years of age) – a period of self-belonging when children experience themselves, especially in a close relationship with their mothers, and learn to take care of themselves or of their own inner child;
- growing up (up to 14 years of age) – a period of belonging to the family when children learn the roles of being a woman/mother/wife and a man/father/husband (a father's activity is important in case of boys) and mature in these roles;
- adolescence (up to 21 years of age) – a period of belonging to school and peer groups when adolescents experience themselves in relations with others and recognise their roles in peer and school groups; and
- adulthood on – a period of belonging to the world, to the human community, to society and, finally, at the later stages of life, to the universe, when people recognise their role in creating and co-creating and in development through giving and receiving.

When child and mother are one

The correct development of a child and then a teenager takes place in four major stages. The first stage encompasses the first three years of life. About two months before birth (in the seventh month of prenatal life), the number of ganglions and the amount of the grey matter in the brain are already optimal. From this point forward, a child learns the rhythm of his/her mother's heartbeat, which calms him/her down in the months following birth. Research confirms that young children calm down at the sound of their mothers' hearts and voices more easily than at their fathers' voices.

The relationship and interactions with the mother, as well as her feminine energy, are most important for children between 1 and 3 years of age. Basically, it seems that children's entire development up to the age of 7 unfolds optimally if they are in the mother's—a woman's—care. She responds intuitively to the information transmitted by the child and, thus, satisfies the child's needs in a visceral way. Contact with the mother sustains the state of soothing and security. This is the period of unconditional love, care, attention and mutual co-feeling between the mother and the child. During this time, the relationship with the self is constructed, and the model of self-love—love of one's own inner child—is produced. This means that the ability of self-soothing, self-care and self-security is fostered and developed for the future.

Children's egocentricity is revealed in that children do not differentiate themselves from their mothers or other people around them. They are convinced that mothers feel and experience exactly the same as they do. If a mother provides secure attachment, she openly expresses emotions and feelings. Sadness, pain, fear and satisfaction are expressed without any restraints. Children prefer being soothed and embraced by their mothers rather than by other people. In the presence of secure mothers, children are eager to explore the environment. Therefore, in the future and if no traumatic experiences befall them, they will grow up into adults capable of selecting safe places for themselves and for supporting others. They will openly express their feelings without being afraid to be hurt, ignored or rejected. They will be convinced that if they need help, they can ask for it without fearing that such requests will be turned down. Children naturally balance between security and autonomy. They explore their surroundings on their own, and when they choose intimacy, they use it for as long as they need to. Adults who experienced secure attachment in childhood accept various human emotions, including sadness and anger, and communicate their emotions to others without fearing rejection. Children who experience secure attachment are direct and empathetic, able to openly communicate their feelings and to take the perspective of others' into account. They are not afraid to approach people who go through difficult experiences. In the future, they become strong, and their strength comes from within. Secure attachment is a secure basis on which children can rely in the future.

Egocentricity also involves defining one's own boundaries, which is expressed, among others, in what is known as a toddler's defiance. Going through this stage, 2- or 3-year-olds may vigorously protest when somebody else plays with their toys or enters their space; they also tend to attempt to monopolise a part of a room or of a sandpit for themselves.

Building self-love, developing self-mindfulness and noticing one's basic needs result from interactions with the mother in this early period. Feminine maternity is characterised by sensitivity to the child's needs and by empathy, if not intuition, in deciphering the child's needs. By highlighting the feminine aspect here, we, in fact, refer generally to people who exhibit feminine modes of behaviour.

Importantly, the information which is imprinted in children's minds during this stage and the later stages will determine their emotional functioning, thoughts and behaviours. Up to the seventh year of age, children fully identify with the labels that they are given. When the mother says 'my son is a poor eater' or 'he hates spinach', the child enacts this pattern and will soon refuse to eat spinach even if mum is not around. At this stage, particularly essential information about attachment and relations with other people becomes imprinted. Traumas that are experienced in this period may determine the entire subsequent development of individuals and haunt them for most of their adult lives, if they do not attempt to identify these and then implement restructuring and reorganisation.

The longer certain information and patterns are reproduced and as long as the same path is followed in coping with challenges, problems and everyday situations, the more permanent and irreversible layering of patterns is instilled in the structure of the person's mind, not only in the 'circulating mind', but also in the information in the body. It will take considerable investments to alter them in adulthood. This is the reason why it is so exigent to ensure optimal development throughout the stages leading to independence.

Why a loving dad must be around

In this period, children distinguish themselves from their mothers and from other people. It is the time when they build themselves, relying on their relationships with both their mothers and their fathers. Interactions with fathers in this period are of particular importance, especially to boys.

The greatest number of neurons develop up to seven years of age. Their considerable proportion (nearly 30%) will be removed between 7 and 14 years of age. This phenomenon is referred to as neural Darwinism, because neurons which are not useful in a given environment disappear. Thus, if learning to draw is more important than communicating with others, the latter connections will be eliminated or diminished. At the same time, the neural connections which are important in this system/in the family will be activated.

In this period, children develop their sense of independence and experience themselves as a person separate from the parent. Children's sexual identity is usually consolidated in the previous developmental phase.

After seven years of age, children begin to learn the roles of man and woman together with the principles of social functioning inscribed in them by watching their mothers and fathers perform these roles. The roles and principles which have long been endorsed in a given system—the family, a partnership and other small social groups—are usually given precedence.

The existing educational models and methods have disjoined and are still disjoining some emotions and behaviours from female and male roles. For example, expressions of sensitivity, fragility, emotion or uncertainty have traditionally been at odds with the model of masculinity, while anger, strength, audacity and resolve have been deemed unbecoming to a woman. Masculinity has been supposed to manifest in prowess, heroic deeds, intelligence, determination and domination, whereas femininity in acquiescence, weakness, sensitivity, submission and nurturance. Males thus tend to cope with difficulties by assuming the position of inaccessibility and withdrawing from communication or even from relationships.

As can easily be imagined, because of such a separation of emotions/the mind from the body, males lack resources to fully communicate with themselves, with each other and with women. A lot of women also adopt the patriarchal functioning modes at work or in relations with others. Men of whom such 'masculinity' has been demanded cannot handle multiple situations in life that call for emotional and authentic self-expression, especially when inaccessibility and domination were priority values within their community/society.

This patriarchal model of functioning entails a considerable level of frustration and stress. Over generations, the lack of communication between the body and the mind has been and still is 'drowned in alcohol' or vented out in gambling and, recently, on the Internet and through video games. Moreover, strength has been 'proven' in common violence. For their part, women all too often avail themselves of criticism instead of power when trying to change this quality in men.

Women's and men's brains differ, as do their world perceptions and the usage of the world in terms of certain emotional and cognitive challenges (Vetulani, 2007). They need differentiated stimuli for their development, but they also need mutual communication in order to produce a new value through the synergy of the feminine and the masculine.

Women's brains are better equipped with white matter while men's brains have, on average, larger grey matter areas (Hoffman et al., 2017).

This different structure does not favour either men or women but, rather, shows the different possibilities of a male and a female mind.

Male brains are optimised for communicating within the hemispheres, whereas female brains are optimised for interhemispheric communication. The difference in male and female brain structures is connected with various abilities, for example, with higher narrative abilities of women (Ingalhalikar et al., 2014; Angelopoulou et al., 2020).

This is another argument supporting the insight that men's psychology and women's psychology should coexist to benefit men, women and entire societies alike.

The model of maleness

Between 7 and 14 years of age, it is imperative that children interact with both parents, and boys especially with their fathers. In this period, boys go through the process of initiation and learning what it means to be male, finding out how maleness is expressed and, ultimately, becoming males.

It seems that this is the best time in men's lives to learn how to express themselves and become confident in their actions.

According to Jung, mature manifestations of masculinity are imaged in the archetypes of King, Warrior, Magician and Lover, whereby their bright and dark sides are likewise acknowledged (Moore and Gilette, 1990). Interestingly, while the former two sound familiar to some men, the latter two are rarely understood. However, when recognised, they prove to be requisite to men for mature self-identification. As boys are initiated into maleness, they are taught how to function in these roles. In fact, none of these identifications is recommendable if it is dissociated from the other ones. An example of a mature combination is bringing together the King's care or paternal care for the entire kingdom, for the home and for the planet, the generosity and wisdom of the Magician, the Warrior's capacity of resolute and loyal action and the Lover's certainty that he is connected to others.

The archetypes on which we can rely have also their dark sides. However, in universal understanding, a warrior cannot be a destroyer, a sadist or a masochist, as he never invests more energy than strictly necessary. Destroying something can only be useful if it leads to the rise of something better, vibrant, fresh and more valuable. If a man has proper access to the Warrior in him, he will exhibit care and compassion he will appreciate and create, and he will take care of others and himself. The Warrior's fight is a good fight in order to make the world a better and more satisfying place for everybody.

A lot of males still mistake controlling and hostile behaviour for strength. In fact, such behaviour originates from the weakness and helplessness of a hurt boy. Few of these boys experienced the care of mature parents.

At home: how children learn from adults

Children acquire different roles in their families. Starting in early childhood, they can learn about the mutual support or rivalry of men and women and programme their minds into certain ways of thinking, feeling and acting. As can be imagined, the strongly imprinted patterns rehearsed over years are difficult to remove.

Parents who themselves did not experience a positive child-raising code can repetitively determine principles/values which they will pass to their children. Certainly, entrenchment in schemas that limit the understanding and feelings of the self and of one's own belonging can result in further problems.

The sense of belonging to the first group system that is family is experienced when a person is noticed and appreciated for what s/he is. That is why ignoring this potential and imprinting other rules through the social reward and punishment system turn out to be a combination that is incompatible with the person in the future and impedes his/her achievement of a rewarding life. This usually calls for intervention/reconstruction and a reorganisation of resources in cooperation with a therapist.

The period called early adolescence is extraordinarily sensitive, and young people are especially vulnerable to developing emotional trauma in this phase. This is caused, for example, by tempestuous hormonal and emotional changes and by disparities in the development of the brain and of other body parts, with the brain only maturing fully in the third decade of life.

We should realise that most traumas experienced by young people are traumas experienced in family environments, as this book has made clear. Emotional trauma is associated with neglect, rejection, deprivation, emotional punishment, ridicule and destructive evaluations. These are among the most serious factors (about 80%) in later developmental, emotional and cognitive deficits.

Trauma results from a person being left helpless in the face of his/her own fear or agitation—being left alone without the possibility of coping with or standing up to the events. When a child has no possibility to respond and no support in a difficult situation, or when s/he realises s/he has been hurt through socially imposed rules, the changes that occur in his/her organism may be long-lasting and linger on, although deeply hidden, over several years of his/her life to come.

Adults who have grappled with their own problems transfer these onto children in an emotional and unaware manner. They try to shelter their children from the experience of failure and prepare them for a life which they consider to be good for their children. Instead of fostering children's self-love and love of others, self-confidence, belief in vitality and agency, they focus on the same schema and, for example, instil competitive thinking in them. Modern adolescents do not make decisions because they are afraid of being evaluated and feel unable to experience their lives fully. Fearing wrong decisions, they make none instead. Fearing the spontaneous, the genuine and the vigorous, they neither relish joy and pleasure nor share what they know with others, while lingering in isolation and seclusion (Twenge, 2017; Moore and Gilette, 1990).

Research findings show that when compassionate and patient support is applied instead of criticism and judgemental evaluations, the brain develops much faster and better. The brains of children who experience emotional violence develop at a slower pace, and many of their regions are disproportionately small or inactive in comparison with the brains of children who experience healthy relationships (De Bellis et al., 1999).

The parents are authority figures for their children until about 14 years of age. In this period, good relations with the parents still matter a lot to children. Given this, the period is the optimum timeframe for experiencing their sexuality, gender roles or roles in the family system in which one can safely express oneself, one's emotions and one's needs and learn how to respect the needs of other people around and how to take care of oneself and others. This is a period in which children want to belong to their families, to have their own place in them, to be noticed and to be considered important the way they are. Only if these conditions are met do children, respecting themselves and others, acquire or imprint rules of family functioning and of their own functioning in the family, which they will use in their adult lives in the future.

Am I worth as much as I matter to my friends?

The period from about 14 to 21 years of age is a time when teenagers chiefly construct themselves in relation to the social world beyond the family.

This is a period when they exert themselves to please the group, test its potential and seek their place in it. People learn what social groups are and what it takes to participate in them. If prior knowledge and experiences give them a stable ground for manifesting themselves in the environment, they will show themselves to the world, verify others' reactions and take their chosen roles in the group. The group mutually adjust to one another by correcting the ways in which people perform in various group roles (Adams and Galanes, 2006).

A person who enters a group with the full potential of the sense of self-belonging and belonging to the family will be more resistant to group difficulties, isolation, group anxiety and to the inaccessibility of group members.

A person with a low sense of belonging, high anxiety and considerable insecurity will learn how to function in order to avoid suffering and another rejection, instead of learning how to benefit from others' potential.

Unfortunately, rejection experienced in one's family translates into rejection by the group. Children with a reduced sense of belonging adopt the roles of group clowns, mascots, kamikazes, outsiders, and, in particular, of scapegoats (Brown and Pehrson, 2006).

For what reasons does the group exclude some kids?

The group and group processes may contribute to the exclusion of an individual. If the group is stalled at an early stage of the development or in the phase of rebellion and conflict, individuals will find it far more difficult to develop trust and feel that they belong to the group. Importantly, in the phase of group conflicts, rejection and exclusion from the group usually afflict strong individuals who differ from others and act as leaders, initiators and inventors. People who have different views and whose thinking and behaviour diverge from those of the group are most likely to face the risk of exclusion. All groups which seek unanimity will exclude individuals who are a hazard to their cohesion and group processes (Corey, Corey and Corey, 2014). Exclusion also affects people who lack features or skills typically shared by others, as well as those who have certain original qualities which the group lacks, such as a particularly high IQ, artistic talents, a brilliant mathematical aptitude, etc.

Groups are also characterised by low tolerance for people who elevate group anxiety. Group anxiety is especially pronounced at the first stage of group formation; if an individual exacerbates group anxiety through his/her attitude, verbal displays or nonverbal communication, the group may seek to eliminate him/her from group activities and prefer other people who release tension, make the group laugh, etc. (Jedliński, 2000). People are rejected in groups that have a low level of organisation, weak leadership and/or incompetent or inattentive educators who do not know the group sufficiently and do not know how to work with them.

Groups also exclude individuals who expect/anticipate exclusion. People who are excluded develop a strong feeling that, usually inexplicably, they are not or cannot be part of a community. They feel maladjusted, which consequently makes them marginalised, overlooked and rejected. The sense of exclusion or the sense of insufficient belonging may be related to the family or school system, or it is a general sense of misalignment within the social system.

Exclusions are effected both by people who have experienced exclusion themselves (and usually do it consciously and intentionally) and by people who have a sense of belonging (and usually do it unintentionally or non-deliberately).

However, groups may be mature, predestined or conducted skilfully enough to be inclusive, compassionate and welcoming to members even if they vary widely.

Processes of inclusion or exclusion take place at different levels within groups. At the first level, group members endeavour to approach a person in various ways, and a lower level of 'exclusion' is characterised by openness to others. Then come consent to inclusion and the state of ambivalence, which forms a dividing line between exclusion and inclusion. Ambivalence means indifference to whether a given individual is excluded from or included in the group. The following processes encompass a gradation of ignoring, avoiding and, finally, physically rejecting and ostracising a person (Leary and Springer, 2001). Despite differences in the intensity of rejection done by the group, an individual being excluded may feel indifference as acutely as ostracism.

School and group structures are very strong and relevant sites of developing the sense of belonging or rejection.

School may generate or reduce stress and anxiety resulting from differences among students (e.g. in their school achievements); it can foster group support through implementing programmes to counteract the passive witness effect and to train students in everyday heroism, such as the Heroic Imagination Project (www.hip.org.pl; www.heroicimagination.org; Zimbardo, 2007). School may exert its influence by fostering a proper climate and promoting the sense of belonging for all students.

Maturity and building one's own life

This is a period of self-reliance in which people integrate their prior experiences, make their own choices in social relations, make autonomous decisions independently of authorities, thereby becoming an authority to themselves, and learn to be adults. Their brains mature in parallel as the prefrontal cortex fully develops its functions and 'catches up' with the other parts of the brain. Individuals are capable of comprehensively using the possibilities of their brains in analytical and creative work, in developing ideas and in self-development.

People feel that they belong to the systems which they co-form (e.g. the family, society, workplace and community) and of which they are a creative part. They respect their environment and the people around, therein themselves. They take care of their natural environment. Performing the roles of a man, a woman or other non-binary roles, people decide to support their own and their partners' potential in this scope. They have opportunities to establish relationships and partnerships which are based on care, compassion, mutual kindness and efforts to make the world a better place for themselves and for future generations.

People follow a mature path when their development unfolds through consecutive phases, from egocentricity to community with others and acting for their own good and the good of others. Children first identify with their mothers, then with significant others (usually family members), subsequently, with their peer groups and, in the end, possibly with the entire humanity. Maturity involves not only the ability of decentering (i.e. adopting the perspective of others and stepping beyond one's own self), but also compassion. One's creative development and experience of soothing are predicated on recognising this fact and developing the deep-rooted belief that 'I am part of a bigger whole and others are likewise part of a bigger whole'. Equally crucial is distancing oneself from one's strong emotional attitudes in order to disarm defences and launch change. Retaining a high potential of vitality/energy through proper nutrition, breathing, outdoor exercises, etc. is the third component (Pritchard, Richardson, Sheffield and McEwan, 2019; Richardson and Sheffield, 2017).

Why may our ancestors' approach to femininity and masculinity help?

Recent observations imply that there is reason to believe that a lot of the reasons for the fear of being hurt and misunderstood are related to engaging in intimate relationships. In their experience of independence, women and men deny the need for being part of a relationship, even though they suffer from loneliness at the same time.

Women would like to learn about their femininity but also want to find out about their inner masculine element and bring the two into a perfect balance. Similarly, men discover their feminine part, which, if harmonised with their masculinity, can be a source of strength for and satisfaction in a relationship with a woman. Women who recognise their masculine part are capable of action, of building their home and of protecting their territory. The feminine part of women entails receptivity and recognition of a man's actions. Men possess similar equivalents of masculinity and femininity. However, people do not find it easy to bring femininity and masculinity in harmony inside and in relationships, whether they engage in heterosexual or non-heterosexual relationships.

At this point, we can usefully refer to Carl Gustav Jung's concepts of femininity and masculinity, which vividly convey what women and men look for in themselves and what facilitates their engagement in a relationship with another person (Jung, 2007).

According to this symbolic approach, the anima (i.e. the inner woman) is a personification of female tendencies in a male's psyche. Jung describes these tendencies as nebulous moods, prophetic insights, susceptibility to irrationality, empathy, intuition and capacity for personal love. The experience of the anima is well represented by shamans who don special garments and paint their bodies to have better contact with the world of the unconscious (spirits). A man's anima is shaped by his mother. If her influence was negative and expressed in irritation, labile moods and insecurity, it will negatively affect the man. For example, he will repeatedly tell himself: 'Others have good lives, but not you', 'I have got no joy', and 'I am nobody'. Other manifestations of a negative anima include sarcastic or weepy comments. If a man is able to overcome the anima's negative impact, it will strengthen his masculinity. A positive anima will help him find an appropriate spouse or partner. Besides this, he will have an opportunity to use empathy and intuition, as well as recognising himself in his inner world of feelings and values. The anima appears in four stages of development: primitive woman, romanticised beauty, love (Eros) and spirituality and wisdom. According to Jung, the last stage of anima development is wisdom which surpasses what is purest and holiest, though it can be experienced by men who treat feelings seriously and preserve them in music, sculpture, writing or other forms of creative practice. This is the stage where the unconscious part is integrated, intellectually and ethically examined and evaluated at the level of feelings.

The animus (i.e. the masculine personification of the unconscious in women) also displays good and bad aspects. The animus is personified in a firm conviction that is expressed in a loud and emphatic voice. It can assume a negative form when a woman becomes a hard and merciless source of power. The animus is fundamentally shaped by a woman's father. He bestows a set of indisputably true beliefs on his daughter's animus. The negative animus discourages women from having deeper relations with real males. It appears in myths and folktales as the demon of death. In this way, it embodies cold and destructive thinking through which a woman goes in the moments of weakness, for example, when she fails to fulfil her emotional engagement. She feels insecure and inferior, believing that she 'is hopeless' and 'there is no point in trying'. Such thoughts can come complete with ruthlessness, frothiness, silence and opposition. The positive side of the animus is embodied in entrepreneurship, courage, trust and, in its highest form, a profound sense of spirituality. The animus has four stages of development: physical prowess and athleticism, a capacity for purposive planning, verbal expression, and the incarnation of sense and meaning. When a woman and a man successfully manage the animus and the anima, respectively, in their development, the next stage involves the development of the Self's unconscious part—the psyche's deeper core.

To be able to build a close relationship with another person, one must recognise one's sexual identification and acknowledge and harmonise its feminine and masculine elements. Whenever one distances oneself from oneself, one also distances oneself from intimacy with another person. A woman and a man who experience emotions and feelings in their relationship and truthfully talk about them with each other can not only improve the quality of their relationship, but also develop themselves on this basis of togetherness.

Is our sense of exclusion imprinted?

The sense of belonging and the sense of exclusion are the first psychological experiences in people's lives. These are mental states essential to human health and life. They manifest later as robust self-beliefs or attitudes which are brought into various social situations. Therefore, they can be regarded in psychological terms both as people's resources/properties and as processes in which these people are involved.

People whose need of belonging has been met usually experience a stable sense of belonging. They do not expect rejection when they make their need of belonging known. They establish relations and respond to other people's behaviour in natural ways. They control their anger, are empathetic and have high self-esteem, which helps them retain a good mood and understand their own and other people's emotions (Wilczyńska, 2013, 2014).

People who experience the sense of exclusion usually expect a potential rejection. They are afraid that others will avoid and ignore them, differ, deregulate or spread rumours and false tales about them and hurt and exploit them (Kerr and Levine, 2008). They do not communicate their need of belonging to others, and if they recognise this need in themselves, they conceal it and are unable to find suitable ways of satisfying it. The level of externally expressed aggression is higher in the excluded parties than in the belonging parties. Self-esteem and mood are lowered in the former. These people experience discrepancies within particular types of emotional intelligence (Mayer, Salovey and Caruso, 2000). When their capacity for co-feeling with others (experiential emotional intelligence) is higher, their control and understanding of their own and others' emotions (strategic emotional intelligence) are usually diminished and vice versa (Wilczyńska, 2013).

In young children, responses to rejection are acute. The pain is keenly felt, unless it is permanent or unmanageable, in which case it is cut off or 'insulated'. People, in a way, abandon themselves through suppressing pain. The point is that if children are rewarded with attention for 'being in accordance with others' wishes' and for 'what they do', rather than for the very fact that 'they are', this other part of the self becomes unwanted. One will only identify with the part of the 'self' which is recognised by others and desirable for others. Not only does the wound of rejecting something so intimate hurt and call for nursing/help, but also people cannot admit that they carry such a wound. This would mean admitting to being unwanted and unfitting, as well as exposing them to the pain of rejection once again.

The further one moves from such hurts, the less acute the pain becomes, because the layers of insulation are put in place to shield people against suffering, shame and guilt. In childhood, this was an 'effective' way to survive, forget, deny or freeze. Yet in adult life, this comes back unseen and unfelt, but nonetheless disrupting life and relations and triggering loneliness, anxiety, depression and diseases. Separated from self-love, people retreat from love for others. In the deep recesses of their minds, they are wounded and confused and possibly losing their will to live. Paradoxically, what is supposed to protect people against being wounded again, in fact, thrashes any hope of recovery (Lowen, 1988).

Such a constellation of experiences, defences and behaviours paralyses individuals' capacities to accept love, care and warmth from others and to offer these to themselves and others. In such circumstances, people often 'prove' with their own lives that they are not relevant and important enough to be loved; their relations fall apart or loosen up, and their relationships are treated as makeshift logistic solutions. Although they crave to be recognised, accepted, important, visible and wanted, even if they are given the coveted attention and love, no durable trace of them remains in their cognitive and emotional structures, because the deeply embedded rules and self-beliefs ('I am not fitting, important, good enough, etc.') make it impossible to retain the information which diverges from the 'logic' of the entire system. The feelings of being accepted, perceived and loved are received with considerable caution or are viewed as threatening, since they are directly associated with the experience of being rejected in the past. There is reason to believe that even infants are programmed and socially adapt to such situations and reactions to which they have been most often exposed. A specific response to rejection or separation is imprinted in respective personality disorders (Johnson, 1994).

People can cognitively understand that they have experienced exclusion, but they cannot cope with it and start living high-quality lives. They simply do not know how to do so, and most of them live with this burden until the end of their days. They do not know in which part of the mind or the body they should invest to help themselves. Mental solutions prove insufficient, for old wounds—much like old unused objects stored up in the attic—have been put away somewhere deep down in the forgotten memory of the mind, but they nevertheless take up room and affect people, because they are there even though they cannot be seen. It is difficult to heal something that is inaccessible, has been forgotten and is not recognised, and the only information about it is inferable from the stiffened-up body or from malfunctions of some of its organs.

In order to feel that one belongs, to regain the sense of being part of a community and to derive joy from it as an important and fitting member, one must reconnect with one's emotions in order to reorganise and change them. One must simultaneously revisit painful feelings and take care of oneself with support from an/other person/people (Cherepanov, 2015; Ivanich, 2020). Taking care of the self or of others entails transmitting concrete memetic information which is comprised of the sensations we receive or communicate to others through words and the senses.

This indicates that we acquire an ingrained sense of exclusion as a result of strong emotional experiences in the early developmental phase and early adolescence. In the following chapter, I will outline a convincing concept of the formation of the systems of memory, mind and nongenetic information transmission.

Chapter 17

Recognising memories, emotions, feelings and thinking

Transformation and thriving

In traditional psychology and psychotherapy, individual self-redesigning and lifelong self-designing are still viewed as a future vision. Scientists work to establish means of augmenting future people through artificial intelligence. As of today, any part of the human body can be substituted with a prosthetic device, so it is believed that, in the future, it will be possible to read people's minds and furnish them with selected attributes, thoughts and feelings. Redesigning means that people who once functioned in a certain way engage in the process of building belonging and, as a result, transform their moods, attitudes, feelings, dreams and plans.

As psychologists, we have learned that we can focus on problem-solving and assuage or remove symptoms of disorders and accompany our patients through their transformation processes. Using computers to intervene in human bodies and minds is regarded as unethical. Several people still believe that computers have limitations that will preclude them from replacing humans, but if we consider the organic computer to be a reality, we must realise that differences between the human and the 'machine' disappear along with mental constraints in this respect. For example, researchers of the ETH Zürich and the University of Basel have already constructed the first biocomputers which are made of living cells and work as simple electronic circuits. Owing to such advancements, a perfect computer may one day become the president of any country. Nevertheless, whether or not such visions of the future ever come true, it is our essential challenge to improve human development by mobilising people's best capacities and promoting their efforts of self-construction, self-rebuilding and harmonising the heart, the mind and the body, especially in the aftermath of stressful and traumatic occurrences.

Instead of repairing people and healing them by means of modern technologies, preventive measures can be applied. If the nurturing and development of all newly born children until adulthood were the sole domain of parents who love looking after children and have predispositions for it or have undergone special training, it certainly would not be a problem for them to treat all children with identical love and mindfulness, irrespective of their biological kinship. In this way, 'IT specialists' would deal with software; 'doctors' would treat all patients, and 'parents' would busy themselves with raising all children. This would certainly help us avoid several problems related to mental health. The memetic and cultural transmission proves stronger than the biological transmission or, at least, counterbalances the genetic one. I am not arguing for child-rearing in which all children are treated in exactly the same way; rather, I am making a case for child-rearing founded on unconditional love and support for every young person's potential for full development.

As shown in the first part of the book, a lot of people across the world are haunted by problems linked to relational traumas accumulated from early childhood and to anxieties and depression resulting from them.

The process of therapy (rebuilding or recovering the sense of belonging) proposed in this book unfolds in three major stages/phases. In the first phase, the individual comes to the realisation of the accumulated past experiences, consisting mainly of traumas, together with the defences and behaviour schemas that have accompanied her/him as 'imprinted' programmes. In the second phase, the person becomes released from these programmes and, thanks to this, makes changes in his/her self-perception so that the burden of the past or old programmes is no longer a factor in it, while self-trust, self-respect and compassion form its new underpinnings. At this stage, people need to disassemble their boundaries and thinking habits. In the third phase, people engage in ongoing creation, investing in their own inner home/themselves through trust and the recognition of their needs to be relevant, recognised and loved. The home (I/Myself) is here a metaphor for a person's inner world—a world of his/her sensitivity, feelings, needs and thoughts which we all wish were part of our coveted family homes. This home is not only a safe place, but also a space in which we receive care and appreciation, as well as being a site where we can fashion and develop ourselves as self-reliant people and make decisions about our own brain work and conscious thinking.

Regrettably, most of our real family homes operate in rather different ways. As children, we are evaluated, compared with others and given ready-made advice that fits other people better. Early life experiences imprint programmes. Parents mistakenly believe that if they set the bar high for their children and motivate them to achieve, their children will enjoy a life of success in the future. In fact, quite opposite effects can be and are indeed produced by this approach, as the young generation, though tolerant and flexible, are now consumed by anxieties about the future and are unwilling to distinguish themselves. Instead of moving from one social success to another, as their parents have planned, young people have considerable difficulty in establishing profound relations with other family members and are socially isolated, afraid of strangers and unwilling to enter into relationships with others for fear of being hurt. They are a generation who understand more and are open, yet they have been, so to speak, obligated to think and be in relations in different ways, because life has been transferred to the Internet. Currently, the rates of depression and anxiety are surging higher than ever before worldwide, an effect that researchers also attribute to the transformations of recent years and months (Twenge and Joiner, 2020).

Emphatically, these three phases actually overlap and interweave, but it is important to explore their distinct objectives separately to clearly delineate the areas that need attention and effort. My approach in this respect is underpinned by my own practical research and psychotherapeutic knowledge.

Today we are witnessing the most intensive development of varied psychological therapeutic models in the history of psychology. I deeply believe that in the coming years we will see a rapid rise of a homogeneous approach grounded on close psychosomatic interdependences that have been discovered and explored in recent years. People's health status is one of the key engines that drives new research and discoveries. American, European and particular Asian populations are now most susceptible not only to circulatory and cardiac diseases, but also to mental diseases. At the same time, the causes of both physical and mental types of disorders are more and more frequently found to be interrelated. The increasing incidence of degenerative diseases, which did not occur in the past, is an unmistakable beacon that our lifestyles are deleterious and that we make serious mistakes, for example, in our daily habits. Across health disciplines, experts perceive a link between diseases of the body and emotional problems. For example, microkinesitherapy—a physiotherapeutic technique developed by the French microkinesitherapist Daniel Grosjean—shows that people activate or release old emotions during a massage triggered by micro-pressure or even by micro-touch of certain points of the body. In this context, Grosjean talks of the 'cell memory' of the body.

Help provision, which has so far been the domain of psychologists and psychotherapists, is likely to become part of our everyday practices soon as a result of people's growing self-awareness and better knowledge of psychology and health support. Psychotherapists and psychologists will face new challenges corresponding to the new discoveries addressed in this book, therein the responsibility for the comprehensive development of people's full potential by supporting their self-belonging as a dimension of a self-conscious human close to others.

Restructuring of defence mechanisms: changes in Boolean gates in the heart

Some psychotherapy schools insist that difficulties in present functioning can be eliminated or reduced, and the quality of life increased only through the discovery and recognition of early childhood experiences.

This corresponds to the first phase of building/recovering the sense of belonging, which I name 'reconstructing'. The restructuring of defence mechanisms, especially disclosing the source of emotions and the cause of thoughts and behaviours, is very difficult for a lot of people, because it demands revisiting painful and/or repressed emotions. Additionally, it requires a separation between real, fresh and authentic feelings from old emotions based on imprinted programmes. This phase focuses on the reconstruction of past memories, emotions and feelings as an origin of destructive or nonadaptive beliefs and prejudices. The chief objective is to retrieve them, reveal their role and deal with them safely so as to maximally curtail their impact on the person's current life.

The restructuring of defences, the expression of sedimented emotions and the identification of their location in the body have come to serve as a means of facilitating the patients' expression of grief and despair (Coughlin Della Selva, 2004). Patients who were rejected and excluded in childhood tend to harbour grief for a long time and have difficulty overcoming these lingering emotions on their own (Bowlby, 1980). However, discovering programmes is very difficult, or in many cases is not possible, because of the strong role played by transmitted and/or unconscious programmes.

Individuals form their self-images on the basis of their past experiences, and if they bear such an unrecognised or repressed burden of experiences, they may function as people of entirely altered personality traits.

The process of recovering the sense of belonging cannot overlook feelings that were involved in past situations of exclusion or ostracism. It is important to acknowledge and admit these sensations from the level of a child who was unable to cope with them or coped with them in a manner that detrimentally affected later development. In all probability, it does not matter for such a person whether the memories s/he retrieves in this process are real or partly invented on the basis of his/her strong emotions and own interpretations. What truly matters is discussing patterns of his/her actions as thoroughly as possible and removing negative emotions saved within the experiences, which are stored in body memory. Therapists usually enquire about particular physical details and sensory memories. During a therapeutic session, patients are encouraged to recall auditory, olfactory and visual impressions which they associated with such events. This happens, for example, during Intensive Short-Term Dynamic Psychotherapy (Coughlin Della Selva, 2004). Reexperiencing past sensations in a safe setting often involves a confrontation with the perpetrator or the person who inadvertently inflicted harm. A relatively mature, even teenage, individual has at his/her disposal other and far more wide-ranging capacities of understanding emotions and situations than a young child does.

This is why although the process of recognising (step I) and releasing (step II) the accrued feelings and emotions is, as a rule, implemented from a child's perspective, it is, in fact, carried out by an aware adult. Given this, longstanding or suppressed experiences from relations with people in the past can be neutralised and released in relief rather than in suffering, which can lead to understanding, forgiveness and a reconciliation of the parties involved (step III).

The treatment method of the Coherence Therapy involves helping people burrow into deep emotional implicit memory and retrieve into direct experience the negative emotional learnings at the root of unwanted moods, behaviours and thoughts. Bruce Ecker and Laurel Hulley (1996) link this method to the neuropsychological study on memory reconsolidation—a naturally occurring phenomenon through which emotional memories can be 'dissolved and erased'.

The process of forgiveness is powerful and forms an inseparable part of crossing another threshold in one's quest to becoming a more self-constituting individual (Luskin, 2007).

According to the concepts discussed above, all mental processes are accompanied by parallel biochemical and electromagnetic processes in the body. Consequently, a restructuring of logic gates is indeed believed to be viable, albeit challenging. Heart lipid rafts are made up of the most basic phospholipids, which means that the information is stored in binary form. For this processes to take place, fatty acid supplementation is recommended, as fatty acids are essential food for our bodies and minds.

We need to resort to new therapeutic strategies to reveal and release the imprinted information that has long restricted the individual. It can happen, for example, under gentle psychotherapeutic guidance during sessions with physiological substances that temporarily facilitate access to this 'black box', with a view to reconfiguring or reconstructing information. There is some evidence that certain substances (e.g. psilocybin, psychedelic substances) may be beneficial to individuals by making the brain, the mind and the body more malleable (Griffiths, 2018).

It is possible to reach the forgotten, 'rigidly' imprinted data together with the functioning schemas based on these if connections among these data (i.e. events, feelings, interpretations, behaviour guidelines in so-called nondeclarative memory) are loosened up. Dispersion characteristic of psychedelic states helps retrieve the desired information on the condition that proper guidance is provided by a therapist in the process. Researchers explain this state by citing heightened entropy in some aspects of the brain's operations or states, which makes it easier to access dispersed data. In such conditions, memories and emotions associated with these are 'unbound' and declassified, becoming accessible to people. By suppressing entropy, people have their everyday consciousness in the conscious states of mind, but this consciousness is of limited quality. The repression of entropy is also said to be associated with metacognitive functions, therein with the testing of reality and with self-awareness (Carhart-Harris et al., 2014).

Research on the therapeutic use of hallucinogenic drugs, therein in depression and anxiety therapies, is becoming increasingly widespread. Therapeutic effectiveness is predicated on competently conducted psychotherapy before, during and after pharmacological interventions. Clinical studies are being carried out in this respect, which is all the more urgent as psychopharmacology has not updated treatment methods for psychiatric patients for quite a while now. Research results are very promising even in healthy individuals. The major question now is whether we are ready for a new paradigm of mental health therapy. I believe that this deserves serious consideration. As shown by studies on MDMA (a classic psychedelic agent known as molly), the drug supports the feeling of security and empathy, for example in PTSD patients. MDMA-supported therapy also reduces symptoms of social anxiety, and patients have reported that the feeling of security helps them reproduce and beneficially work through their traumas (Mithoefer et al., 2018; Danforth et. al., 2018; Johnson, 2019).

Recent placebo-controlled trials in psychologically distressed cancer patients have shown that psilocybin causes a decrease in anxiety and depression and an increase in the quality of life. This state persists for at least a month and possibly six months or more (Griffiths et al., 2016; Grob et al., 2011; Ross et al., 2016).

Reconstruction entails reordering and restructuring the primary data in the appropriate way for a given person. Grown-up and self-aware individuals rank past memories differently and are capable of unburdening themselves of responsibility for some early childhood events, of guilty feelings and of stigmas.

It is becoming increasingly obvious that mental therapy supported by proper diets or/and new neurochemical treatment may help one become the champion of one's own life.

Reorganisation: how the mind organises behaviour change

The second stage or the reorganisation of the schemas of thinking and feeling is a complex step in people's current lives. Events and experiences are analysed and worked through 'here and now'. Everything occurs in the system in which the individual lives, learns and works. Essentially, the feelings and emotions one experiences are the first reliable and genuine source of information, even before the cognitive and evaluative process is initiated.

This stage of building or recovering the sense of belonging consists in changing previous patterns and schemes of reacting as a prelude to self-development. This venture requires exceptional self-discipline and motivation for implementing new rules and continuing to be mindful, without ever losing sight of one's 'path'. This is of key importance, because people who have developed a set of their own 'survival strategies', as a rule, very easily fall back onto old habits and schemas, which thwarts further development.

The individual's task is to replace the old schema of acting, feeling and thinking with a new model. To simplify, in reality, it is often an inverted pattern in which the person practises mindfulness, self-appreciation, self-gratitude and self-care, instead of self-evaluation, self-blame and focus on risks. Seeing to their own needs and their expression, individuals give themselves a leeway to activate emotions, feel compassion and be receptive to new experiences with new people while respecting their own and others' limits. Examples of previous schemas are: 'men/women cause problems', 'one must work whether one likes one's job or not', 'I cannot trust others', 'I cannot rely on my colleagues', 'time flies', 'one must meet others' expectations', 'successexpectations', 'success is long in the making' 'I am lonely and left to fend off for myself', etc. They can be replaced with people's own choices in which they resolve, for example, that they are not constrained by time, that they decide about their relationships on their own, and that it is up to them whether or not they feel grateful. People make their own decisions and accept that whatever happens in their lives happens at the right moment, that they determine what their lives are like, that life can be/is easy and joyful, that an individual is part of a whole that approves of him/her. Besides, by designing their lives, they consciously control their attention, choose opulence above restrictions, give up on relationships which have been/are destructive and decide that they can learn easily. They use their own creative potential and the potential of their brains to transgress the previous limits of thinking. In this way, they create their reality anew.

The process of coming to experience oneself in an entirely new fashion is exceptionally difficult, especially if the same entrenched patterns have been repeatedly mobilised over years. This demands alertness to and mindfulness of signals from one's own body, feelings, emotions and all other beacons from inside.

The new ways of experience are not straightforward and can be unclear at the beginning of the process. The person learns these as they emerge, concomitantly and consistently with discovering the truth about him/herself, his/her sensations and needs

Some strategies employed in the second phase resemble mindfulness training (Kabat-Zin) with elements of compassion, i.e. mindful compassion (Gilbert, 2010; Gilbert and Choden, 2014). The British researcher Paul Gilbert (2010) recommends Compassion-Focused Therapy to develop skills of coping with everyday stressful situations, trauma and depression. In this way, the mind undergoes remodelling.

This process is incessantly reenacted at the neurochemical and psychophysical levels. All changes in feelings, thoughts and spoken words are associated with changes in the electromagnetic potential transmitted by the red blood cells. In fact, the healing process is permanent and affects people's current feelings and thoughts.The red blood cells use cell membrane phospholipids to detect the new information (informions) and transport it constantly to both the heart and the brain memory and back.

Self-awareness and readiness for thriving

The third stage is devoted to self-flourishing, that is, self-development. It consists in building oneself anew upon the foundation of what has been achieved in the two previous phases. The outcomes of processes unfolding at this stage are supposed to change the person's quality of life into what the person has self-consciously envisaged and designed.

This is the stage in which people embark on designing their own lives in conformity with their self-aware will. People's free choices in life have the power to modify or alter the resources of the mind. As the second phase of changes involves reorganisation, that is, the liberation of the mind from pogrammes and constraining schemas, the third phase entails replacing them with people's own choices made at their highest potential or with unrestricted access to their full resources and without the sense of deficit or limitation.

Emphatically, the processes that occur in these three phases overlap and, rather than terminating, spirally trigger new sequences. They extend over long periods in people's lives, if not throughout their lives. Once commenced, they offer a chance of living a meaningful and more satisfying life. If awareness is involved, these processes become more and more inclusive, corresponding to the individual's growing consciousness and progressing development. The subsequent processes of reconstruction, reorganisation and growth are mobilised and repeated time and again.

The third stage entails self-building in regard to the sense of belonging to a system or self-belonging. Depending on the person's age, maturity and readiness, this phase can be more focused either on belonging to an external system or on belonging to oneself. At this stage, the person's cognitive and creative capacities are restored, and s/he again derives pleasure and joy from his/her rediscovered roles—those of child, woman, man, mother, father, wife, husband or partner, whereby these roles intersect and are closely interconnected. How each of these roles is performed depends on the person's new formulation of his/her needs and expectations towards him/herself, the world and other people. This is a phase in which one builds overall self-trust and trust in one's life, based on one's self-trust constructed in the dimensions of man/woman, child/mother, lover/lover, etc.

Self-formation in a given role which is symbolic and archetypal brings comfort and relief. The notion of the archetype is deliberately evoked here, as it engenders the feeling that we are a fractal element of a whole and that, as such, we carry unconscious collective and individual experiences that are simply discovered at this stage. As a pathfinder, we possess the 'potential of all pathfinders'. As a woman, we can realise the potential of all women. Unconscious properties are made conscious, which affects the ways in which people function.

The proposal above builds, among others, on the collective consciousness, which all people fall back on. In this way, they can learn foreign languages or know how to be the mother of a newborn baby. In the same fashion, they can use the available information resources, such as information about generational trauma, and make choices that open up new possibilities, rather than shutting these down. In fact, limiting behaviour is caused by emotion, thought or unrecognised programmes founded on them.

The entrenchment of such changes in the body is not only supported mainly by the brain (CPU processor), which solves problems and is creative, but also and first and foremost by the mind and the parts of the body in which the information is coded/imprinted. The heart, the blood and all of the cells of our bodies are composed of chemical compounds that make the memetic recording possible. Allylic double bonds which are found in fatty acids formed throughout evolutionary selection are fully adapted to registering the temporal-structural cyclicity of all developments that take place in and affect biological life on the Earth, starting from the genesis of RNA, DNA, proteins, lipids and hydrocarbons, and ending with their combining into living systems, such as we are. It is cell membrane fatty acids in all human bodies that have the capacity to capture information concerning time, space and experiences within them.

Personal and social harmony

This concept chiefly differs from other psychological frameworks and therapeutic ideas, because its central axis lies in individual and collective resources and the analytical source used by the individual changes. Individuals first discern themselves and their environment as supportive to them in this journey. Then, they rely on connecting to beneficial personal resources which they have themselves accumulated or have gained as descendants of a family and members of a community. The knowledge and belief that one is part of a bigger whole in time-space—a component of the universe in the physical sense and an element of humanity in the temporal dimension—are key factors. Each and every one of us bears what is called memetic memory, a concept discussed in this book. Ancestors transmit their experiences to the following generations through memetic memory. The more they achieve, the better memetic information they hand down to their successors, such as easy and quick solutions and pleasures derived from experiencing life, rather than traumas and conflicts. The way one is guided by one's own needs and principles is the benchmark for accomplishing such a development. This is how self-belonging and autonomous, independent human functioning in respect of the self and others could be described.

Crucially, the process of self-building and developing self-belonging can take place only if the person perceives and wants changes in his/her life.

If this challenge is taken up with deep belief that change is possible and reality is ready for change, this change indeed happens. This often unfolds in meditation, visualisation or a combination of the two through which the need, desire and readiness for change are expressed. This readiness can also concern therapy in which unconscious processes become recognised, and thereby change is commenced. Carl Gustav Jung claimed that inner conviction was enough, whereby he meant inner consent to connect to the unconscious or a point where individuation begins (Jung, 2007). The path to this inner change of individuation is difficult to predict at particular stages. What is at stake here, however, is the understanding, general as it may be, of the processes of restoring or building the self and self-belonging.

Individuals who are mentally healthy and derive joy and satisfaction from life are aware that they themselves have chosen their life paths, or they trust that they are in a good position in this world. Crises that seem difficult and overwhelming can, in fact, serve as starting points of new paths if only these are used to promote people's mental development. According to Jung, this is a process in which unconscious components of the self become recognised, integrated with and included in life. Having new data and research findings at our disposal today, we know how this process works for individuals and how it is expressed in and through bodily signs. Relevant measurements can be carried out at various levels, starting from examining the composition and proportions of fatty acids and ending with observing cardiovascular variability, brain waves and/or ectodermal responses.

The sense of belonging entails self-experience through gratitude and feeling valued as an important person who is a recipient of care and compassion, as well as a fractal part of the total system. 'Fractal' is a particularly important notion, because the experience of being part of a system furnishes individuals with elements of this system so that they can subsequently function as self-reliant people. The fuller one's experience of gratitude, appreciation, care and compassion is, the more mature and self-contained one becomes both as a partner in relationships and as an individual who undergoes further professional and personal development.

Chapter 18

Conclusion

A brighter psychology for tomorrow

Academic textbooks and psychological literature have not taught us about Lamarck's theory. It was passed over because Darwin's theory claimed the chief position in explaining phenomena in psychology and related disciplines. This is why the contemporary *Homo sapiens* has difficulty imagining a world without hierarchies, divisions, rivalries and consumerism. However, the dissemination of social life and leadership based on natural selection breeds and is bound to continue to breed the sense of exclusion in people. Loneliness and the increasing incidence of mental disorders and degenerative diseases afflict the contemporary 'dying-out' *Homo sapiens* more commonly than ever before. We see numerous people opposing genetic programming, without even realising that they are being programmed memetically all the time. Nevertheless, two types of information—natural and cultural—contribute to phenotypic changes in people. Environmental informions have access to the genes and set the tone of gene expression (genomics) and evolution (genetics).

Medical and psychological knowledge about the human blood is far from perceiving transfusion as a form of 'the transfer of the mind'. Admittedly, there are insufficient research results in this respect yet, but for years there have been cases of patients changing their likes and preferences after transplantations or transfusions. I believe that the concepts laid out in this book will inspire further research.

The significance of phospholipids, which are, among others, the main component of the brain, the nervous system and all of the cell membranes, has been and still is the most ignored theme in research, and not just in the psychological field. For over two decades now, we have had reliable research findings at our disposal which show that cholesterol is the basis of, rather than a threat to, the correct functioning of the brain, the body and the mind. The point is to retain proper proportions of certain fatty acids, instead of avoiding them (De Meester, 2009; Wilczyńska, De Meester, Singh and Bargiel-Matusiewicz, 2010).

In the course of our journey together, we have learned that the sense of belonging and the sense of exclusion are the first strong experiences in human life and that they are experienced together with fundamental emotions, which affect further development through imprinting information in the lipid structures of the heart—the Boolean logic gates. So far, mental/psychic processes have predominantly been located in the human brain. Several scholars have even insisted that 'change begins in the brain'. In fact, information is collected in the body and in the brain. Therefore, the body is the space to be discovered. The processes which take place in the brain are an outcome of the maturing of certain structures that are only fully ready to reedit information in adult life. With the help of their brains, people can make cognitive efforts to modify the meaning of non-cognitive information. But what if information from the body does not reach the brain, for example, information related to the sense of security and affiliation? Inferably, the brain can find out what these are and how these work exclusively from the information obtained from the external world. It can also produce various speculations about these, which are beneficial or not to people. One can also try and reach these, but not necessarily through the brain. Usually, the brain and logical thinking do not lead to the source of the very primary emotions.

Erythrocytes (RBC) as vehicles of the mind or memes mutually teach each other and other parts of the body. The return to historical analyses will soon be real science, and ways of retrieving this information in people will hopefully result in improved effects of psychotherapy. However, other kinds of knowledge will also be indispensable, ranging from nutrigenetics/genomics[1] (diet/physical activity) to psychonomy (psychology/psychiatry) and the studies of phenotypes that depend on them.

Systems of emotional regulation are treated as life-saving systems, and they certainly served this function in the past. Today, however, we can view them differently as a superfluity or a vestige inherited from our ancestors—as automatic and intuitive information imprinted in the Boolean gates, which impede human creative functioning.

Still, identity can be created; however, not on the basis of what has been inscribed, but rather on the basis of what the human being will write/record about him/herself. That is why pointing at the mind in the nature/culture dispute is a groundbreaking hypothesis: 'Information—the mind—was first and will be last... *Homo sapiens*—"the poor of spirit"—is facing that reality as we speak. It is becoming a problem, environmentally and socially. Humility and fierce resolve or leadership are *Homo modestis* assets to keep climbing the Ladder' (De Meester, 2020, p. 9).

The human being of the future—*Homo Modestis*—can survive by means of cultural selection based on deep humanism, compassion, care and tenderness and by offering support to him/herself and the world. This liberates one from beliefs that wreck the sense of belonging. Cognitive development, acting and planning the future are possible owing to self-awareness and care when feeling that one belongs to the community that is humanity, our planet and the universe.

Separation versus community and development

As an advocate of pragmatic psychology of the future, I realise that psychonomy/psychology will soon be one of the most needed and fastest developing disciplines. Having access to a considerable amount of thought-provoking hypotheses and studies that provide new knowledge, we can discover the mind and the functions of the brain from an entirely different perspective and rely on these in designing new forms of therapy.

Exclusion means not only being rejected by others, but also being isolated from one's true self and then dissociating oneself from other people. The incompleteness and the inauthenticity of the self result in separation from one's own body, which is treated as a foreign object. Besides, the individual blocks away some difficult emotions which make his/her experience of life complete. As a consequence, s/he becomes isolated, separated and distanced from other people, an outcome propelled by his/her belief in his/her individuality, maladjustment or exceptionality. In this way, the individual functions as if s/he dangled in the void without any grounding, denying his/her relations with other creatures and feeling above or beneath others. Such attempts at taking control of 'his/her own life' paradoxically sever him/her from this life.

The loss of contact with the world as a whole, in its global human dimension, has occurred through the process of desensitisation. People are overstimulated, tense and cut off from themselves, from each other and from the place they inhabit. They are lonely and atomised, and they themselves sustain the illusion of being separated from others by self-excluding or excluding others.

Working with the imagination, which helps people find their bearings in the shared world again, is an important aspect of support. Openness to experiences coming from the body and the focus on developing an awareness of the body and the senses have so far proven an effective way of retrieving information inscribed in the body. Although currently available therapies cannot yet read the code of this record, clients often find the effects of such psychotherapy satisfying.

Workshops and group meetings serve to reproduce once-natural modes of group living, where the members obtained support and experienced mutuality. Women's groups, men's circles and involvement in support groups for men and women which reinstate communal life and reciprocal support are observably becoming increasingly popular.

Such practices can also be individually undertaken as part of self-development. This involves learning mindful feeling, listening and examining the signals from one's own body and from the outside, as well as opening up to the sensations of both pleasure and discomfort. This entails permitting oneself to experience reality the way it is, within sight and 'within hand's reach' or 'here and now'. Difficult emotions and experiences associated with them, which foster recurrent thought schemas, can be released when they are perceived, discovered, recognised, released and replaced. Attempts to avoid suffering cause even greater suffering. The recognition and the reinforcement of a person's sensitivity to him/herself and to the world around kindle a wish to belong and then the sense of belonging and free development.

Furnished with new ideas, we can now stand up to scholarly and personal challenges to study and more accurately describe the interconnections among the body, the mind and the brain. Another challenge for us is to develop carefully designed support programmes for each of these separately and study their interplays for the benefit of humanity.

Notes

1. As written previously, a diet rich in fatty acids is especially important for people's health and prevention of the further development of degenerative diseases.

References

Abu-Hassan, K., Taylor, J. D., Donati, E., Bortolotto, Z. A., Indiveri, G., Paton, J., Nogaret, A. (2019). Optimal solid state neurons. *Nature Communications, 10*(5309), 1–13.

Adams, K., Galanes, G. J. (2006). *Communicating in Groups: Applications and Skills*. New York: McGraw-Hill.

Ahmed, A. (2017). A new era of TV watching behavior: Binge-watching, depression and loneliness. Is there a relationship? *Media Watch, 8*(2), 192–207.

Aghakhani, H., Main, K. J. (2019). Can two negatives make a positive? Social exclusion prevents carryover effects from deceptive advertising. *Journal of Retailing and Consumer Services, 47*, 206–214.

Ainsworth, M., Blehar, M., Waters, M., Wall, S. (1978). *Patterns of Attachment: A Psychological Study of the Strange Situation*. Hillsdale, NJ: Erlbaum.

Aldridge, R. W., Story, A., Hwang, S., Nordentoft, M., Luchenski, S., Hartwell, G., Tweed, E., Lewer, D., Katikireddi, S. V., Hayward, A. (2018). Morbidity and mortality in homeless individuals, prisoners, sex workers, and individuals with substance use disorders in high-income countries: A systematic review and meta-analysis. *The Lancet, 391*, 241–250.

Allen, M. T., Crowell, M. D. (1989). Patterns of autonomic response during laboratory stressors. *Psychophysiology, 26*, 603–614.

Amos, M. P., McCaskill, J., Rasmussen, S. (2011). Biological and chemical information technologies. *Procedia Computer Science, 7*, 56–60.

Angelopoulou, G., Meier, E. L., Kasselimis, D., Pan, Y., Tsolakopoulos, D., Velonakis, G., Karavasilis, E., Kelekis, N. L., Goutsos, D., Potagas, C., Kiran, S. (2020). Investigating gray and white matter structural substrates of sex differences in the narrative abilities of healthy adults. *Frontiers in Neuroscience, 13*, 1424.

Annalect Primary Research & Insights Group. (2014). Tune in: The impact of binge-viewing. Retrieved from https://www.annalect.com/impact-binge-viewing/, accessed 28 September 2018.

Ansbacher, H. L., Ansbacher, R. R. (Eds.). (1956). *The Individual Psychology of Alfred Adler*. New York: Basic Books, Inc.

Argyle, M. (1987). *The Psychology of Happiness*. London: Methuen.

Aronson, E., Wilson, T. D., Akert, R. M. (1997). *Psychologia społeczna, serce i umysł*. Poznań: Zysk i S-ka.

Barker, R., Dembo, T., Lewin, K. (1941). Frustration and regression: An experiment with young children. *University of Iowa Studies: Child Welfare*, *18*(1), xv+314.

Barnard, L. K., Curry, J. F. (2011). Self-compassion: Conceptualiazations, correlates and interventions. *Review of General Psychology*, *15*(4), 289–303.

Barsalou, L. W. (1999). Perceptual symbol systems. *Behavioral and Brain Sciences*, *22*, 577–609.

Bartholomew, K. (1990). Avoidance of intimacy: An attachment perspective. *Journal of Social and Personal Relationships*, *7*, 147–178.

Baum, R. (2013). Transgenerational trauma and repetition in the body: The groove of the wound. *Body Movement and Dance in Psychotherapy*, *8*(1), 34–42.

Baumeister, R. F. (1991). *Escaping the Self: Alcoholism, Spirituality, Masochism, and Other Flights from the Burden of Selfhood*. New York: Basic Books.

Baumeister, R. F. (2005). *The Cultural Animal: Human Nature, Meaning, and Social Life*. Oxford University Press, 464 pages.

Baumeister, R. F., Brewer, L. E., Tice, D. M., Twenge, J. M. (2007). The need to belong: Understanding the interpersonal and inner effects of social exclusion. *Social and Personality Psychology Compass*, *1*, 506–520.

Baumeister, R. F., DeWall, C. N., Ciarocco, N. J., Twenge, J. M. (2005). Social exclusion impairs self-regulation. *Journal of Personality and Social Psychology*, *88*, 589–604.

Baumeister, R. F., Leary, M. R. (1995). The need to belong: Desire for interpersonal attachments as a fundamental human motivation. *Psychological Bulletin*, *117*, 497–529.

Baumeister, R. F., Twenge, J. M., Nuss, C. K. (2002). Effects of social exclusion on cognitive processes: Anticipated aloneness reduces intelligent thought. *Journal of Personality and Social Psychology*, *83*, 817–827.

Becker, H. S. (1963). *Outsiders: Studies in the Sociology of Deviance*. New York: The Free Press.

Becker, R. O., Selden, G., Guarnaschelli, M. D. (1998). *The Body Electric: Electromagnetism and the Foundation of Life*. New York: William Morrow Paperback.

Benenson, J. F., Markovits, H., Thompson, M. E., Wrangham, R. (2011). Under threat of social exclusion, females exclude more than males. *Psychological Science*, *22*(4), 538–544.

Bentler, P. M. (1990). Comparative fit indices in structural models. *Psychological Bulletin*, *2*, 238–246.

Berkowitz, L. (1989). Frustration-aggression hypothesis: Examination and reformulation. *Psychological Bulletin*, *106*(1), 59–73.

Berkowitz, L. (1993). Pain and aggression: Some findings and implications. *Motivation and Emotion*, *17*, 277–293.

Bernardi, L., Sleight, P., Bandinelli, G., Cencetti, S., Fattorini, L., Wdowczyc-Szulc, J., Lagi, A. (2001). Effect of rosary prayer and yoga mantras on autonomic cardiovascular rhythms: Comparative study. *British Medical Journal*, *323*(7327), 1446–1449.

Bonanno, G. A. (2004). Loss, trauma, and human resilience: Have we underestimated the human capacity to thrive after extremely aversive events? *American Psychologist*, *59*, 20–28.

Bonanno, G. A., Mancini, A. D. (2008). The human capacity to thrive in the face of potential trauma. *Pediatrics*, *121*, 369–375.

Bosquet Enlow, M., Egeland, B., Blood, E. A., Wright, R. O., Wright, R. J. (2012). Interpersonal trauma exposure and cognitive development in children to age 8 years: A longitudinal study. *Journal of Epidemiology and Community Health*, *66*(11), 1005–1010.

Bowbly, J. (1969). *Attachment and Loss. Vol. 1: Attachment.* New York: Basic Books.

Braden, G. (2017). *Human by Design.* New York: Hay House Inc.

Brooks, S. K., Webster, R. K., Smith, L. E., Woodland, L., Wessely, S., Greenberg, N., Rubin, G. J. (2020). The psychological impact of quarantine and how to reduce it: Rapid review of the evidence. *Lancet*, *395*, 912–920. https://doi.org/10.1016/S0140-6736(20)30460-8.

Brown, R., Pehrson, S. (2019). *Group Processes: Dynamics within and Between Groups, Third Edition.* New York: John Wiley & Sons.

Brown, K. W., Ryan, R. M. (2003). The benefits of being present: Mindfulness and its role in psychological well-being. *Journal of Personality and Social Psychology*, *84*(4), 822–848.

Browne, M. W., Cudeck, R. (1993). Alternative ways of assessing model fit. In: *Testing Structural Equation Models,* Bollen, K. A., Long, J. S. (Eds.). Newbury Park, CA: Sage, 136–162.

Buckley, K., Winkel, R., Leary, M. R. (2004). Reactions to acceptance and rejection: Effects of level and sequence of relational evaluation. *Journal of Experimental Social Psychology*, *40*, 14–28.

Byrne, R. W., Russon, A. E. (1998). Learning by imitation: A hierarchical approach. *Behavioral and Brain Science. 21*(5), 667–684.

Cacioppo, J. T., Hawkley, L. C., Berntson, G. G. (2003). The anatomy of loneliness. *Current Directions in Psychological Science*, *12*, 71–74.

Cacioppo, J. T., Hawkley, L. C., Ernst, J. M., Burleson, M., Berntson, G. G., Nouriani, B., Spiegel, D. (2006). Loneliness within a nomological net: An evolutionary perspective. *Journal of Research in Personality*, *40*(6), 1054–1085.

Cacioppo, J. T., Patrick, W. (2009). *Loneliness: Human Nature and the Need for Social Connection.* New York: W.W. Norton & Company, Inc.

Calamassi, D., Pomponi, G. P. (2019). Music tuned to 440 Hz versus 432 Hz and the health effects: A double-blind cross-over pilot study. *Explore (NY)*, *15*(4), 283–290.

Cannon, W. B. (1970). *Bodily Changes in Pain, Hunger, Fear and Rage.* Boston: Appleton Century.

Carey, N. (2012). *The Epigenetics Revolution: How Modern Biology is Rewriting Our Understanding of Genetics, Disease and Inheritance.* London: Icon Books Ltd.

Carhart-Harris, R., Leech, R., Hellyer, P., Shanahan, M., Feilding, F., Tagliazucchi, E., Chialvo, R., Nutt, D. (2014). The entropic brain: A theory of conscious states informed by neuroimaging research with psychedelic drugs. *Frontiers in Human Neuroscience*, *8*(1), 1–22.

Carmichael, M. (2009). Who says stress is bad for you? *Newsweek*, *153*(8), 14.

Carroll, D., Turner, J. R., Hellawell, J. C. (1986). Heart rate and oxygen consumption during active psychological challenge: The level of difficulty. *Psychophysiology*, *23*, 174–181.

Cassidy, J., Parke, R. D., Butskovsky, L., Braungart, J. M. (1992). Family-peer connections: The roles of emotional expressiveness within the family and children's understanding of emotions. *Child Development*, *63*, 603–618.

Cherepanov, E. (2015). Psychodrama of the survivorship. *The Journal of Psychodrama, Sociometry, and Group Psychotherapy*, *63*(1), 19–31.

Chudzicka-Czupała, A., Grabowski, D., Wilczyńska. A. (2017). Mobbing and discrimination in companies: The importance of prevention. *Polish Journal of Applied Psychology*, *15*(1), 79–92.

Chomsky, N. (2000). *New Horizons in the Study of Language and Mind*. Cambridge: Cambridge University Press.

Chomsky, N. (2002). The faculty of language: What is it, who has it, and how did it evolve? *Science*, *22*(298), 1569–1579.

Cierpiałkowska, L., Sęk, H. (Eds.). (2011). *Psychologia kliniczna*. Warszawa: PWN.

Cohen, J. (1977). *Statistical Power Analysis for the Behavioral Sciences*. New York: Academic Press.

Cochran, M., Bo I. (1989). The social network, family involvement, and pro- and antisocial behavior of adolescent males in Norway. *Journal of Youth and Adolescence*, *18*, 377–398.

Coie, J. D., Dodge, K. A., Kupersmidt, J. B. (1990). Peer group behavior and social status. In: Asher, S. R., Coie, J. D. (Eds.), Cambridge studies in social and emotional development. Peer rejection in childhood (p. 17–59). Cambridge University Press.

Cohen, D. B. (2006) "Family constellations": An innovative systemic phenomenological group process from Germany. *The Family Journal*, *14*(3), 226–233.

Compas, B., Connor-Smith, J. K., Saltzman, H., Harding Thomsen, A., Wadsworth, M. E. (2001). Coping with stress during childhood and adolescence: Problems, progress, and potential in theory and research. *Psychological Bulletin*, *127*, 87–127.

Compas, B. E., Malcarne, V. L., Fondacaro, K. M. (1998). Coping with stressful events in older children and young adolescents. *Journal of Consulting and Clinical Psychology*, *56*(3), 405–411.

Connor-Smith, J. K., Compas, B. E., Wadsworth, M. E., Thomsen, A. H., Saltzman, H. (2000). Responses to stress in adolescence: Measurement of coping and involuntary stress responses. *Journal of Consulting and Clinical Psychology*, *68*(6), 976–992.

Corey, M. S., Corey, G., Corey, C. (2014). *Groups Process and Practice Group Dynamics*. Belmont, CA: Brooks/Cole.

Corr, P. J. (2005). Social exclusion and the hierarchical defense system: A comment on McDonald and Leary. *Psychological Bulletin*, *131*, 231–236.

Coughlin Della Selva, P. (2004). *Intensive Short Therm Dynamic Psychoterapy: Theory and Technique*. New York: Wiley.

Courtin, E., Knapp, M. (2017). Social isolation, loneliness and health in old age: A scoping review. *Health & Social Care in the Community*, *25*, 799–812.

Courtois, C. A., Ford, J. D. (Eds.). (2009). *Treating Complex Traumatic Stress Disorders: An Evidence-Based Guide*. New York: Guilford Press.

Coyne, J. C., Rohrbaugh, M. J., Shoham, V., Sonnega, J. S., Nicklas, J. M., Cranford, J. A. (2001). Prognostic importance of marital quality for survival of congestive heart failure. *The American Journal of Cardiology*, *88*(5), 526–529.

Crawford, M. A., Bazinet, R. P., Sinclair, A. J. (2009). Fat intake and CNS functioning: Ageing and disease. *Annals of Nutrition and Metabolism*, *55*, 202–228.

D'Andrea, A. (2010). *Czas oczekiwania. Jak przeżywają oczekiwanie na adopcję: dziecko, para małżeńska, profesjonaliści?* Poznań: Wyższa Szkoła Pedagogiki i Adminstracji w Poznaniu.

Dalai Lama (1995). *The World of Tibetan Buddhism*, Jinpa, G. T. (Ed.) Somerville, MA: Wisdom Publications.

Danieli, Y., Norris, F. H., Engdahl, B. (2016). Multigenerational legacies of trauma: Modeling the what and how of transmission. *American Journal of Orthopsychiatry*, *86*(6), 639–651.

Danieli, Y., Norris, F. H., Engdahl, B. (2017). A question of who, not if: Psychological disorders in Holocaust survivors' children. *Psychological Trauma: Theory, Research, Practice, and Policy*, *9*(Suppl 1), 98–106.

De Bellis, M. D., Keshavan, M. S., Clark, D. B., Casey, B. J., Gieddd, J. N., Boring, A. M., Frustaci, K., Ryan, N. D. (1999). Developmental traumatology. Part II: Brain development. *Biological Psychiatry*, *45*(10), 1271–1284.

Deci, E. L., Ryan, R. M. (1991). A motivational approach to self: Integration in personality. *Nebraska Symposium on Motivation: Perspectives to Motivation.* Lincoln, NE: University of Nebraska Press, 38, 237–288.

De Couck, M., Caers, R., Musch, L., Fliegauf, J., Giangreco, A., Gidron, Y. (2019). How breathing can help you make better decisions: Two studies on the effects of breathing patterns on heart rate variability and decision-making in business cases. *International Journal of Psychophysiology*, *139*, 1–9.

DeJong, H., Fox, E. (2019). Does rumination mediate the relationship between attentional control and symptoms of depression? *Journal of Behavior Therapy Experimental Psychiatry*, *63*, 28–35.

DeLongis, A., Folkman, S., Lazarus, R. S. (1988). The impact of daily stress on health and mood: Psychological and social resources as mediators. *Journal of Personality and Social Psychology*, *54*, 486–496.

De Meester, F. (2018a). From body (Columbus) to mind (Tsimtsoum) concept. *Psychologia w Praktyce*, 7. https://psychologiawpraktyce.pl/artykul/identyfikowanie-i-lokalizowanie-umyslu.

De Meester, F. (2018b). Psychology in practice. *Annals of Psychiatry and Mental Health*, *6*(3), 1135. https://www.jscimedcentral.com/Psychiatry/psychiatry-6-1135.pdf.

De Meester, F. (2019). Tomorrow's medicine: Psychology from a quantum physics perspective. *Psychologia w Praktyce, 13*. https://psychologiawpraktyce.pl/artykul/medycyna-jutra; *International Journal of Psychiatry Research* (2019), 2(7), 1–5. http://scivisionpub.com/pdfs/psychology-from-a-quantum-physics-perspective-tomorrows-medicine-1017.pdf; *Annals of Psychiatry and Mental Health* (2020), *8*(1), 1143. https://www.jscimedcentral.com/Psychiatry/psychiatry-8-1143.pdf, https://www.jscimedcentral.com/Psychiatry/vol8issue1.php.

De Meester, F. (2020). The mind is a transient mathematical matrix imprint at cell membrane fatty acids level. *Psychologia w Praktyce*, *19*, 8–19. https://psychologiawpraktyce.pl/artykul/umysl-jako-przejsciowa-matryca-matematyczna-wdrukowana-na-poziomie-kwasow-tluszczowych-blony-komorkowej; *Annals of Psychiatry and Mental Health* (2020), *8*(1), 1144. https://www.jscimedcentral.com/Psychiatry/psychiatry-8-1144.pdf.

De Meester, F. (2009). Progress in lipid nutrition: The Columbus concept addressing chronic diseases. In: *A Balanced Omega-6/Omega-3 Fatty Acid Ratio, Cholesterol and Coronary Heart Disease*, Simopoulos, A. P., De Meester, F. (Eds.). Basel: Karger, 100, 110–121.

De Meester, F. (2013). From Columbus to TsimTsoum concepts: A Kyoto-type approach. In: *Omega-6/3 Fatty Acids: Functions, Sustainable Strategies and Perspectives*, De Meester, F., Watson, R. R., Zibadi, S. (Eds.). New York: Humana Press, Springer Science & Business Media, 397–416.

De Meester, F., Wilczyńska, A., Singh, R. B., Wilson, D. W., Pella, D., Fedacko, J., Siegelova, J., Fiser, B., Galli, C., Cornelissen, G., Halberg, F. (2011). The chronomics trial: Report of a 3-month pilot study. In: *Non-Invasive Methods in Cardiology 2011: Symposium Proceedings*, Halberg, F., Kenner, T., Siegelová, J. (Eds.). Brno: Masaryk University, Faculty of Medicine, 141–161.

De Meester, F., Wilczyńska, A., Singh, R. B., Wilson, D. W. (2011). Why the TsimTsoum concept is essential to human health? In: *Nutraceutics, Biomedical Remedies and Physiotherapeutic Methods for Prevention of Civilization-Related Diseases*, Podbielska, H., Trziszka, T. (Eds.). *Biomedical Engineering Acta*, *4*, 41–42.

Dennett, D. (2016). *Od bakterii do Bacha. O ewolucji umysłów*. Kraków: Copernicus Center Press.

DePaulo, B. M. (2007). *Singled Out: How Singles Are Stereotyped, Stigmatized, and Ignored, and Still Live Happily Ever After*. New York: St Martin's Griffin.

Depue, R. A., Morrone-Strupinsky, J. V. (2005). A neurobehavioral model of affiliative bonding: Implications for conceptualizing a human trait of affiliation. *The Behavioral and Brain Sciences*, *28*(3), 313–350, discussion: 371–395.

DeWall, C. N., Anderson, C. A., Bushman, B. J. (2011). The general aggression model: Theoretical extensions to violence. *Psychology of Violence*, *1*(3), 245–258.

DeWall, C. N., Baumeister, R. F. (2006). Alone but feeling no pain: Effects of social exclusion on physical pain tolerance and pain threshold, affective forecasting, and interpersonal empathy. *Journal of Personality and Social Psychology*, *91*, 1–15.

Dixon, H. C., Overall, N. C. (2016). Regulating fears of rejection: Dispositional mindfulness attenuates the links between daily conflict, rejection fears, and destructive relationship behaviors. *Journal of Social and Personal Relationships*, *35*(2), 159–179.

Drozdowski, L., Weigl, B. (Eds.). (2011). *Rodzinne domy dziecka – opieka, wychowanie, terapia*. Warszawa: Fundacja ORLEN-Dar Serca.

Dubey, P., Kumar, Y., Singh, R., Jha, K., Kumar, R. (2019). Effect of music of specific frequency upon the sleep architecture and electroencephalographic pattern of individuals with delayed sleep latency: A daytime nap study. *Journal of Family Medicine and Primary Care*, *8*(12), 3915–3919.

Dudek, D., Grabski, B., Siwek, M. (2003). Trening Pozytywnych Doznań: nowa propozycja terapeutyczna w kompleksowym leczeniu depresji. *Psychoterapia*, *4*, 47–57.

Dzwonkowska, I. (2013). Współczucie wobec samego siebie a inne wymiary osobowości oraz emocjonalne funkcjonowanie ludzi. *Czasopismo Psychologiczne*, *19*(2), 303–313.

Dzwonkowska, I., Lachowicz-Tabaczek, K., Łaguna, M. (2008). *Samoocena i jej pomiar. Polska adaptacja skali SES M. Rosenberga. Podręcznik*. Warszawa: Pracownia Testów Psychologicznych.

Eccles, J. C. (1992). *Evolution du cerveau et création de la conscience*. Paris: Fayard.

Eck, J., Schoel, C., Greifeneder, R. (2017). Belonging to a Majority Reduces the Immediate Need Threat from Ostracism in Individuals with a High Need to Belong. *European Journal of Social Psychology*, *47*, 273–288.

Eck, J., Schoel, Ch., Greifeneder, R. (2016). Coping with or buffering against the negative impact of social exclusion on basic needs: A review of strategies. In: Riva, P., Eck, J. (Eds.): *Social exclusion: Psychological approaches to understanding and reducing its impact*. 2016. Springer.

Ecker, B., Hulley, L. (1996). *Depth Oriented Brief Therapy: How to Be Brief When You Were Trained to Be Deep and Vice Versa*. San Francisco, CA: Jossey-Bass.

Edmunds, S., Brown, G. (2010). Effective small group learning: AMEE Guide No. 48. *Medical Teacher*, *32*(9), 715–726.

Eisenberger, N. I., Liebermann, M. D., Williams, K. D. (2003). Does rejection hurt? An fMRI study of social exclusion. *Science*, *302*(5643), 290–292.

Ekman, P., Cordaro, D. (2011). What is meant by calling emotions basic. *Emotion Review*, *3*, 364–370.

Emler, N., Reicher, S. (1995). *Social Psychology and Society. Adolescence and Delinquency: The Collective Management of Reputation*. Blackwell Publishing.

Emoto, M. (2005). *The Hidden Messages of Water*. New York: Simon and Shuster. 67–83.

Estévez, E., Emler, N. P., Cava, M. J., Inglés, C. J. (2014). Psychosocial adjustment in aggressive popular and aggressive rejected adolescents at school. *Psychosocial Intervention*, *23*(1), 57–67. https://doi.org/10.5093/in2014a6.

Eysenck, H. J., Eysenck, S. (1975). *Manual of the Eysenck Personality Questionnaire*. San Diego, CA: EdITS.

Feliksiak, M., Omyła-Rudzka, M. (2018). *Depresja w doświadczeniach i opiniach. Komunikat z badań, Centrum Badania Opinii Społecznej*. Warszawa: Centrum Badania Opinii Społecznej.

Felnhofer, A., Kafka J. X., Hlavacs, H., Beutl, L., Kryspin-Exner, I., Kothgassner, O. D. (2018). Meeting others virtually in a day-to-day setting: Investigating social avoidance and prosocial behavior towards avatars and agents. *Computers in Human Behavior*, *80*, 399–406.

Ferris, L. J., Jetten, J., Hornsey, M. J., Bastian, B. (2019). Feeling hurt: Revisiting the relationship between social and physical pain. *Review of General Psychology*, *23*(3), 320–335.

Frith, Ch. (2011). *Od mózgu do umysłu. Jak powstaje nasz wewnętrzny świat*. (A. Binder, M. Binder, Trans.). Warszawa: Wydawnictwa Uniwersytetu Warszawskiego.

Flayelle, M., Maurage, P., Vögele, C., Karila, L., Billieux, J. (2019). Time for a plot twist: Beyond confirmatory approaches to binge-watching research. *Psychology of Popular Media Culture*, *8*, 308–318.

Folkman, S., Moskowitz, J. T. (2004). Coping: Pitfalls and promise. *Annual Review of Psychology*, *55*, 745–774.

Fontani, G., Corradeshi, F., Felici, A., Alfatti, F., Migliorini, S., Lodi, L. (2005). Cognitive and physiological effects of Omega-3 polyunsaturated fatty acid supplementation in healthy subjects. *European Journal of Clinical Investigation, 35*, 691–699.

Frydenberg, E., Lewis, R. (1993). Boys play sport and girls turn to others: Age, gender and ethnicity as determinants of coping. *Journal of Adolescence, 16*, 252–266.

Frydenberg, E., Lewis, R. (1996). A replication study of the structure of the adolescent coping scale: Multiple forms and applications of a self-report inventory in a counselling and research context. *European Journal of Psychological Assessment, 12*(3), 224–235.

Frydenberg, E., Lewis, R. (2000). Coping with stresses and concerns during adolescence: A longitudinal study. *American Educational Research Journal, 37*(3), 727–745.

Frydenberg, E., Lewis, R. (2002). Adolescent wellbeing: building young people's resources. In: *Beyond Coping: Meeting Goals, Vision and Challenges*, Frydenberg, E. (Ed.). Oxford: Oxford University Press, 175–194.

Garbarino, J. (1992). *Children and Families in the Social Environment*. New York: Random House.

Garbarino, J. (1999). *Lost Boys: Why Our Sons Turn Violent and How We Can Save Them*. New York: Random House.

Gardner, W. L., Pickett, C. L., Brewer, M. B. (2000). Social exclusion and selective memory: How the need to belong influences memory for social events. *Personality and Social Psychology Bulletin, 26*, 486–496.

Gardner, W. L., Pickett, C. L., Jeffries, V., Knowles, M. (2005). On the outside looking in: Loneliness and social monitoring. *Personality and Social Psychology Bulletin, 31*(11), 1549–1560.

Gerson, S. (2019). The enduring psychological legacies of genocidal trauma: Commentary on "The intergenerational transmission of Holocaust trauma: A psychoanalytic theory revisited". *The Psychoanalytic Quarterly, 88*(3), 501–511.

Gazzaniga, M. S. (2009). *Human: The Science Behind What Makes Us Unique (1st ed.)*. New York: Harper Perennial.

Gazzaniga, M. S. (2013). *Kto tu rządzi – ja czy mój mózg? Neuronauka a istnienie wolnej woli*. (A. Nowak, Trans.). Sopot: Smak Słowa, 220.

Gazzaniga, M. S., Ivry, R. B., Mangun, G. R. (2009). *Cognitive Neuroscience: The Biology of the Mind (3rd ed.)*. New York: W.W. Norton.

Germer, Ch. K. (2009). *The Mindful Path to Self-Compassion*. New York: The Guilford Press.

Gerritsen, R. J. S., Band, G. P. H. (2018). Breath of life: the respiratory vagal stimulation model of contemplative activity. *Frontiers in Human Neuroscience, 12*, 397.

Gesch, C. B., Hammond, S. M., Hampson, S. E., Eves, A., Crowder, M. J. (2002). Influence of supplementary vitamins, minerals and essential fatty acids on the antisocial behavior of young adult prisoners: Randomised, placebo-controlled trial. *British Journal of Psychiatry, 181*, 22–28.

Gilbert, P. (2005). Compassion and cruelty: A biopsychosocial approach. In: *Compassion: Conceptualisations, Research and Use in Psychotherapy*. Gilbert, P. (Ed.), London: Routledge, 9–74.

Gilbert, P. (2010). *The CBT Distinctive Features Series. Compassion Focused Therapy: Distinctive Features*. New York: Routledge/Taylor & Francis Group.

Gilbert, P. (2014). The origins and nature of compassion focused therapy. *British Journal of Clinical Psychology*, *53*, 6–41.

Gilbert, P., Choden. (2014). *Mindful Compassion: How the Science of Compassion Can Help You Understand Your Emotions, Live in the Present, and Connect Deeply with Others*. Oakland, CA: New Harbinger Publications.

Gilbert, P., McEwan, K., Matos, M., Rivis, A. (2011). Fears of compassion: Development of three self-report measures. *Psychology and Psychotherapy: Theory, Research and Practice*, *84*, 239–255.

Goetz, J., Keltner, D., Simon-Thomas, E. (2010). Compassion: An evolutionary analysis and empirical review. *Psychological Bulletin*, *136*, 351–374.

Goffman, E. (1986). *Stigma: Notes on the Management of Spoiled Identity*. New York, London and Toronto: Simon and Schuster Inc.

Golberstein, E., Wen, H., Miller, B. F. (2020). Coronavirus disease 2019 (COVID-19) and mental health for children and adolescents. *Journal of the American Medical Association Pediatrics*. Advance online publication. https://doi.org/10.1001/jamapediatrics.2020.1456.

Goleman, D. (2007). *Inteligencja emocjonalna*. (A. Janowski, Trans.). Poznań: Media rodzina.

Goossens, L., Lasgaard, M., Luyckx, K., Vanhalst, J., Mathias, S., Masy, E. (2009). Loneliness and solitude in adolescence: A confirmatory factor analysis of alternative models. *Personality and Individual Differences*, *47*(8), 890–894.

Gore, C., Figuereido, J. B. (2003). Wykluczenie społeczne i polityka przeciwdziałania ubóstwu. *Problemy Polityki Społecznej*, *5*, 18.

Goryńska, E. (2005). *Przymiotnikowa Skala Nastroju UMACL Geralda Matthewsa, A.Grahama Chamberlaina, Dylana M. Jonesa. Podręcznik*. Warszawa: Pracownia Testów Psychologicznych Polskiego Towarzystwa Psychologicznego.

Gould, S. J. (1991). *Niewczesny pogrzeb Darwina*. (N. Kancewicz-Hoffman, Trans.). Warszawa: PIW.

Górska, I. (2019). Mózg i tajemnice jego aktywności elektrycznej. Jak za pomocą treningu fal mózgowych rozwinąć jego ukryte zdolności? *Psychologia w Praktyce*, *5*(17).

Gray, J. A. (1982). *The Neuropsychology of Anxiety: An Enquiry into the Functions of the Septo-Hippocampal System*. Oxford: Oxford University Press.

Griffiths, R. R., Johnson, M. W., Richards, W. A., Richards, B. D., Jesse, R., MacLean, K. A., Barrett, F. S., Cosimano, M. P., Klinedinst, K. A. (2018). Psilocybin-occasioned mystical-type experience in combination with meditation and other spiritual practices produces enduring positive changes in psychological functioning and in trait measures of prosocial attitudes and behaviors. *Journal of Psychopharmacology*, *32*(1), 49–69.

Groarke, J., Berry, E., Wisener, L., McKenna-Plumley, P., McGlinchey, E., Armour, C. (2020, June 24). Loneliness in the UK during the COVID-19 pandemic: Cross-sectional results from the COVID-19 psychological wellbeing study. https://doi.org/10.31234/osf.io/j2pce.

Grosjean, D. (2011). *Recherche de l'étiologie en microkinésithérapie*. Pont-à-Mousson: Editions Maisonville.

Grosjean, D. (2020). Mikrokinezyterapia a psychoterapia. *Psychologia w praktyce*, *19*, 58–62.

Grosjean, D., Benini, P. (2002). Traité pratique de microkinésithérapie, Tome 2, Le système nerveux. Les muqueuses. 2e éd. rev, corr. et complétée. Pont-à-Mousson: C.F.M.

Guttmann-Steinmetz, S., Crowell, J. A. (2006). Attachment and externalizing disorders: A developmental psychopathology perspective. *Journal of the American Academy of Child and Adolescent Psychiatry*, *45*(4), 440–451.

Hagerty, B. M., Lynch-Sauer, J., Patusky, K. L., Bouwsema, M., Collier, P. (1992). Sense of belonging: A vital mental health concept. *Archives of Psychiatric Nursing*, *6*(3), 172–177.

Hagerty, B. M. K., Patusky, K. L. (1995). Developing a measure of sense of belonging. *Nursing Research*, *44*, 9–13.

Hagerty, B. M., Williams, R. A., Coyne, J. C., Early, M. R. (1996). Sense of belonging and indicators of social and psychological functioning. *Archives of Psychiatric Nursing*, *10*(4), 235–244.

Halberg, F., Cornélissen, G., Spector, N. H., Sonkowsky, R. P., Otsuka, K., Baciu, I., Hriscu, M., Schwartzkopff, O., Bakken, E. E. (2003). Stress/strain/life revisited: Quantification by blood pressure chronomics: benetensive, transtensive or maletensive chrono-vasculo-neuro-immuno-modulation. *Biomedicine & Pharmacotherapy*, *57*(1), 136–163.

Hańczak, M. (2017). *Zaakceptuj siebie. O sile samowspółczucia.* Warszawa: Wydawnictwo Samo Sedno, Warszawa.

Hedderman, E., O'Doherty, V., O'Connor, S. (2020). Mindfulness moments for clinicians in the midst of a pandemic. *Irish Journal of Psychological Medicine*, 1–4. doi:10.1017/ipm.2020.59.

Heller, L., LaPierre, A. (2012). *Healing Developmental Trauma: How Early Trauma Affects Self-Regulation, Self-Image, and the Capacity for Relationship.* New York: North Atlantic Books.

Helversen von, B., Wilke, A., Johnson, T., Schmid, G., Klapp, B. (2011). Performance benefits of depression: Sequential decision making in a healthy sample and a clinically depressed sample. *Journal of Abnormal Psychology*, *120*(4), 962–968.

Herman, B. H., Panksepp, J. (1978). Effects of morphine and naloxone on separation distress and approach attachment: Evidence for opiate mediation of social affect. *Pharmacology Biochemistry & Behavior*, *9*(2), 213–220.

Hess, Y. D., Valdman, T. L., Knowles, M. L. (2019). Interpersonal and intrapersonal approach and avoidance motives after social rejection. *Comprehensive Results in Social Psychology*, *3*(3), 201–223.

Hirst, W., Yamashiro, J. K., Coman, A. (2018). Collective memory from a psychological perspective. *Trends in Cognitive Sciences*, *22*(8), 737.

Hoffecker, J. F. (2009). *The Spread of Modern Humans in Europe.* Washington, DC: National Academy of Science.

Hofmann, K., Rodriguez-Rodriguez, R., Gaebler, A., Casals, N., Scheller, A., Kuerschner, L. (2017). Astrocytes and oligodendrocytes in grey and white matter regions of the brain metabolize fatty acids. *Scientific Reports*, *7*(1).

Holt-Lunstad, J. (2015). Loneliness and social isolation as risk factors for mortality: A meta-analytic review. *Perspectives on Psychological Science*, *10*(2), 227–237.

Howie, H., Rijal, C. M., Ressler, K. J. (2019). A review of epigenetic contributions to post-traumatic stress disorder. *Dialogues in Clinical Neuroscience, 21*(4), 417–428.

Hofstede, G. H. (1997). *Cultures and Organizations: Software of the Mind.* New York: McGraw-Hill.

Hu, L.-T., Bentler, P. M. (1998). Fit indices in covariance structure modeling: Sensitivity to underparameterized model missspecification. *Psychological Methods, 3*(4), 424–453.

Hu, L.-T., Bentler, P. M. (1999). Cutoff criteria for fit indices in covariance structure analysis: Controventional criteria versus new alternatives. *Structural Equation Modeling, 1*, 1–55.

Ingalhalikar, M., Smith, A., Parker, D., Satterthwaite, T. D., Elliott, M. A., Ruparel, K., Hakonarson, H., Gur, R. E., Gur, R. C., Verma, R. (2014). Sex differences in the structural connectome of the human brain. *Proceedings of the National Academy of Sciences of the United States of America, 111*(2), 823–828.

Ivanich, J. D., Mousseau, A. C., Walls, M. et al. (2020). Pathways of adaptation: Two case studies with one evidence-based substance use prevention program tailored for indigenous youth. *Prevention Science, 21*, 43–53.

Jaworowska, A., Matczak, A., Ciechanowicz, A., Stańczak, J., Zalewska, E. (2005). *Popularny Kwestionariusz inteligencji emocjonalnej.* Pracownia Testów Psychologicznych Polskiego Towarzystwa Psychologicznego.

Jazaieri, H., Jinpa, T. L., McGonigal, K., Rosenberg, E., Finkelstein, J., Simon-Thomas, E., et al. (2013). Enhancing compassion: A randomized controlled trial of a compassion cultivation training program. *Journal of Happiness Studies, 14*, 1113–1126.

Jazaieri, H., McGonigal, K., Lee, I. A., Jinpa, T., R. Doty, J. R., Gross, J. R., Goldin, P. R. (2018). Altering the trajectory of affect and affect regulation: The impact of compassion training. *Mindfulness, 9*(1), 283–293.

Jedliński, K. (2000). *Trening Interpersonalny.* Warszawa: Wydawnictwo W.A.B.

Jodorowsky, A. (2014). *Metagenealogy: Self Discovery through Psychomagic and the Family.* Tree Park Street Press, Inner Traditions Bear and Company, 640.

Johnson, S. M. (1994). *Character Styles.* New York: W. W. Norton & Company.

Johnson, M. W., Hendricks, P. S., Barrett, F. S., Griffiths, R. R. (2019). Classic psychedelics: An integrative review of epidemiology, therapeutics, mystical experience, and brain network function. *Pharmacology & Therapeutics, 197*, 83–102.

Jorge, R. E., Robinson, R. G., Moser, D., Tateno, A., Crespo-Facorro, B. Arndt, S. (2004). Major depression following traumatic brain injury. *Archives of General Psychiatry, 61*, 42–50.

Jöreskog, K. G., Sörbom, D. (1984). *LISREL-VI User's Guide (3rd ed.).* Mooresville, IN: Scientific Software.

Juczyński, Z., Ogińska-Bulik, N. (2009). *Narzędzia pomiaru stresu i radzenia sobie ze stresem.* Warszawa: PWN.

Jung, C. G. (2007). *Man and His Symbols.* Zurich: Foundation of the works of C.G. Jung.

Kabat-Zinn, J. (2003). *Clinical Psychology: Science and Practice.* Wiley Online Library.

Kabat-Zinn, J. (2013). *Życie – piękna katastrofa.* (R. Skrzypczak, Trans.). Warszawa: Wydawnictwo Czarna Owca.

Kanarek, R. B., Carrington, C. (2004). Sucrose consumption enhances the analgesic effects of cigarette smoking in male and female smokers. *Psychopatology, 173*, 57–63.

Katayama, M., Kubo, T., Yamakawa, T., Fujiwara, K., Nomoto, K., Ikeda, K., Mogi, K., Nagasawa, M., Kikusui, T. (2019). Emotional contagion from humans to dogs is facilitated by duration of ownership. *Frontiers in Psychology, 10*, 1678.

Kehoe, P., Blass, E. M. (1986). Opioid-mediation of separation distress in 10-day-old-rats: Reversal of stress with maternal stimuli. *Developing Psycholobiology, 19*, 385–398.

Kerr, N. L., Levine, J. M. (2008). The detection of social exclusion: Evolution and beyond. *Group Dynamics: Theory, Research, and Practice, 12*(1), 39–52.

Kielcolt-Glaser, J. K., Garner, W., Speicher, C. E., Penn, G., Glaser, R. (1984). Psychosocial modifiers of immune competence in medical students. *Psychosomatic Medicine, 46*, 7–14.

Kirkpatrick, L. A., Waugh, C. E., Valencia, A., Webster, G. D. (2002). The functional domain specificity of self-esteem and the differential prediction of aggression. *Journal of Personality and Social Psychology, 82*(5), 756–767.

Klengel, T., Dias, B. G., Ressler, K. J. (2016). Models of intergenerational and transgenerational transmission of risk for psychopathology in mice. *Neuropsychopharmacology, 41*(1), 219–231.

Kłosiński, M. (2017). W stronę hermeneutyki gier komputerowych. *Teksty Drugie, 3*, 51–68.

Kojder, A. (1980). Co to jest teoria naznaczania społecznego? *Studia Socjologiczne, 3*, 46.

Kozlowska, K., McLean, L. M., Walker, P., Carrive, P. (2015). Fear and the defense cascade: Clinical implications and management. *Harvard Review of Psychiatry, 23*(4), 263–285.

Kornienko, O., Ha, T., Dishon, T. (2020). Dynamic pathways between rejection and antisocial behaviour in peer networks: Update and test of confluence model. *Development and Psychopathology, 32*(1), 175–188.

Kurzweil, R. (2006). *The Singularity Is Near: When Humans Transcend Biology*. New York: Penguin Books, 672.

Lacey, J. I. (1967). Somatic response patterning and stress: Some revisions of activation theory. In: *Psychological Stress: Issues in Research*, Appley, M. H., Trumbull, R. (Eds.). New York: Appleton-Century-Crofts, 14–44.

Lai, Y-H. Carr, S. (2018). A critical exploration of child-parent attachment as a contextual construct. *Behavioral Science, 8*(12), 112–128.

Larsen, W., Dhem, A. (2003). *Embryologie Humaine (2e éd)*. Bruxelles: De Boeck.

Layous, K., King, L., Lyubomirsky, S., Wang, L., Doraiswamy, P. M. (2011). Delivering happiness: Translating positive psychology intervention research for treating major and minor depressive disorders. *Journal of Alternative and Complementary Medicine, 17*(8), 675–683.

Lazarus, R. S., DeLongis, A. (1983). Psychological stress and coping in aging. *American Psychologist, 38*, 245–254.

Lazarus, R. S., Folkman, S. (1984). *Stress, Appraisal, and Coping*. New York: Springer.

Liem, A., Wang, C., Wariyanti, Y., Latkin, C. A., Hall, B. J. (2020). The neglected health of international migrant workers in the COVID-19 epidemic. *Lancet Psychiatry*, 7(94), e20, 10.1016/S2215-0366(20)30076-6.

Leary, M. R. (2004). The function of self-esteem in terror management theory and sociometer theory: Comment on Pyszczynski et al. *Psychological Bulletin*, *130*, 478–482.

Leary, M. R., Baumeister, R. F. (2000). The nature and function of self-esteem: Sociometer theory. In Zanna, M. P. (Ed.), *Advances in experimental social psychology*, Vol. 32, 1–62. Academic Press, 32, .

Leary, M., Kowalski, R. M. (2001). *Lęk społeczny*. Gdańsk: GWP.

Leary, M. R., Springer, C. A. (2001). *Hurt Feelings: The Neglected Emotion. W: Aversive Behaviors and Interpersonal Transgression*, Kowalski, R. (Ed.). Washington, DC: American Psychlogical Association, 51–175.

Leary, M. R., Tambor, E. S., Terdal, S. K., Downs, D. L. (1995). Self-esteem as an interpersonal monitor: The sociometer hypothesis. *Journal of Personality and Social Psychology*, *68*, 518–530.

Leary, M. R., Tate, E. B., Adams, C. E., Allen, A. B., Hancock, J. (2007). Self-compassion and reactions to unpleasant self-relevant events: The implications of treating oneself kindly. *Journal of Personality and Social Psychology*, *92*(5), 887–904.

Leary, M. R., Twenge, J. M., Quinvilan, E. (2006). Interpersonal rejection as a determinant of anger and aggression. *Personality and Social Psychology Review*, *10*, 111–132.

Lee, A., Hankin, B. L., (Mar. 2009). *Insecure attachment, dysfunctional attitudes, and low self-esteem predicting prospective symptoms of depression and anxiety during adolescence. Journal of Personality and Social Psychology*, *38*(2), 219–231.

Lee, A., Hankin, B. (2009). Insecure attachment, dysfunctional attitudes, and low self-esteem predicting prospective symptoms of depression and anxiety during adolescence. *Journal of Personality and Social Psychology*, *38*(2), 219–231.

Lehrer, E. (2014). The Netflix effect. *Weekly Standard*, 19, 24(3). Retrieved from http://www.weeklystandard.com/articles/netflix-effect_782745.html, accessed 28 September 2015.

Levine, A., Heller, R. (2012). *Attached: The New Science of Adult Attachment and How It Can Help You Find—and Keep—Love*. New York: Penguin Random House.

Levitas, R. (2005). *Inclusive Society? Social Exclusion and New Labour (2nd ed.)*. London: Palgrave.

Levitas, R., Pantazis, C., Fahmy, E., Gordon, D., Lloyd, E., Patsios, D. (2007). *The Multi-Dimensional Analysis of Social Exclusion*. Bristol: Department of Sociology and School for Public Policy, University of Bristol.

Lieberman, M. D., Eisenberger, N. I. (2008). The pains and pleasures of social life: A social cognitive neuroscience approach. *NeuroLeadership Journal*, *1*(1), 38–43.

Long, C. R., Averill, J. R. (2003). Solitude: An exploration of benefits of being alone. *Journal for the Theory of Social Behaviour*, *33*, 21–44.

Lowen, A. (1988). *Love, Sex and Your Heart*. New York: MacMillan.

Luskin, F. (2007). *Forgive for Love: The Missing Ingredient for a Healthy and Lasting Relationship*. New York: HarperCollins.

Lyubomirsky, S., King, L., Diener, E. (2005). The benefits of frequent positive affect: Does happiness lead to success? *Psychological Bulletin*, *131*(6), 803–855.

Macdonald, G., Leary, M. R. (2005). Why does social exclusion hurt? The relationship between social and physical pain. *Psychological Bulletin*, *131*, 202–223.

Macroen, A., Goossens, L. (1993). Loneliness, attitude toward aloneness, and solitude: Age differences and developmental significance during adolescence. In Jackson, S., RodriguezTome, H. (Eds.), *Adolescence and its social worlds* (pp. 197-227). Hove, UK: Erlbaum.

Maddi, S. R. (1999). The personality construct of hardiness: I. Effects on experiencing, coping, and strain. *Consulting Psychology Journal: Practice and Research*, *51*(2), 83–94.

Main, M., Solomon, J. (1986). Discovery of an insecure-disorganized/disoriented attachment pattern. In: *Affective Development in Infancy*, Brazelton, T. B., Yogman, M. W. (Eds.) Norwood, NJ: Ablem, 95–124.

Makransky, J. (2003). Compassion in Buddhist psychology. In: *Wisdom and Compassion in Psychotherapy*, Germer, C. K., Siegel, R. D. (Eds.) New York: Guilford Press, Chapter 4.

MarketCast Study Finds TV "Binge-Viewing" Creates a More Engaged Viewer for Future Seasons and Not a Bingeing Habit. (2020).

Markus, H. R., Conner, A. (2014). *Clash! How to Thrive in a Multicultural World.* New York: A Plume Book.

Markus, H. R., Kitayama, S. (2010). Culture and selves: A cycle of mutual constitution. *Perspectives on Psychological Sciences*, *5*, 420–430.

Martin, P. (1997). *The Sickening Mind: Brain, Behaviour, Immunity and Disease.* Scarborough, 320.

Maslow, A. H. (1954). *Motivation and Personality.* New York: Harper.

Matrix, S. (2014). The Netflix effect: Teens, binge watching, and on-demand digital media trends. *Jeunesse*, *6*(1), 119–138. Retrieved from http://dx.doi.org/10.1353/jeu.2014.0002, accessed 28 September 2015.

Matthews, G., Jones, D. M., Chamberlain, A. G. (1990). Refining the measurement of mood: The UWIST mood adjective checklist. *British Journal of Psychology*, *81*, 17–42.

Mayer, J. D., Gaschke, Y. N. (1988). The experience and meta-experience of mood. *Journal of Personality and Social Psychology*, *55*, 102–111.

Mayer, J. D., Salovey, P. (1997). What is emotional intelligence? In: *Emotional Development And Emotional Intelligence: Educational Implications*, Salovey, P., Sluyter, D. J. (Eds.). New York: Harper Collins.

Mayer, J. D., Salovey, P., Caruso, D. (2000). Models of emotional intelligence. In: Sternberg, R. J. (Ed.), *Handbook of intelligence.* (p. 396–420). Cambridge University Press.

McCracken, G. (2013). From Arrested Development to Dr. Who, binge watching is changing our culture. *Wired*, 23 May. Retrieved from www.wired.com/2013/05/beyond-arrested, accessed 28 September 2015.

McCraty, R., Atkinson, M., Tomasino, D., Bradley, R. T. (2009). The coherent heart: Heart-brain interactions, psychophysiological coherence, and the emergence of system-wide order. *Integral Review*, *5*(2).

McQuail, D. (2010). *McQuail's Mass Communication Theory (6th ed.).* Thousand Oaks, CA: Sage.

Menzies, D., Davidson, B. (2002). Authenticity and belonging: The experience of being known in the group. *Group Analysis*, *35*(1), 43–55.
Moeller, R. W., Seehuus, M., Peisch, V. (2020). Emotional intelligence, belongingness, and mental health in college students. *Frontiers in Psychology*, 11–93.
Molden, D. C., Lucas, G. M., Gardner, W. L., Dean, K., Knowles, M. (2009). Motivations for prevention or promotion following social exclusion: Being rejected versus being ignored. *Journal of Personality and Social Psychology*, *96*, 415–431.
Moore, R., Gilette, D. (1990). *King, Warrior, Magician, Lover: Rediscovering the Archetypes of the Mature Masculine*. New York: HarperCollins.
Moretti, M. M., Peled M (2004). Adolescent-parent attachment: Bonds that support healthy development. *Pediatrics Child Health*, *9*(8), 551–555.
Myers, D. (1985). *The Pursuit of Happiness*. New York: William Morrow & Co.
Najwyższa Izba Kontroli (NIK). (2018). *Depresja - jak pomóc sobie i innym?* Retrieved from https://www.nik.gov.pl/aktualnosci/uwaga-depresja.html, accessed 28 September 2018.
Napoli, M., Marsiglia, F., Kulis, S. (2003). Sense of belonging to school as a protective factor against drug abuse among Native American urban adolescents in the Southwest. *Journal of Social Work Practice in the Addictions*, *3*(2), 25–42.
Naranjo, J. R., Fuentes, J. A. (1985). Association between hypoalgesia and hypertension in rats after short-term isolation. *Neuropharmacology*, *24*, 167–171.
Neff, K. D. (2003a). Self-compassion: An alternative conceptualization of a healthy attitude toward oneself. *Self and Identity*, *2*, 85–100.
Neff, K. D. (2003b). The development and validation of a scale to measure self-compassion. *Self and Identity*, 2, 223–250.
Neff, K. D., Germer, C. (2017). Self-compassion and psychological wellbeing. In: *Oxford Handbook of Compassion Science*, Doty, J. (Ed.). Oxford: Oxford University Press, Chapter 27.
Newcomb, A. F., Bukowski, W. M., Pattee, L. (1993). Children's peer relations: A meta-analytic review of popular, rejected, neglected, controversial, and average sociometric status. *Psychological Bulletin*, *113*, 99–128.
Newman, K. S. (2004). *Rampage: The Social Roots of School Shootings*. Contributors: Fox, C., Harding, D., Mehta, J., Roth, W. New York: Basic Books.
Nisbett, R. E. (2003). *The Geography of Thought: How Asians and Westerners Think Differently ... and Why*. New York: Simon & Schuster Inc.
Nitsun, M. (1996). *The Anti-Group Destructive Forces in the Group and Their Creative Potential*. London: Routlege.
Nordgren, L. F., Banas, K. I., MacDonald, G. (2011). Empathy gaps for social pain: Why people underestimate the pain of social suffering. *Journal of Personality and Social Psychology*, *100*(1), 120–128.
Nutt, D. (2019). Psychedelic drugs – a new era in psychiatry? *Dialogues in Clinical Neuroscience*, *21*(2), 139–147.
Obrist, P. A. (1976). The cardiovascular-behavioral interaction – as it appears today. *Psychophysiology*, *13*, 95–107.
O'Keeffe, P. (2013). A sense of belonging: Improving student retention. *C College Student Journal*, *47*, 605–613.
Ogawa, S., Lee, T. M., Kay, A. R., Tank, D. W. (1990). Biophysics brain magnetic resonance imaging with contrast dependent on blood oxygenation (cerebral blood

flow/brain metabolism/oxygenation). *Proceedings of the National Academy of Sciences of the United States of America*, *87*, 9868–9872.

Pauly, T., Lay, J. C., Scott, S. B., Hoppmann, C. A. (2018). Social relationship quality buffers negative affective correlates of everyday solitude in an adult life-span and an older adult sample. *Psychology and Aging*, *33*(5), 728–738.

Peisah, C., Byrnes, A., Doron, I., Dark, M., Quinn, G. (2020). Advocacy for the human rights of older people in the COVID pandemic and beyond: A call to mental health professionals. *International Psychogeriatric*, *33*(5), 728.

Pena, L. L. (2015). *Breaking Binge: Exploring the Effects of Binge Watching on Television Viewer Reception*. Syracuse, NY: Syracuse University.

Perel, E. (2006). *Mating in Captivity: Unlocking Erotic Intelligence*. New York: Harper.

Phillips, J. M., Gatchel, R. J. (2000). Extraversion-introversion and chronic pain: Locus of control in the patient with chronic pain. In: *Personality Characteristics of Patients with Pain*, Gatchel, R., Weisberg, J. (Eds.). Washington, DC: American Psychological Assiciation, 181–202.

Pincus, D. B., Friedman, A. G. (2004). Improving children's coping with everyday stress. *Clinical Child & Family Psychology Review*, *7*(4), 223–240.

Pittman, M., Sheehan, K. (2015). Sprinting a media marathon: Uses and gratifications of binge-watching television through Netflix. *First Monday*, *20*(10).

Pritchard, A., Richardson, M., Sheffield, D., McEwan, K. (2020). The relationship between nature connectedness and eudaimonic well-being: A meta-analysis. *Journal of Happiness Studies*, *21*, 1145–1167.

Porges, S. W. (2003). Social engagement and attachment: A phylogenetic perspective. *Roots of Mental Illness in Children, Annals of the New York Academy of Sciences*, *1008*, 31–47.

Proulx, C. M., Snyder-Rivas, L. (2013). The association between individual health and trajectories of marital happiness and problems. *Journal of Family Psychology*, *27*, 194–202.

Putnam, R. D. (2000). *Bowling Alone: The Collapse and Revival of American Community*. New York: Simon & Schuster.

Raymond, J. M., Sheppard, K. (2018). Effects of peer mentoring on nursing students' perceived stress, sense of belonging, self-efficacy and loneliness. *Journal of Nursing Education and Practice*, *8*, 16–23.

Reijntjes, A. H. A., Dekovic, M., Vermande, M. M., Telch, M. J. (2008). Predictive validity of the Children's Attributional Styles Questionnaire: Linkages with reactions to an in vivo peer evaluation manipulation. *Cognitive Therapy and Research*, *32*, 247–260.

Ribner, N. (2005). *Terapia nastolatków*. (O. Waśkiewicz, Trans.). Gdańsk: GWP.

Richardson, M., Sheffield, D. (2017). Three good things in nature: Noticing nearby nature brings sustained increases in connection with nature. *Journal PsyEcology*, *8*(1), 1–32.

Robles, T. F., Slatcher, R. B., Trombello, J. M., McGinn, M. M. (2014). Marital quality and health: A meta-analytic review. *Psychological Bulletin*, *140*(1), 140.

Rosenberg, M. (1965). *Society and the Adolescent Self-Image*. Princeton, NJ: Princeton University Press.

Rutkowski, K., Dembińska, M. (2015). Post-war research on post-traumatic stress disorder. Part II – 1989 onwards. *Psychiatria Polska*, *22*, 1–15.

Rutter, M. (1987). Psychosocial resilience and protective mechanisms. *American Journal of Orthopsychiatry*, *57*(3), 316–331.

Ryan, R. M., Deci, E. L. (2000). Self determination theory and the facilitation of intrinsic motivation, social development and well-being. *American Psychologist*, *55*(1), 68–78.

Salovey, P., Mayer, J. D., Caruso, D. (2004). Pozytywna psychologia inteligencji emocjonalnej. In: *Psychologia pozytywna*, Czapiński, J. (Ed.). Warszawa: PWN, 380–398.

Sapolsky, R. (2004). Social status and health in humans and other animals. *Annual Review Anthropology*, *33*, 393–418.

Sapolsky, R. (2010). *Dlaczego zebry nie mają wrzodów*. (M. Guzowska-Dąbrowska, Trans.). Warszawa: PWN.

Scaer, R. (2014). *The Body Bears the Burden: Trauma, Dissociation, and Disease (3rd ed.)*. New York: Routledge/Taylor & Francis Group.

Schaan, V. S., Schultz, A. Rubel, J. A., Bernstein, M., Domes, G., Schächinger, H., Vögele, C. (2019). Childhood trauma affects stress-related interoceptive accuracy. *Frontiers in Psychiatry*. *10*. Article 750.

Schore, A. N. (2002). Advances in neuropsychoanalysis, attachment theory, and trauma research: Implications for self psychology. *Psychoanalytic Inquiry*, *22*(3), 433–484.

Schore, A. N. (2009). Relational trauma and the developing right brain. An interface of psychoanalytic self psychology and neuroscience. *Annals of the New York Academy of Science*, *1159*(1), 189–203.

Schutte, N. S., Malouff, J. M., Hall, L. E., Haggerty, D. J., Cooper, J. T., Golden, C. J., Dornheim, L. (1998). Development and validation of a measure of emotional intelligence. *Personality and Individual Differences*, *25*, 167–177.

Schutzenberger, A. A. (2014). *The Ancestor Syndrome Transgenerational Psychotherapy and the Hidden Links in the Family Tree*. London: Routledge.

Schwarz, G. E., Higgins, J. D. (1971). Cardiac activity preparatory to overt and covert behavior. *Science*, *173*, 1144–1145.

Schwerdtferger, A., Friedrich-Mai, P. (2009). Social interaction moderates the relationship between depressive mood and heart rate variability: Evidence from an ambulatory monitoring study. *Health Psychology*, *28*(4), 501–509.

Siegel, D. J., Bryson, T. P. (2020). *The Power of Showing Up: How Parental Presence Shapes Who Our Kids Become and How Their Brains Get Wired*. New York: Ballantine Books.

Sillivan, S. E., Vaissière, T., Miller, C. A. (2015). Neuroepigenetic regulation of pathogenic memories. *Neuroepigenetics*, *1*(1), 28–33.

Silver, H. (2006). Social exclusion. *Blackwell Encyclopaedia of Sociology*. Oxford: Blackwell, 4411–4413.

Simpson, J. A., Overall, N. C. (2014). Partner buffering of attachment insecurity. *Current Directions in Psychological Science*, *23*, 54–59.

Singer, T., Engert, V. (2019). It matters what you practice: Differential training effects on subjective experience, behavior, brain and body in the ReSource Project. *Current Opinion in Psychology*, *28*, 151–158.

Sosen, R. J. M., Van der Molen, M. W., Jennings, J. R., van Beek, B. (2000). Wisconsin card sorting in adolescents: Analysis of performance, response times and heart rate. *Acta Psychologica, 104*, 227–257.

Sosnowski, T. (2002). *Zadania umysłowe a aktywność sercowo-naczyniowa.* Gdańsk: Gdańskie Wydawnictwo Psychologiczne.

Stanik, J. (2012). *Psychologia sądowa. Podstawy. Badania. Aplikacje.* Warszawa: PWN.

Stokes, J. E. (2016). Marital quality and loneliness in later life: A dyadic analysis of older married couples in Ireland. *Journal of Social and Personal Relationships, 34*(1), 114–135.

Stora, J. B. (2015). *A New Body-Mind Approach: Clinical Cases.* London: Routlege.

Strycker, N. (2014). *The Thing With Feathers: The Surprising Lives of Birds and What They Reveal about Being Human.* New York: Riverhead Books.

Szarfenberg, R. (2005a). Marginalizacja i wykluczenie społeczne – stare problemy w nowej rzeczywistości. *PULSS Kujawsko-Pomorski.* Toruń: ROPS.

Szarfenberg, R. (2005b). Od trzech elementarnych strategii badawczych do programu badań wykluczenia społecznego. In: *Wykluczenie społeczne*, Frąckiewicz, L. (Ed.) . Katowice: Uniwersytet Ekonomiczny.

Szarfenberg, R. (2007). Ubóstwo, marginalność i wykluczenie społeczne. In: *Polityka społeczna*, Firlik-Fesnak, G., Szylko-Skoczny, M. (Eds.). Warszawa: PWN. 317–331.

Szymczak, M. (1992). *Słownik języka polskiego.* Warszawa: Wydawnictwo Naukowe, 108.

Śmieja, M. (2018). Bycie w związku a dobrostan. Jakie funkcje psychospołeczne pełnią bliskie relacje. *Psychologia w praktyce, 12*, 3–6.

Ten Have-de Labije, J., Neborsky, R. J. (2017). *Intensywna krótkoterminowa psychoterapia dynamiczna dla praktyków.* Warszawa: Wydawnictwo Harmonia.

Teppers, E., Klimstra, T. A., Damme, C. V., Luyckx, K., Vanhalst, J., Goossens, L. (2013). Personality traits, loneliness, and attitudes toward aloneness in adolescence. *Journal of Social and Personal Relationships, 30*(8), 1045–1063.

Thornhill, R., Thornhill, N. W. (1989). The evolution of psychological pain. W: *Sociobiology and the Social Sciences,* Bell, R. (Ed.). Lubock: Texas Tech University Press, 73–103.

Todman, L. C., Taylor, J. S., Cochrane, K., Arbaugh-Korotko, J., Berger, J., Burt, E., Caponi, M., Houston, E., Hahn, A. K., Mandeleew, D. (2009). Social exclusion indicators for the United States. *Journal of Individual Psychology, 65*(4), 330–359.

Tugade, M., Fredrickson, B., Feldman Barret, L. (2004). Psychological resilience and positive emotional granularity: Examining the benefits of positive emotions on coping and health. *Journal of Personality, 72*(6), 1161–1190.

Tumin, D. (2017), Does marriage protect health? A birth cohort comparison. *Social Science Quarterly, 99*, 626–643.

Twenge, J. M. (2002). Birth cohort, social change, and personality: The interplay of dysphoria and individualism in the 20th century. In: *Advances in Personality Science,* Cervone, D., Mischel, W. (Eds.). New York: The Guilford Press, 196–218.

Twenge, J. M. (2017). *iGen: Why Today's Super-Connected Kids Are Growing Up Less Rebellious, More Tolerant, Less Happy and Completely Unprepared for Adulthood.* New York: Atria Books.

Twenge, J. M., Baumeister, R. F., Dewall, C. N., Ciarocco, N. J., Bartels, J. M. (2007). Social exclusion decreases prosocial behavior. *Journal of Personality and Social Psychology, 92*, 56–66.

Twenge, J. M., Baumeister, R. F., Tice, D. M., Stucke, T. S. (2001). If you can't join them, beat them: Effects of social exclusion on aggressive behavior. *Journal of Personality and Social Psychology, 81*, 1058–1069.

Twenge, J. M., Catanese, K. R., Baumeister, R. F. (2002). Social exclusion causes self-defeating behavior. *Journal of Personality and Social Psychology, 83*, 606–615.

Twenge, J. M., Catanese, K. R., Baumeister, R. F. (2003). Social exclusion and the deconstructed state: Time perception, meaninglessness, lethargy, lack of emotion, and selfawareness. *Journal of Personality and Social Psychology, 85*, 409–423.

Twenge, J., Joiner, T. E. (2020). Mental distress among U.S. adults during the COVID-19 pandemic. https://doi.org/10.31234/osf.io/wc8ud.

Ulriken de Vinar, M. (2012). Political violence: Transgenerational inscription and trauma. *International Journal of Applied Psychoanalytic Studies*, 9(2), 95–108.

Van der Kolk, B. A., Pelcovitz, D., Roth, S., Mandel, F. S., Farlane, M. C., Herman, J. L. (1996). Dissociation, somatization, and affect dysregulation: The complexity of adaptation of trauma. *The American Journal of Psychiatry, 153*(7), 83–93.

Verlinden, S., Hersen, M., Thomas, J. (2000). Risk factors in school shooting. *Clinical Psychology Review, 20*, 3–56.

Vetulani, J. (2013). Early maternal separation: A rodent model of depression and a prevailing human condition. *Pharmacological Reports, 65*(6), 1451–1461.

Vetulani, J., Mazurek, M. (2007). *Bez ograniczeń. Jak rządzi nami mózg.* Warszawa: PWN.

Vetulani, J. (2017). *Trauma dziecięca a rozwój mózgu-prof. dr hab. Jerzy Vetulani,* Retrieved from https://www.youtube.com/watch?v=tZkBZxqZUlY, accessed 28 September 2019.

Wang, F., Pereira, A. (2016). Neuromodulation, emotional feelings and affective disorders. *Mens Sana Monographs, 14*, 5–29.

Warr, P. (2004). Psychologiczne skutki długotrwałego bezrobocia. In: *Człowiek w społecznej przestrzeni bezrobocia*, Chirkowska-Smolak, T., Chudzicka, A. (Eds.) Poznań: Wydawnictwo UAM, 137–153.

Weisz, J. R., Mccabe, M. A., Denning, M. D. (1994). Primary and secondary control among children undergoing medical procedures: Adjustment as a function of coping style. *Journal of Consulting and Clinical Psychology, 62*, 324–332.

Wesselmann, E. D., Williams, K. D. (2017). Social life and social death: Inclusion, ostracism, and rejection in groups. *Group Processes & Intergroup Relations, 20*(5), 693–706.

Wheeler, K. S. (2015). The relationships between television viewing behaviors, attachment, loneliness, depression, and psychological well-being. *University Honors Program Theses*. Georgia Southern University. Retrieved from https://digitalcommons.georgiasouthern.edu/honors-theses/98, accessed 28 September 2015.

WHO (2017). *Depression and Other Common Mental Disorders: Global Health Estimates*. Retrieved from https://apps.who.int/iris/bitstream/handle/10665/254610/WHO-MSD-MER-2017.2-eng.pdf, accessed 28 September 2018.

Wilczyńska, A. (2013). *Radzenie sobie młodzieży w sytuacjach zagrożenia wykluczeniem społecznym*. Katowice: Wydawnictwo UŚ.

Wilczyńska, A. (2016). Hedonistic vs. eudaimonistics interventions in preventing a sense of exclusion in young people. In: *Applied Psychology of Time*, Tokarska, U. (Ed.) Warszawa: PWN, 213–233.

Wilczyńska, A. (2019). Fatty acids in human diet and their impact on cognitive and emotional functioning. In: *The Role of Functional Food Security in Global Health,* Singh, R. B., Watson, R. R., Takahashi, T. (Eds.). London: Elsevier.

Wilczyńska, A., De Meester, F. (2011). Parametry emocjonalne i pomiar pracy serca w prerehabilitacji osób zagrożonych chorobami cywilizacyjnymi związanymi ze stresem. In: *Oblicza rehabilitacji,* Pisula, E., Margiel-Matusiewicz, K., Walewska, K. (Eds.). Warszawa: MediPage, 289–305.

Wilczyńska, A., De Meester, F., Singh, R. B., Bargiel-Matusiewicz, K. (2010). Heart rate and blood pressure in the context of nutritional and psychological analysis: A case study. *European Journal of Medical Research*, *15*, 217–223.

Wilczynska A., Januszek M. (2014). Właczenie versus wykluzcenie młodzieży-wyniki badań. In: *Młodzież na biegunach życia społecznego,* Wilczyńska, A. (Ed.) Warszawa: PWN. 233–260.

Wilczyńska, A., Januszek, M., Bargiel-Matusiewicz, K. (2015). The need to belong and sense of belonging versus effectiveness of coping. *Polish Psychological Bulletin*, *46*(1), 72–81.

Wilczyńska, A., Piękoś, J. (2014). Scenariusze interwencji psychologii pozytywnej w pracy z młodzieżą. In: *Młodzież na biegunach życia społecznego,* Wilczyńska, A. (Ed.) Warszawa: PWN. 212–232.

Wilczyńska-Kwiatek, A., Bargiel-Matusiewicz, K. (2008). Contemporary picture of women's unemployment: Personality conditioning of unemployment and its consequences for psychic health. *Archives of Psychiatry and Psychotherapy*, *10*(4), 63–68.

Wilczyńska-Kwiatek, A. (2009) Psychologiczne aspekty zagrożenia wykluczeniem społecznym młodzieży. In: *Wybrane zagadnienia z psychologii klinicznej i osobowości. Psychologia kliniczna nastolatka*, Szewczyk, L., Talik, E. (Eds.). Lublin: TN KUL, 149–170.

Wilczyńska-Kwiatek, A., Bargiel-Matusiewicz, K., Łapiński, Ł. (2009). Asthma, allergy, mood disorders, and nutrition. *European Journal of Medical Research*, *14*(4), 248–254.

Wilczyńska-Kwiatek, A., De Meester, F., Singh, R. B., Łapiński, Ł. (2010). Western diet and behaviour: The Columbus concept. In: *Modern Dietary Fat Intakes in Disease Promotion*, De Meester, F., Zibadi, S., Watson, R. R. (Eds.). New York: Humana Press, 3–29.

Wilson-Mendenhall, C. D., Barrett, L. F., Barsalou, L. W. (2013). Neural evidence that human emotions share core affective properties. *Psychological Science*, *24*, 947–956.

Weerdmeester, J., Lange, W-G. (2019). Social anxiety and pro-social behavior following varying degrees of rejection: Piloting a new experimental paradigm. *Frontiers in Psychology*, 10.

Yehuda, R., Lehrner, A. (2018). Intergenerational transmission of trauma effects: Putative role of epigenetic mechanisms. *World Psychiatry*. *17*(3), 243–257.

Zhang, J., Lu, H., Zeng, H., et al. (2020) The differential psychological distress of populations affected by the COVID-19 pandemic. *Brain, Behaviour and Immunity, 87*, 49–50. doi:10.1016/j.bbi.2020.04.031.

Zhong, C. B., Leonardelli, J. G. (2008). Cold and lonely: Does social exclusion literally feel cold? *Psychological Science, 19*(9), 838–842.

Zillmann, D. (1979). *Hostility and Aggression*. New York: Taylor & Francis Group.

Zimbardo, Ph. G. (2007). *The Lucifer Effect: Understanding How Good People Turn Evil*. New York: Random House.

Zimbardo, Ph. G. (2008). *The journey from the Bronx to Stanford to Abu Ghraib. Journeys in Social Psychology: Looking Back to Inspire the Future*, 85–104.

Zimbardo, Ph. G., Boyd, J. (2009). *The Time Paradox: The New Psychology of Time That Will Change Your Life*. New York: Atria Books.

Zimbardo, Ph. G., Sword, R. M., Sword, R. K. M. (2012). *The Time Cure: Overcoming PTSD with the New Psychology of Time Perspective Therapy*. San Francisco: Jossey-Bass.

Zimbardo, Ph. G., Coulombe, N. (2015). *Gdzie ci mężczyźni?* Warszawa: PWN.

Zimmer, B. (2013). Keeping a watch on 'binge watching'. *Visual Thesaurus*, 9 Aug. Retrieved from https://www.visualthesaurus.com/cm/wordroutes/keeping-a-watch-on-binge-watching, accessed 28 September 2019.

Index

www.ingramcontent.com/pod-product-compliance
Ingram Content Group UK Ltd.
Pitfield, Milton Keynes, MK11 3LW, UK
UKHW022022180926
475701UK00005B/989
9780367627898